CRAFTING NOVELS & SHORT STORIES

WritersDigest.*com*
Cincinnati, Ohio

CRAFTING NOVELS & SHORT STORIES

The Complete Guide to Writing Great Fiction

FROM THE EDITORS OF WRITER'S DIGEST

FOREWORD BY JAMES SCOTT BELL

 Published by Writer's Digest Books, an imprint of F+W Media, Inc., 10151 Carver Road, Suite # 200, Blue Ash, OH 45242. (800) 289-0963. First edition.

For more resources for writers, visit www.writersdigest.com/books.

To receive a free weekly e-mail newsletter delivering tips and updates about writing and about Writer's Digest products, register directly at www.writersdigest.com/enews.

15 14 13 12 11 5 4 3 2 1

Distributed in Canada by Fraser Direct
100 Armstrong Avenue
Georgetown, Ontario, Canada L7G 5S4
Tel: (905) 877-4411

Distributed in the U.K. and Europe by F&W Media International
Brunel House, Newton Abbot, Devon, TQ12 4PU, England
Tel: (+44) 1626-323200, Fax: (+44) 1626-323319
E-mail: postmaster@davidandcharles.co.uk

Distributed in Australia by Capricorn Link
P.O. Box 704, Windsor, NSW 2756 Australia
Tel: (02) 4577-3555

Edited by Melissa Wuske
Designed by Claudean Wheeler
Production coordinated by Debbie Thomas

TABLE OF CONTENTS

PART 2: PLOT & CONFLICT:
YOUR STORY'S ACTION & SUSPENSE

PART 3: POINT OF VIEW:
THE VOICE OF YOUR STORY

PART 5: DIALOGUE:

WHAT YOUR CHARACTERS SAY TO EACH OTHER

PART 6: DESCRIPTION & WORD CHOICE:

WHAT YOU TELL READERS

PART 7: REVISION:

HOW YOUR STORY COMES TOGETHER

FOREWORD

BY JAMES SCOTT BELL

When I was a freshly scrubbed law school graduate I went to work for a big civil litigation firm in Beverly Hills. I wanted to be a trial lawyer and, having won my law school's coveted trial advocacy award, I was raring to go. Thought I knew it all right out of the gate.

So the day came when one of the senior associates had a dinky little trial coming up and didn't want to be bothered. He asked me if I wanted to take it. Take it? This was my big moment!

It was indeed a relatively small bench trial (one judge, no jury) but I treated it like the Trial of the Century. When I showed up at the courthouse the other attorney met me, shook my hand, and suggested in collegial tones that perhaps we could settle this thing here and now. He asked to see the new evidence I was going to present, which consisted of a few letters, and I showed him. He conferred with his client and came back and made a settlement offer that was way too low. The lawyer actually said he was now going to take this to trial. He obviously didn't know I was the second coming of Clarence Darrow.

When the trial got under way there was a moment when the opposing lawyer stood up and addressed the judge. He told the judge I was withholding evidence from the court. "I have seen this evidence and Mr. Bell is trying to deceive you, Your Honor," he said.

I was furious. I babbled incoherently. It threw me off my game. And even though I won this one-day trial, the amount gained for my client was less than what I thought it should be.

I complained angrily to the senior associate about how I was treated. He snorted and sat me down. "Don't you know the first rule of trial work? Don't ever trust the other lawyer."

So simple. So pithy. It was advice I needed to hear before I walked into a courtroom.

There is nothing so instructive in any endeavor of life as having an experienced hand give you the benefit of his wisdom. Which is why I appreciate the writing instruction presented in a good craft book like this one. It's like having that seasoned professional sit down with you and tell you things you could only learn on your own after lots of trial and error, if you learn them at all.

When I was first trying to figure out how to write, I devoured the fiction column in *Writer's Digest*, then inked by the great Lawrence Block. I read it every month as if it were a sacred page, underlining what jumped out at me. I still have binders full of those back issues and have turned to them nostalgically on occasion, always picking up a fresh tip or being reminded of one that I'd first read there.

Likewise, I have an entire floor to ceiling bookcase with nothing but writing books, all of them highlighted to one degree or another.

My philosophy has always been if I can learn just one thing from an article or book on writing, it's worth it. If there is one tip or technique that will lift my writing to another level, I want to know it. I don't ever want to rest as a writer. Books like the one you are holding your hand are your friends in that regard.

The fact that it is a collection from a number of brilliant teachers of the craft is a huge benefit. It's like you get to sit at a large table for coffee with a group of skilled instructors and listen to their insights while you take notes. In fact, it's better. You don't have to pause and ask them to repeat something. You can linger over a section of the book as long as you want.

But you must do more than that. You must put into practice what you learn. When you read something that strikes you as relevant to your own writing journey, figure out a way to practice it. Make up a writing exercise for yourself.

You'll find many exercises already in the book, waiting for you. Don't know what to write? Try Elizabeth Sims's "Random Sentence Kick-Start" on page 129.

Are your characters not coming to life as you'd like? Give them dreams, as suggested by Nancy Kress on page 25.

If time to write is a problem, drink in Sage Cohen's essay on how to be most productive (page 236).

In fact, drink in this whole book. Linger over it. Keep it handy. You'll find yourself turning to it when you need to, and even before you need to. What you have here is instructional gold. Mine it, refine it, use it. And follow three simple rules:

1. Keep learning.
2. Keep writing.
3. Never trust the other lawyer.

—James Scott Bell

INTRODUCTION

Writing fiction requires grit and sensitivity. It's an elusive craft. You chase it and chase it, and you sometimes feel like you'll never master it. The subtleties of character, word choice, and revision make it imperative to stay in tune with every element of your work, even as you relentlessly battle the writer's self-conscious subconscious.

It's daunting to say the least.

By picking up this book, you've taken a decisive step to prove your dedication to the craft. In these pages you'll find the know-how your need to fuel your determination. That's what this book is for. It pulls together the expert writers, editors, and agents to give the best advice for every aspect of fiction writing. With their wisdom, you'll find your confident, compelling voice.

Whether you're writing flash fiction, a short story, a novel, or an epic trilogy, you'll come away with a game plan for chasing the craft. With each chapter, you'll build your stamina and sharpen your fiction instincts.

THE TOOLS YOU NEED

Each part of the book will lead you through a focused look at one element of strong storytelling. You'll learn tips from experts that will give your work the power to stand out.

- **PART 1** helps you define and refine your characters.
- **PART 2** provides the tools to make your plot and conflict high-energy and intense.
- **PART 3** guides you as your hone your story's point of view.
- **PART 4** gives a framework for weaving setting and backstory.
- **PART 5** helps you create dialogue that rings true.

- **PART 6** guides you as you select the right words and descriptions throughout your story.
- **PART 7** is a complete guide to revising your story to perfection.

Each section gives you insights to help you find what works and what doesn't work in your story.

The Focus on the Writing Life sections will help you integrate your skills into a balanced, productive, and fulfilling career.

Start at the beginning and read to the end or search for chapters that meet the needs of the moment. Either way, your writing will be transformed.

Plus, at the end of the book you'll find genre descriptions to help you classify your work and a list of resources to help you delve further into the craft.

Let the voices in *Crafting Novels & Short Stories* be your guide as you develop the grit and sensitivity to become a fiction master.

FOCUS ON THE WRITING LIFE:

GETTING STARTED

GET OFF YOUR BUTT & WRITE

BY THE EDITORS OF WRITER'S DIGEST

"So, what do you do?" asks the fellow dad at the soccer match, glancing over at you while he keeps an eye on his daughter, the star forward.

"I'm a writer," you announce proudly.

"That's fascinating! Anything I would recognize?" he asks, while you both cheer a save by your team's goalie.

"Not yet," you admit. "I haven't had much luck yet in getting published." There is a pause while he makes a sympathetic-sounding cluck. "Actually, I haven't been writing much lately at all," you continue. "Being home with the kids takes so much of my energy that by the time they're in bed at the end of the day all I want to do is watch television. Plus, writing is so discouraging when you can't get someone to even look at your work."

There is a beat while he processes this. "But, you're a writer, right? How can you be a writer without actually *writing*?"

This scene may cause you to chuckle with recognition or possibly to hang your head in shame. Real writers *write*. Successful writers find the time every day to hone their craft and meet their writing obligations—whether those obligations are external (from editors) or internal (from an incontestable desire to write). What usually separates good writers from bad ones (and often, published writers from unpublished ones) is a strong work habit. That's it. That's the big secret. Real writers work hard. In fact, most work ridiculously hard.

Professional writers know there's nothing like a looming deadline to make them focus on their work. In fact, the real problem for beginning writers is usually not scrambling to meet a deadline, but simply organizing their time efficiently enough to find time to write at a productive pace. All writers feel this way from time to time. As other commitments encroach on our days, writing is often pushed aside like an unpleasant chore.

Accomplishing your writing goals requires making a writing plan, which is a time schedule that lists what you need to do and when.

CHOOSE TO WRITE

Everybody on the planet has the same amount of time every day. How we choose to use that time makes some of us writers and others of us short-order cooks. If you are a short-order cook who wants to write, however, you should probably take a bit of time to think about how you use your time.

Sandra Felton, who has written more than a dozen books on how to get organized, including *Neat Mom, Messie Kids*, and *The New Messies Manual*, points to prioritizing and dedication as helpful organizational tools for writers. "I think the whole answer is focus," she says. "I think what focus means is you have to decide what you want to do and lob off other stuff that you also want to do. Because you want to write more."

Note that the choice is not between writing and doing something else that you don't want to do. The choice is among a nearly overwhelming array of things that seem appealing: checking in with your friends on Facebook, reading for pleasure, or having people over for dinner. Then there's going to movies and the theater and the opera and family get-togethers and on trips and watching way too much television. Sometimes people would even rather do laundry and dishes than write. (All writers have days like that, but if that's your constant M.O., you may wish to rethink a literary vocation.) Faced with so many options, people tend to choose too many and feel like they're short of time.

Some people actually can use stray snippets of free time to write, penning novels on the back of envelopes while waiting in the checkout line at the grocery store. If they have ten minutes between helping a child with homework and driving her to flute lessons, they use those ten precious minutes to write or polish a small chunk of prose. Such people are the envy of the rest of us. For the rest of us, writing for publication requires larger pieces of time to research, ponder, draft, rewrite, and polish.

MAKE WRITING A HABIT

Finding writing time requires a modicum of organization, but using it productively demands dedication. The theme of virtually every article about getting organized to write is straightforward: *Just do it.* Wanting to write and writing itself are cousins, not identical twins. Psychological research indicates that writing every day, whether your muse is whispering in your ear or has deserted you, produces not only more writing but also more ideas for future writing.

The writing habit, like the exercise habit, is its own reward. When you don't do it, you feel as if you're cheating yourself. Real writers don't sit around and wait for inspiration to strike before they put fingers to keyboard; they put fingers to keyboard and know that somewhere during those hours they will discover small nuggets of inspiration. The fingers-to-keyboard, butt-in-the-chair pose is like exercise for the writer. In a way, this is just like real runners who pound the pavement or the treadmill in all weather, whether they are busy with work or on vacation. Like physical exercise, writing is often not enjoyable while you're doing it, though occasionally an endorphin or two will spark and the serotonin does its thing. Most of the time, though, writing is just a matter of discipline, plain and simple. Discipline comes more easily to some people than to others, but it is certainly a skill that can be cultivated.

"The only thing I can tell you I do that's inviolate is when I have to write, I get up in the morning and literally go straight to the typewriter," says Stephanie Culp, who has written books on organization and time management. "Any little distraction that takes me away from my desk kills it. When I'm writing something large, it takes about three fitful days, and then I'm in the rhythm of it, and I write it. I can still write a book in three weeks."

Here are some tips for getting into a writing habit.

- Start by setting aside an hour or a half hour every day to write.
- Or make a goal to write a set number of words each day.
- Try to write at the same time every day so it will feel peculiar to do something else at that time.
- Write even if you feel uninspired, even if you don't feel ready to write. If you want to be a writer, you must write.

YOUR WRITING PLAN

Often, getting started on a writing project is the hardest part. Most writing jobs, however, can be viewed as a sequence of doable tasks that follow the same general path from beginning to end. If you accomplish each task in order, you can follow the plan to a finished piece. The more you write, the more you will be able to anticipate how much time a particular project will take you.

The planning guidelines below help you break your book project into smaller tasks. Start with individual chapters, and break down the chapters into component parts. Schedule your writing project into your day at specific times, and, with a little luck but more hard work, you'll finish your pieces on time.

If you're a person who resents and resists scheduling, remember that creating a writing plan is intended to help you, not restrict you. The goal is to relieve some stress, organize your life, and make your writing process more efficient. Meeting even mini deadlines can lift your spirits and bolster your confidence. Simply crossing items off to-do lists feels so good that the act in itself becomes a reward and keeps you writing.

Take a look at the following guidelines, which will help you better organize your writing time and, in turn, finish your projects.

1. SET REASONABLE, MEASURABLE GOALS. Even if you're not writing to someone else's external deadline, give yourself your own deadline and treat it seriously. Because you understand the power of the written word, write down a specific goal, with a due date: "Finish chapter by [whatever date]." Some people even establish a punishment and/or reward if they meet or don't meet their self-imposed deadlines: "If I complete chapter five by Friday, I can go to see a movie; if I don't finish on time, I will force myself to scrub the toilets as penance." Well, you don't have to clean the toilets, but a *little* self-flagellation is probably good for you.

2. DIVIDE AND CONQUER. View your writing project not as an overwhelming monolith, but a compilation of many smaller items. The reason hard jobs get bypassed is that they often seem too daunting if they're written as one entry on your list of goals. For example, "Write a book in the next year" can be overwhelming. The scope of the project is so big, and the deadline so far away, that achieving the goal seems impossible. Instead, focus on smaller tasks to do today, tomorrow, this week, and this month to help you reach that goal. You're likelier to accomplish smaller tasks in the near future than a vague goal in the abstract faraway. The tasks help you reach that distant goal step-by-step.

3. CREATE A PLAN OF ORDERED TASKS. Writing down tasks in the order in which they should be done keeps you focused, as well as frees your mind to concentrate on the important things—rather than wasting mental energy trying to remember all the niggling details that must be done each day. Break the task down into manageable steps.

4. SELECT DATES AND STICK TO THEM. "Someday, I'm going to write a book." How many times have we all thought this? Turn your lofty dream into an actual accomplishment by adopting a workable schedule. For example, choose a date on your calendar for beginning your writing project. Make it today. You'll be surprised by how much more quickly you'll work with deadlines, especially if they come with positive and negative consequences. For example, if you miss your deadline at a major magazine, you may never be hired again and may in fact not see your piece in print, which are both negative consequences. But if you make your deadline, determine that you will give yourself a real day off, a massage, an entire chocolate cake, or what have you. Enlist other people to hold you accountable.

5. WORK BACKWARD. The most important step in planning the time for your writing project is this one: On your calendar, mark the story's final due date. (If you don't have a deadline from a publisher, give yourself a reasonable one.) Then figure out when each of the specific items, in reverse order, must be completed if you are to meet that deadline. Allow a little wiggle room in your calendar for the delays that inevitably happen: an interviewee gets the flu and has to postpone by a few days, the computer crashes, etc.

Next to each item on your list, write the time you think it will take to accomplish it and the deadline for completing it. People commonly put far too many items on their to-do list and, as a result, feel defeated when they have to copy uncompleted items from day to day. As William James once wrote, "Nothing is so fatiguing as the eternal hanging on of an uncompleted task." So jot down what you can reasonably expect to accomplish in a day. Some people have success using online organizational websites to help them stay on track. For example, on www.Toodledo.com, users can create goals for themselves, color code them, assign themselves deadlines, prioritize the tasks in a "hotlist," and keep track of the time spent on each project. There are other similar sites as well, including many that are compatible with PDAs and smart phones. (Of course, the old-fashioned system of a pen and a sticky note works fine, too.)

YOUR NOVEL BLUEPRINT

BY KAREN S. WIESNER

Writing a novel and building a house are pretty similar when you think about it. For instance, most builders or homeowners spend a lot of time dreaming about their ideal houses, but there comes a time when they have to wake up to the reality of building by analyzing what they expect from a house and whether the plans they've selected will meet their needs. Architects argue that it's better to build from the inside out.

This is where a home plan checklist comes in handy. This list assembles the key considerations to keep in mind when deciding on a plan, including what are called external monologues, which relate primarily to the outside of a house and its environment, and internal (interior) monologues. (The word monologue, in building, refers to a single facet of overall composition on the inside or outside of a house, such as flooring material or landscaping aspects.) Writers spend a lot of time dreaming about their ideal story. Eventually they have to face reality and analyze whether or not the story will work. Authors, too, usually build from the inside out—in other words, they know what they want at the heart of their stories and they build around that.

This is where a story plan checklist becomes essential, because it targets the key considerations necessary when building a cohesive story that readers will find unforgettable. The checklist has basic external and internal monologues. Monologue, in writing, refers to a single facet of overall composition concerning the internal or external elements, such as conflict and motivation. Generally, these are composed individually in free-form summaries, but they need to develop and grow cohesively.

The story plan checklist can ensure cohesion between character, setting and plot. This checklist connects all the dots between internal and external conflicts, and goals and motivations, thereby guaranteeing the cohesion all stories require. In its most simplified form, a story plan checklist includes free-form summaries (or monologues) covering each of the following:

PART I: THE BASICS

- Working Title
- Working Genre(s)
- Working Point-of-View Specification
- High-Concept Blurb
- Story Sparks
- Estimated Length of Book/Number of Sparks

PART II: EXTERNAL MONOLOGUES

- Identifying the Main Character(s)
- Character Introductions
- Description (outside POV)
- Description (self POV)
- Occupational Skills
- Enhancement/Contrast
- Symbolic Element (character and/or plot defining)
- Setting Descriptions

PART III: INTERNAL MONOLOGUES

- Character Conflicts (internal)
- Evolving Goals and Motivations
- Plot Conflicts (external)

While you're in the beginning stages of forming a story plan, sit down and figure out some of the working details (which may change throughout the process).

THE BASICS OF A STORY CHECKLIST

Title and Genre Specification

First, come up with a preliminary title. All you need here is something to reference the project. While you don't want to lock in your genre too early (stories evolve in unpredictable ways), get started with genre specification. For now, list all the genres this story *could* fit into.

POV Specification

Now start thinking about what point of view you want to use for your book. It's very important to start your story plan checklist with this because the identities of your main characters will play a huge part in your characterization and, subsequently, each of the areas you'll be summarizing on your checklist. Most stories spark with a character who may end up becoming your main character. Your best bet for deciding which character's viewpoint to use: In any scene, stick to the view of the character with the most at stake—the one with the most to lose or gain.

High-Concept Blurb

The high-concept blurb is a tantalizing sentence—or a short paragraph with up to four sentences (one or two is ideal)—that sums up your entire story, as well as the conflicts, goals, and motivations of the main character(s). It's no easy task. Here's a simplified explanation of what your sentence needs to contain:

> (name of character) wants (goal to be achieved) because (motivation for acting), but she faces (conflict standing in the way).

Story Sparks

At this point in the checklist, we've established the basics of the story and we're ready for the beginning spark—so crucial to drawing a reader's interest—followed by the initial external and internal monologues on the story plan checklist. Here you'll begin the cohesive development of your story.

A story spark is something intriguing that ignites a story scenario and carries it along toward fruition. It's that "aha!" moment when a writer thinks up something that completely captures his imagination, and he must see how it unfurls and concludes. I dare say there's not a writer alive who hasn't come up with one idea that blows the mind. However, most don't realize that a story has to have more than one of these sparks to sustain it. A story spark must infuse and reinfuse the story, and a new one must be injected at certain points in order to support the length and complexity of the story.

Most novels up to 75,000 words have three story sparks: one for the beginning, one for the middle, and one for the end. The beginning spark sets up the conflict. The middle spark (or possibly more than one middle spark) complicates the situation. Finally, the end spark resolves the conflict and situation. Short stories, flash fiction, and novellas usually have only one or two sparks (beginning and ending). All of these sparks absolutely must be cohesive to ensure a solid story.

Estimated Length of Book/Number of Sparks

The more sparks you include, the longer and more complex your book will be. It's hard to get around that, so plan accordingly. With that in mind, a story of more than 75,000 words may have an excess of three basic sparks, especially in the middle, because a longer story needs complexity to sustain it. A middle story spark can appear anywhere after the beginning one—before the end—though it usually appears somewhere toward the halfway mark of the book.

To give you a basic idea of how many sparks you'll need for a novel, you can figure that if you have an estimated 250 words per page:

- up to 75,000 words = 300 pages (3 sparks)
- 90,000 words = 360 pages (4 sparks)
- 100,000 words = 400 pages (4+ sparks)

You might also make a note about where you want to place the extra spark(s). In general, extra sparks should come in the beginning or middle of the book.

EXTERNAL MONOLOGUE

Identifying the Main Character(s)

If you have no idea who your main characters are, chances are this particular story needs a lot more brainstorming. Even if your story is more plot oriented than character oriented, brainstorming on your characters until you can fully envision them will help immensely.

In this section of the checklist, simply list the names of the main characters. While a complex book will have more primary and secondary characters, most 75,000- to 90,000-word stories have, at least in terms of main characters, a hero, a heroine, and/or a villain.

Character Introductions

The introduction of a character in the story plan checklist is a springboard into finding out more about him. It's like meeting someone for the first time—you say your name and a few pertinent details about yourself. In the checklist, you list a name and the character's role in the story. Each of your main characters will have particular skills that are shaped specifically for the plot, and that's really what you're introducing in this section of the checklist. Some of these could and should be carefully selected occupational skills, but most will go far deeper than that.

Character Descriptions From Outside Viewpoints

If you're using a third-person omniscient POV, chances are your main characters will be described by other characters. Although this kind of description can include physical appearances, it should always incorporate *impressions* made by your characters upon the ones around them. You can describe the main characters from *each* individual viewpoint in the book. Or your summary can simply encompass the most basic impressions without ascribing them to the person offering them.

Character Descriptions From Self Viewpoint

Very few people describe themselves the same way others do. That makes it even more important for main characters to describe themselves, because the reader gets a strong sense of who your players are with both outside and inside descriptions. In essence, these are like mini first-person profiles. The characters talk about themselves and sometimes give their impressions of others.

Character Occupational Skills

Especially in a work of fiction, what the characters do is pivotal to their personalities and motivations. Just about everything hinges on these interests, hobbies, or jobs. What the character does for a living (or doesn't do, if he doesn't have a job), gives him the necessary skills to deal with the conflicts he's facing in the story. To build the form of cohesion we've been talking about, the character's skills should be directly related to either his internal or external conflicts. In the best-case scenario, his skills will connect to both in some way.

Enhancement/Contrast

If you want to create a truly unique character—and what writer doesn't?—the best way to do so is by providing her personality with enhancements and contrasts. Enhancements are the subtle, balanced, or extreme elements that complement what the writer has already established as traits for that character. Enhancements are personality traits that make a character uniquely larger than life. A writer can't create a truly average Joe because he would be boring to read. In the fictional world, an author may present a hero who seems ordinary at first glance, but something makes him stand apart. This something may not be revealed until later, when his quality is tested.

A contrast, which can also be subtle and quite nuanced, balanced or extreme, is an element that's in opposition to what the writer has already established as traits for that character. A personality contrast is one of the best and most frequently used ways of making a character rise memorably to the spotlight. Few readers want to know a hero who advertises "Hero for Hire—Inquire Within" on a sign outside his office. The hero who's optimistic to a fault, whiter than snow and perfect in every way, is dull.

Flawed (but likeable!) characters are the ones readers root for, because a character without flaws or fears is a character without conflicts. Readers know that true courage is facing what you fear most, pursuing your goals, and not giving up even when there's little chance of success. Readers go crazy for a rough and raw, imperfect hero, with more baggage (of the emotional kind) than a pampered socialite. An eternal pessimist, she wants nothing to do with the title, let alone the job; she's only forced into it by an oft-buried sense of nobility or because something or someone she cares about deeply is in danger.

One way to develop a main character is by introducing another main, secondary or minor character (love interest, family member, friend, or villain) who either enhances or contrasts his personality. You'll see the saving-herself-for-marriage woman paired with a slutty best friend. The street-smart guy with the 4.0 GPA buddy. The happily married accountant with 2.5 kids, living vicariously through his footloose, unfettered college buddy who's been to every corner of the globe on one hair-raising adventure after another.

As a general rule, a character who's an extremist in any regard (whether hard, obsessive, ruthless, or something else) will need someone or something to soften her. In a character who's more balanced, an enhancement or contrast may be more subtle, but should be just as effective. Whatever you do, choose characteristics that'll be necessary at some point in the book, that don't hit the reader over the head, and that advance each story element.

Symbolic Element

Another effective means of developing character is to give him a symbol that defines him, defines the situation he's in, or both. These symbols are sometimes called by the music term *leitmotif*. In the writing world, we use them to associate characters, objects, events, and emotions. Each appearance makes them more intense and meaningful.

Whether you make symbols subtle or well defined, they take on layers of meaning each time they're mentioned, and they become an integral part of the story. As a general rule, every character should have only one associated symbol, but if you have a total of two in the book, one of them should be subtle, while the other should be well defined. The point is to enhance or contrast, not take over the story so the symbol becomes the focal point when you have no desire for it to be.

The symbol can be tangible, in the form of something that defines the character, setting, and plot in some way—a piano, pet, flower, key, map, or necklace—but it doesn't *have* to be. It can be a trait or mannerism the character uses frequently that says something about him and/or develops the character, setting, and plot. It can also be a hobby or vice, or a disability or disfigurement, such as a scar. This tangible or intangible symbol also must be cohesive and not thrown in for the fun of it. In one way or another, it has to enhance or contrast—and thereby develop—your story in deeper ways.

Build in symbols to make your plot, setting, and characters a seamless trinity. The nice thing about incorporating cohesive symbols is that while it's ideal to do this *before* you begin writing the book, it's never too late to come up with them.

Setting Descriptions

Your setting is a basis for building your story—it enhances the characters, conflict, and suspense, and provides a place for all three to flourish. If your setting doesn't match the other elements, you'll work harder at creating fitting characters and plots. Additionally, it will be hard to create the appropriate mood. In any case, you'll have to find a skillful way to play against the contrast of setting.

The importance of creating a setting cohesive with character and plot can be illustrated by imagining different settings for classic novels. What if *Moby Dick*, instead of being set at sea, had been set in, say, a lighthouse? *Moby Dick* wouldn't have been the novel that's become so well known if the setting had been anywhere else but where the author put it.

Describe your setting in such a way that it not only becomes evident how the characters and plot fit there, but supercharges your whole story. What does the setting reveal about the character's personality? What in the setting means the most to him? How will this setting create the stage for conflict and suspense? How can you make it so real that your reader will believe the place actually exists?

The purpose in writing setting descriptions is to allow the reader to "see" what the main character sees, as well as to give a sense of the characters. Very few characters will notice every detail of their surroundings. A character notices the things in his setting that are important to him at the moment. In other words, *focus* the description. Describe only what means the most to the character, what enhances the mood you're attempting to create. If the description doesn't advance some part of the character, setting, or plot development, it's probably unnecessary.

INTERNAL MONOLOGUE

The crucial need for cohesive character, setting, and plot becomes boldly evident in these next steps—which are truly the heart of your story. Life is conflict, and fiction even more so. Without conflict, you don't have a story. For every spark your story has, you'll check off one of each of the following items for all the major characters. This is optional for secondary and minor characters.

Character Conflicts (Internal)

Internal character conflicts are emotional problems brought about by *external* conflicts that make a character reluctant to achieve a goal because of her own roadblocks. They keep her from learning a life lesson and making the choice to act.

In fiction, character conflicts are why plot conflicts can't be resolved. Simply put, the character can't reach his goal until he faces the conflict. The audience must be able to identify with the internal and external conflicts the character faces in order to be involved and to care about the outcome. Character growth throughout the story is key to a satisfactory resolution.

Keep in mind that clearly defined conflicts are ones that won't hit your reader over the head or frustrate her. If you as the writer don't quite understand the conflicts in your story, your instinct will be to compensate by bombarding the story with unfocused ideas. The reader won't find it any easier to sort through them and identify the true conflict. Vaguely defined conflicts usually lead to the reader putting down a book for good.

Your first story spark will usually suggest what the character's conflicts are, and they're almost always based on someone or something threatening what the character cares about passionately. In some instances, a loved one is in jeopardy or something the character wants, needs, or desires above all is at risk of being lost. It's your job to give the character incentives not to give up until everyone is safe and he has what he's fighting for.

Internal and external conflicts depend on each other, and therefore they need to be cohesive. Internal conflicts are all about characters, and external conflicts are all about plot. But keep this in mind, lest confusion creep in: Both internal and external plots belong to the main character(s). After all, if both didn't affect him in some profound way, they wouldn't be conflicts, and therefore wouldn't even be part of his story.

Evolving Goals and Motivation

Goals are what the character wants, needs, or desires above all else. Motivation is what gives her drive and purpose to achieve those goals. Goals must be urgent enough for the character to go through hardship and self-sacrifice.

Multiple goals collide and impact the characters, forcing tough choices. Focused on the goal, the character is pushed toward it by believable, emotional, compelling motivations that won't let him quit. Because he cares deeply about the outcome, his anxiety is doubled. The intensity of his anxiety pressures him to make choices and changes, thereby creating worry and awe in the reader.

Goals and motivations are constantly evolving (growing in depth, intensity, and scope) to fit character and plot conflicts. Your character's goals and motivations will evolve every time you introduce a new story spark because she's modifying her actions based on the course her conflicts are dictating.

Beginning goals and motivations don't generally *change* as much as they become *refined* to the increasing intensity of the conflicts—though they must be clarified in the case of complex novels, especially mysteries that must include red herrings and foils to keep the reader guessing.

Plot Conflicts (External)

External plot conflict is the tangible central or outer problem standing squarely in the character's way. It must be faced and solved. The character wants to restore the stability that was taken from him by the external conflict, and this produces his desire to act. However, a character's internal conflicts will create an agonizing tug-of-war with the plot conflicts. He has to make tough choices that come down to whether or not he should face, act on, and solve the problem.

Plot conflicts must be so urgent as to require immediate attention. The audience must be able to identify with both the internal and external conflicts the character faces in order to be involved enough to care about the outcome. Plot conflicts work hand in glove with character conflicts. You can't have one without the other, and they become more intense and focused the longer the characters struggle. The stakes are raised, choices are limited, and failure and loss are inevitable.

The first layer of a story is created when you plan for and lay the foundation. By using a checklist and analyzing the monologues, you'll be prepared to craft an extremely strong initial layer—one capable of supporting everything you build on it afterward.

KAREN S. WIESNER is the author of *First Draft in 30 Days, From First Draft to Finished Novel,* and more than fifty other titles.

PART 1:

CHARACTERS:

THE STAKEHOLDERS IN YOUR STORY

CHAPTER 1

DRAW CHARACTERS FROM THE STRONGEST SOURCES

BY NANCY KRESS

Every drama requires a cast. The cast may be so huge, as in Leo Tolstoy's *Anna Karenina*, that the author or editor provides a list of characters to keep them straight. Or it may be an intimate cast of two. (In "To Build a Fire," Jack London managed with one person and a dog.) But whatever the size of your cast, you have to assemble it from somewhere.

Where do you get these people? And how do you know they'll make good characters?

You have four key sources: yourself, real people you know, real people you hear about, and pure imagination.

YOURSELF AS CHARACTER: STRAIGHT FROM THE SOURCE

In one sense, every character you create will be yourself. You've never murdered, but your murderer's rage will be drawn from memories of your own extreme anger. Your love scenes will contain hints of your own past kisses and sweet moments. That scene in which your octogenarian feels humiliated will draw on your experience of humiliation in the eighth grade, even though the circumstances are totally different and you're not even consciously thinking about your middle-school years. Our characters' emotions, after all, draw on our own emotions.

Sometimes, however, you will want to use your life more directly in your fiction, dramatizing actual incidents. Charles Dickens used his desperate stint as a child laborer in Victorian England to write *David Copperfield*. Nora Ephron, best-selling author of *Heartburn*, was frank about basing her story of adultery and desertion on her own experiences with husband Carl Bernstein (fiction as public revenge).

Should you create a protagonist based directly on yourself? The problem with this—and it is a very large problem—is that almost no one can view himself objectively on the page. As the writer, you're too close to your own complicated makeup.

It can thus be easier and more effective to use a situation or incident from your life but make it happen to a character who is not you. In fact, that's what the authors cited earlier largely have done. Rachel Samstat, Ephron's heroine, is sassier and funnier than any real person whose husband left her would be. You can still, of course, incorporate aspects of yourself: your love of Beethoven, your quick temper, your soccer injuries. But by applying your own experience to a different protagonist, you can take advantage of your insider knowledge of the situation, and yet gain an objectivity and control that the original intense situation, by definition, did not have.

PEOPLE YOU KNOW AS CHARACTERS: BORROWING TRAITS

Many famous characters are based, in part, on real people. The key words here are in part. Like characters based on yourself, fictional creations based on others seem to be most effective when they're cannibalized. Using people exactly as they are can limit both imagination and objectivity. So instead of using your Uncle Jerome as is, combine his salient traits with those of other acquaintances or with purely made-up qualities. This has several advantages.

First, you can craft exactly the character you need for your plot. Suppose, for instance, that your actual Uncle Jerome is quick tempered and cuttingly witty when angered and remorseful later about the things he said. But your character would work better if he were a stranger to remorse, staying angry in a cool, unrepentant way. Combine Uncle Jerome with your friend Don, who can really hold a grudge. Combining characters gives you flexibility.

This is how Virginia Woolf created Clarissa Dalloway (*Mrs. Dalloway*). Her primary source, according to biographer Quentin Bell, was family friend Kitty Maxse. But Woolf also wrote in her diary that she drew on Lady Ottoline Morrell for Clarissa: "I want to bring in the despicableness of people like Ott." Similarly, Emma Bovary (Gustave Flaubert's *Madame Bovary*) and spymaster George Smiley (John le Carré's series) are composites of people their creators knew.

STRANGERS AS CHARACTERS: ONE SMALL SPARK

In addition to composites of people you know, you can also base characters on people you have only heard or read about. This can work well because you're not bound by many facts. You're making up the character, with the real person providing no more than a stimulus for inspiration.

Say you read about a woman whose will leaves $6 million to a veterinary hospital she visited only once, forty years earlier, with her dying cat. You never met this woman. All you have is the newspaper story. But something about the situation has caught your attention. What kind of person would do that? You begin to imagine this woman: her personality and history, what that cat must have meant to her, why there were no other people important enough to her to leave them any inheritance.

Before long, you've created a full, interesting, and poignant character, someone you might want to write about. Yes, you started with secondhand information—but now the character is fully yours.

As Charlotte Brontë famously remarked, reality should "suggest" rather than "dictate" characters.

CHARACTERS FROM IMAGINATION: FANCY RUNS FREE

Creating purely invented characters is similar to basing characters on strangers. With strangers, a small glimpse into another life sparks the imagination. Made-up characters, too, usually begin with the spark of an idea. The writer then fans the spark into a full-blown person.

William Faulkner, for example, had a sudden mental image of a little girl with muddy drawers up in a tree. That image became Caddy in *The Sound and the Fury*.

EXERCISES

1. Write mini bios for your dream cast

Make a list of characters you either might want to write about or have begun to write about. Three or four will do. Fill out a mini bio for each, listing the basics: age, name, marital status, family ties, occupation, appearance, and general thoughts and feelings.

Now study each mini bio, imagining that character as the star of your story. He will receive the most attention from you and the readers, the highest word count, the emotional arc (if there is one), and the climactic scene. How does the story change when you recast it?

2. Draw inspiration from the news

Read today's newspaper and look for people who spark your imagination. When you find one, write down everything you actually know about this person. Next, fill out a mini bio similar to those you created in the previous exercise, inventing answers to the questions you don't know. Is this someone you'd like to build a story around?

3. Recast a classic

Pick a novel or story you like and know well, and list the major characters. Look at each one and think how different the story would be with a different star. Take, for instance, *Sleeping Beauty*. If the princess were not the heroine but instead a featured player (maybe even a bit player), who might star? Perhaps the prince, with the story becoming his struggle to find a bride. Or perhaps the bad fairy who put a spell on the princess—whatever happened to her? In fact, some of these stories have been written. Same plot, different stars.

FINAL THOUGHTS ON CREATING A PROTAGONIST

Characters usually present themselves encased in at least the rudiments of a fictional situation. Caddy is up in a tree (why?). The deceased lady has left $6 million to an animal hospital. You have something here to work with. Your next task is to look hard at this character/situation in order to decide if the character is strong enough to sustain a story.

NANCY KRESS is the author of twenty-eight books, including *Write Great Fiction: Characters, Emotion & Viewpoint*. Her work has garnered her four Nebula Awards and two Hugo Awards.

CHAPTER 2

EMOTION-DRIVEN CHARACTERS

BY DAVID CORBETT

The source and exact nature of the curious phenomena we refer to as *characters* remains something of a mystery, but the craft of characterization is not.

Although it's clearly a cause for celebration—or at least relief—when a character appears in the mind's eye fully formed, the reality is that for most of us, this is a rare occurrence. Certain techniques are required to will our characters to life. We need to draw on the unconscious, memory, the imagination, and the Muse until our characters quicken, assume clear form, and with hope, begin to act of their own accord.

Can this process—so inherent to the success of any novel—really be condensed into a single method? In my experience as both writer and writing instructor, the answer is, to some extent, yes. The key is first to understand what your characters require from you in order to come to life and then to determine how you can draw on your best available resources to give them what they need.

The most compelling characters are those who appear internally consistent and yet are capable of surprise. In my own work, I've found that the art of crafting such fully realized characters can be boiled down to four crucial elements: a driving need, desire, ambition, or goal; a secret; a contradiction; and vulnerability. Let's take a closer look at each one.

A DRIVING NEED, DESIRE, OR AMBITION

The fundamental truth to characterization is that characters must want something, and the stronger the want, the more compelling the resulting drama. This is because desire intrinsically creates *conflict*, the primordial goo in which character is formed.

Take, for example one of the most memorable characters in American literature—Blanche Dubois, from Tennessee Williams' *A Streetcar Named Desire*. At the start of the story, Blanche has lost her family home and has been left with nowhere to stay. Desperate, she has come to New Orleans to find her sister, Stella, and ask to be taken in.

This is a perfect demonstration that simply by giving the character a deep-seated need or want, you can automatically create conflict, for the world is not designed to answer our desires as easily as we might hope.

A SECRET

For your character, a secret is that inclination or trait (such as a psychological disposition to dishonesty, violence, sexual excess, or the abuse of alcohol or drugs, to name a few) or an incident from the past that, if revealed, would change forever the character's standing in her world, among co-workers, neighbors, friends, family, lovers. Secrets inform us of what our characters have to lose, and why.

Drawing on the example of Blanche Dubois, her secret is that through drink and illicit sexual liaisons, she has become so emotionally and physically dissipated she could not hold on to the family home.

We are our own best source for understanding secrets. We know our own, and if we're insightful, we understand how they affect our behavior—specifically, how they make us afraid.

A CONTRADICTION

We all know people who are both shy and rude, cruel but funny, bigoted but protective. This complexity, which seems to particularly manifest itself during times of stress or conflict, is what can make a person inherently unpredictable, setting the stage for the kind of surprising behavior that can keep readers enthralled, wondering what might happen next.

Our senses and minds are tuned to focus on irregularities—the thing that doesn't quite fit, doesn't make sense, or is simply changing. This is an evolutionarily adaptive trait; it helps in analyzing the environment for threats. But it also attunes us to whatever is unusual in what we perceive; contradictions reveal what we couldn't predict, the enigma, the surprise.

Again, let's look at how this applies to Blanche Dubois: She is desperate and weak, hopelessly vain, with an alcoholic's capacity for denial and delusion—but she is also fiercely proud and resourceful with a surprising steeliness. It's contradictions like these that can automatically pique a reader's interest.

VULNERABILITY

Nothing draws us into a character more than her vulnerability. When people appear wounded or in need of our help, we are instantly drawn to them—it's a basic human reflex. We may also sometimes be repelled or frightened, but either way, the fact of the matter is that injury to another person instantly triggers a strong response.

Obviously vulnerability may be the result of the character's secret: He is afraid of being found out. Or it may come from the intensity of his need or want—because, as we all know, desire can render us naked in a fundamental way. For your character, the ambition and focus inherent in a strong desire can imply some form of inner strength, while at the same time rendering the character vulnerable to being deprived of what he most wants.

Blanche's desperation to find a safe place makes her vulnerable, as does the tawdry nature of her secrets, which threaten to shame her beyond redemption if revealed. In other words, needs or desires, secrets, contradictions, and vulnerability are almost always interconnected.

DEEPENING CHARACTERIZATIONS

Often our characters first appear to us as we flesh out the idea for a story. But characters who emerge from story ideas can often be flat or two-dimensional; this is because at that early stage, they serve the purpose of filling a role, rather than acting as independent beings with needs and fears and affections and concerns "outside the story."

Compelling characters are not cogs in the machine of your plot; they are human beings to whom the story happens.

Some stories *begin* with the characters, of course, and the narrative emerges from an exploration of their needs, their defenses, their secrets and contradictions, or some problem they face. The trick in those cases is making sure the narrative doesn't meander, creating, as writer Philip Larkin called it, "a beginning, a muddle, and an end."

But more often in mainstream fiction and especially genre fiction, the novel begins with a story idea, and the characters need to be fleshed out to keep them from being stock players in the drama. We might wonder how many uniquely memorable world-weary detectives there can be, for example—and yet every year at least one more seems to emerge from the wave of crime novels crashing onto bookstore shelves. It takes skill and insight to breathe life into stock characters, something too often dismissed by those who disdain genre fiction as inferior.

So how do we flesh out our characters when they arise from the needs of our stories or when they otherwise lack the specificity, uniqueness, or power necessary to engage a reader (or the writer)? The best inspiration often comes from within us—and from our experiences with the people in our lives.

Real-Life Characters

Near the end of his life, John Updike wrote a poem titled "Peggy Lutz, Fred Muth," in which he thanked his childhood friends and classmates—the "beauty" and "bully," the "fatso" and others—"for providing a sufficiency of human types ... all a writer needs."

Whether we know it or not, our minds and hearts are populated by all the characters we will ever need—though we may disassemble them and rearrange the parts into composites for variation.

To fully tap this potential, begin by reflecting upon the following real people in your life—jot down their names, fix them in your mind, remember a few details about their lives, their physical appearances, the effect they've had on you, and anything else you think would be important if you were to describe them to someone who didn't already know them.

Include in your exploration:

- A family member you feel particularly close to
- A family member you particularly dislike, or from whom you're estranged
- Your closest friend from childhood with whom you've lost touch
- Your closest friend from childhood with whom you're still in contact
- A stranger whose path crossed yours this past week
- A person you know personally and admire
- A person you know personally and fear
- The love who got away
- The love you wished had gotten away
- Your first love
- Your greatest love
- Your greatest childhood nemesis
- Your greatest adulthood nemesis
- The person from childhood who annoyed you the most
- The person who annoys you the most now
- Your favorite neighbor
- Your least-favorite neighbor
- Your favorite co-worker
- Your least-favorite co-worker
- Your postman or someone else you deal with on a "business" level daily

- An older person who has inspired you
- A child who fascinates you
- Someone for whom you harbor a secret crush or feel sexual attraction
- Someone you believe has a crush on you
- A person who believed in you
- A person who thought you would never amount to anything
- A person whose life you would never trade for your own

The list can go on, of course; it's limited only by one's own inventiveness. But writing out such a list provides a larger cast of characters than we originally might have realized we possessed. We can sometimes unwittingly get into ruts, writing variations on the same character over and over—the overbearing parent, the needy lover, the insufferable phony, the lonely aunt. The value of using people we know to inspire our characters is that we already see them so vividly and specifically.

Emotional Triggers

Of course, we know a great deal about the people in our lives, but we don't know everything—and this is why real people provide excellent but not perfect source material for characters. We will also have to draw on our own lives, at least as a starting point, to fathom a character's inner world.

It often surprises me how frequently writers, especially young writers, fail to explore the rich veins of emotion they possess in their own lives, so they can translate that to their characterizations.

The most important emotional incidents to explore in a character's life—and one's own—are:

> **THE MOMENT OF GREATEST FEAR**: This is perhaps the most important emotional trigger, because almost all of our limitations, failures, frustrations, and disappointments—and thus our secrets and vulnerabilities—can be traced back to or relate to some fundamental fear.

THE MOMENT OF GREATEST COURAGE: This may be physical valor, moral isolation, or simply persisting in the face of some dread.

THE MOMENT OF GREATEST SORROW: Death, grief, loss.

THE MOMENT OF GREATEST JOY: It's strange how nebulous moments of joy can seem—and what a loss. At what stage in your character's life (or in your own) did the golden moment occur? What's happened since?

THE WORST FAILURE: Ouch, I know, but don't shun this moment; from a writer's point of view, it's golden (as are all our travails, sorrows, embarrassments, and screwups—embrace them).

THE MOMENT OF DEEPEST SHAME: Shame is connected to self-image, and this moment will be when that image was seriously undermined in a particularly personal way in front of others.

THE MOMENT OF MOST PROFOUND GUILT: This involves some violation of a moral code. It may also make us ashamed, but guilt involves having knowingly done something wrong.

THE MOMENT OF MOST REDEMPTIVE FORGIVENESS: If you've been forgiven for some serious wrong, it's not likely you've forgotten it. It's permitted you to regain your place with some crucial loved one.

When performing this exercise, my students sometimes get caught up on trying to think of the "greatest" such moments. Don't fall into this needless trap. Instead think merely of one moment (presumably of many) of particularly strong impact in any one category.

TAPPING YOUR EMOTIONAL TRIGGERS

The following are some additional prompts to key significant emotional moments—some in the form of memories, and others in the form of statements that may have been said either by you or to you—that can help enrich your characterizations.

- First time as an adult you said, "I love you."
- A time you said, "I love you," and wished you hadn't.
- A time you were struck, beaten, or defeated.
- A time you struck, beat, or defeated someone else.
- Best time you ever spent with a family member.
- Best time you ever spent with a stranger.
- "Please stop. I'm scared."
- "Don't hurt me."
- "Give that to me."
- "I'm telling."
- "Do as you're told."
- "I can't believe I just said/did that."
- "I could kill you."
- "I'm not that kind of person."
- "You can't ask me to do that."

It's important to be as specific as possible in fleshing out these scenes. The devil is in the details, as they say. And in this instance, the devil is your friend.

Obviously plumbing your own life will not provide access to the whole of your characters' inner lives (unless your characters inhabit the same world you do). Rather these moments provide touchstones, points of access to begin the exploration into similar moments in your characters' lives—a necessary but not sufficient precondition for a compelling portrayal.

Each of these triggers a vulnerability or a secret, perhaps a desire, maybe even a contradiction, depending on context. By envisioning these scenes in your characters' lives, after first exploring them in your own, you gain key insights into the formative episodes in their emotional lives, and, with hope, begin to see them more vividly in your mind's eye, the better to render them on the page.

The key is to intuit the character so distinctly she seems capable of acting on her own volition. Once this happens—and as I said at the outset, it's a mystery how or why it does—you're capable of beginning the dialogue that will form your story, asking your character: Where are you going? Why? How will you get there? With whom? And who will you have become when the journey is over?

DAVID CORBETT (davidcorbett.com) is the author of four critically acclaimed novels, most recently *Do They Know I'm Running?* His story "Pretty Little Parasite" was selected for *Best American Mystery Stories 2009.*

CHAPTER 3

DEPICTING CONVINCING RELATIONSHIPS

BY ELIZABETH SIMS

The very first novel I, aged twenty-something, wrote, is unpublished and will stay that way. An ensemble coming-of-age story of four teenagers, its weaknesses are legion: tame story line, thin action, unimaginatively rendered settings, hackneyed themes (though I will say the dialogue wasn't bad). Having now published seven novels, I look back on that manuscript and realize that underlying the shortcomings I just mentioned lies its principal flaw: poor character development. The kids just don't pop.

So I've been pleased to read reviews of my latest novels (the Rita Farmer mysteries) that praise the characterization—and I've been struck by the number of them that cite the realism of my characters' relationships. While plot is important, good characters can make or break your book. And the best characters are those who relate convincingly not just to their world, but to one another.

Let's consider, to start, the categories of relationships we might write in our fiction:

- Romantic
- Parent/Child
- Siblings
- Aggressor/Victim
- Rivals/Adversaries
- Best Friends

- Boss/Employee
- Caregiver/Receiver
- Cop/Criminal
- Partners (in business, crime, etc.)
- Slave/Master
- Human/Environment
- Human/God
- Human/Pet
- Casual Acquaintances
- ... and so many more.

Everybody has relationships. In your fiction—as in life—you want to take those connections beyond the obvious. Like descriptions, relationships can lapse into cliché. Think of the hero and his wisecracking sidekick, the frustrated housewife and the handsome neighbor, the befuddled father and his precocious child, the renegade cop and the stupid chief.

When you create your characters, go ahead and give them meaty biceps or thin shanks, blue eyes, hemophilia, courage, a ranch, neuroses, penchants for vegetarianism or anarchy or Lawrence Welk or scuba. Do this until you know who they are.

Then explore who they are beyond themselves.

Here's how.

1. MAKE THEM STOP AND THINK

Introspection is the easiest and clearest way to develop your characters' relationships. Make your characters think about their bonds; make them challenge their own thoughts and feelings. *I love him, but why? What's the real reason I hate her? What needs to happen so I can get over this?*

Shakespeare was one of the first masters of introspection, via his soliloquies. When Hamlet considers the pros and cons of avenging his father's murder, you think and feel right along with him. You ask yourself the same moral questions. Your heart catches when he fails to take action, and it catches again when he does act. The central issue to him is honor, and only in the context of alliances can honor exist.

Today's introspective scenes might not be as easily identifiable as those soliloquies were, but they've evolved right along with storytelling styles over the years. Take, for example, Michael Chabon's novelette *The Final Solution*, which merges the Holocaust with British-style crime busting through an elderly Sherlock Holmes (though the character remains unnamed throughout the story). In Sir Arthur Conan Doyle's mysteries, the original Holmes never reveals himself at all; we come to know him only through the eyes of Dr. Watson, the first-person narrator. But in *The Final Solution*, Chabon affords himself complete license to the great detective's brain and heart simply by choosing the third-person point of view. In his portrayal, we see that Holmes is a particularly introspective hero, less self-assured than he used to be (though no less sharp), beset by doubts and petty worries, struggling with old age and the tropes of contemporary life. Most important, we see how hungry he is for human connections: *Will they like me? Will they understand me? Who am I against? Who am I for?* These questions motivate him as the story progresses.

So take a little time to tell your readers what your characters are thinking about the others. Say you're writing a story in which a son kills his abusive father. What agonies would he go through, if the act were premeditated? And if it weren't, what hell would he experience afterward?

Instead of having the son stand next to a tree and tell it his troubles, you might write something like this:

> Roger Jr. fingered the five-dollar bill in his pocket and decided to buy the breakfast burrito instead of two Hostess fruit pies, same price. As he paid the zit-faced clerk, he wondered if he would meet his father in hell. If, after tonight, a bus ran over him, Roger Jr., would he go to hell instantly or would there be some kind of processing period? Would the pain of

being dragged under a bus be worse than waking up in hell? Do they drag people under buses in hell? Would his father be the one to drive the bus, even? Drive the bus around and around the lake of fire or whatever. Roger Sr. would rightly go to hell for what he'd done—for what he'd done for so many years, over and over—but maybe he could work his way out someday. After half of infinity, maybe. Whereas Roger Jr. would stay in hell forever because he'd be a murderer. "You're still the dumbest one in the family," his dad would say in hell, one more time, crookedly, what with half of his face blown off. Let's at least be sure to blow off the full face tonight.

2. GIVE THEM STRONG OPINIONS

Some writers seem reluctant to give their characters strong opinions—maybe because we don't like to seem overbearing ourselves. True, being overbearing may be a flaw, but in fiction, flaws are good. Give your characters flaws that can be fatal. For my series protagonist Rita Farmer, it's her tendency to lose her temper. Her anger flares, and before you know it she's doing something she'll regret. On the other hand, her anger can save her—if it comes up at just the right time. And her fury has much to do with her opinions.

In the opening pages of Ernest Hemingway's *The Sun Also Rises*, the protagonist, Jake Barnes, does nothing but tell all about another character, Robert Cohn, giving opinion after opinion. From the way Jake describes Robert and his accomplishments, we learn some things about Robert, but we learn a lot more about the way Jake thinks. He clearly despises Robert, yet we soon see that the men are also friends, at least of a sort. We sense that they may become rivals. Why? We want to keep reading to find out.

Much of the story's power comes from the feelings the characters have for—and against—one another. We identify with their love, and we're appalled by their callousness. We are also educated by it. *This is how some people live*. Is it shallow, or perhaps deeper than it really seems? Desirable or undesirable? We hold ourselves up to its mirror.

In your own work, remember that every narrator has a personality. Let that narrator's opinions inform her character. And by all means, let characters gossip among themselves. An exchange as simple as this one between two teenagers can paint a sharp little picture:

> "Jeanette has zero self-respect," said Wendy, shoving two skinny sixth-graders aside so she could be first in the cafeteria line.
>
> "Yeah," agreed Dani, crowding behind her, giving an extra shove to one of the littler kids, then looking to Wendy for approval. Then, after a pause, "I saw her making out with Tony after the game Friday."
>
> Wendy whipped around. "Why didn't you tell me? He told me he went home!"
>
> It wasn't true, but Dani did stuff like this over and over. She didn't know why, except that it felt good to get other people in trouble.

3. PLAY A GAME OF RISK

Make one character sacrifice or risk something for another. Countless spiritual scriptures, myths, classics, and modern tales exploit the heart-clutching moment of a character dying to save others, or for a cause. But equally compelling can be a character merely *risking* his life for another.

In Margaret Mitchell's *Gone With the Wind*, Scarlett O'Hara puts everything at stake by remaining in Atlanta as Sherman's army advances, in order to help her sister-in-law Melanie Wilkes through a near-fatal childbirth. The day drags on, it's hot as hell, Melanie writhes in pain, the doctor is busy with thousands of wounded soldiers, most everybody else has fled the city, and the Yankees are coming. Scarlett doggedly mops the pain sweat from Melanie's body as the fear sweat from her own soaks her dress. Mitchell could have cut this scene without really impacting her main plot, but instead she positively *hammers* us with it. Why? Because *it's a test of Scarlett's character.*

Granted, Scarlett had promised Melanie's husband, Ashley, to look after her while he was away fighting. But at the risk of her own life? After all, Scarlett wants Ashley for herself. How easy it would be to let Melanie and the unborn baby, well, sort of die!

No. We need to know that Scarlett wouldn't abandon Melanie even when her own life is at stake, because we need to know that Scarlett isn't merely a hard bitch who gets what she wants. If that was all there was to her, she'd be fine as a stereotype in a soap opera, but she wouldn't be an immortal character. We would not root for her in spite of her flaws.

Make one of your characters willing to die for another, and put him in position where that could happen. Your readers will curse their alarm clocks in the morning.

4. ADD A HYPOTENUSE

Make triangles. Did you notice something about the relationships I listed earlier? They're all dyads. Most relationships start out that way, but too often writers stay stuck on dyadic relationships to the exclusion of more complex ones. Consider F. Scott Fitzgerald's *The Great Gatsby.* Gatsby's relationship with Daisy is memorable only because of the huge hulking reason they can't be together: Daisy's husband, Tom Buchanan.

A lesser author than Fitzgerald might have skimmed over the character of Tom. The very fact of his existence, plus the fact that Daisy took a vow to be true to him, should be enough—and it would've been, for a dime novel of the day. But it wasn't enough for Fitzgerald. He enlarged the character of Tom by giving him a relationship with the narrator, Nick Carraway. Old college acquaintances, their relationship intensifies during the novel, and it's through Nick's eyes that we see Tom's strength, his selfishness, his cruelty and—in a powerful moment when he tries to win Daisy's heart back from Gatsby—his tenderness.

Our emotions are not rational, and our relationships aren't, either. This is why romantic obsession is a terrifically handy tool for the writer (sexual attraction being the great motivator of millions of bad decisions—and sometimes, of course, of salvation, when it works out). Consider adding a sturdy hypotenuse to your two main characters and see what happens. The third party doesn't even have to be human—it can be an animal, a career, an addiction, a call to adventure, an obligation—anything that gets in the way of the cozy pairing you began with.

5. LEVERAGE THE GROUP

As a writer, you're a student of human nature. When I was a retail store manager (prior life), I learned that the two games groups like to play the most are Ain't It Awful and Kill the Leader. People behave differently in groups than they do otherwise, the most obvious and horrifying example being a mob, which is capable of violence far beyond the natural inclination of most individuals because the mob serves not merely as a shield, but as an excuse. The relationships between individuals in a group—whether a clique of three or an organization of thousands—are endlessly varied, shifting, and fascinating.

Three works that use group dynamics to gripping effect are the novels *A High Wind in Jamaica* by Richard Hughes, *The Help* by Kathryn Stockett and the play *Glengarry Glen Ross* by David Mamet. In the first, a group of children fall into the clutches of pirates, and what follows between them serves to illustrate that the veneer of civilization is thinner than most of us can bear to admit. In the second, protagonists from both sides of the divide in segregated Mississippi demonstrate that while groups can greatly influence individuals, the right individual can exercise great power over a group.

And Mamet's play reinforces all of those messages while giving us a spectacle of testosterone-fueled ruthlessness, set in a Chicago real estate office. Competition for money and success drives the men to cruelty, lying, and thieving as one aligns himself against the other, pairs align against individuals, and the group alternately pits itself against the boss, then casts itself in profane servility to him.

One small, subtle moment (which was expanded in the film version of the play) shows how even a passing reference to a relationship can deepen a character's motivation. Levene, a struggling salesman, is desperate to get better customer leads, and in pleading with his boss, he finally says, "My daughter …" and trails off.

That's it. No manipulative words beyond that. Just the simple mention of a relationship—a family obligation, the obligation of a father to a daughter, the obligation perhaps freighted by some special, unnamed circumstance about the daughter—helps the audience understand where Levene is coming from. He is needy, and he isn't above exploiting his own pain.

How can group dynamics deepen your characters? The key is to remember that in a group, relationships and alliances are ever changing, depending on circumstances. And we know circumstances never remain the same. Figure out how the underdog might transform into a tyrant, or how a fun little secret can become a public threat.

6. BEFRIEND AMBIGUITY

If we wish to write clearly, how can ambiguity be okay? I think Patricia Highsmith is just about the best there is when it comes to harnessing ambiguity in relationships. In her Edgar-winning novel *The Talented Mr. Ripley*, the relationship between the two main characters is sexually nebulous, and the same goes for her *Strangers on a Train*.

This was likely due in part to the mores of the time (both were published in the 1950s), but this strangely explicated ambiguity works well to make things feel unsettled, ulterior. Tom Ripley murders Dickie Greenleaf out of a twisted sense of possession, if not love. This is so much more compelling than if Tom had merely murdered Dickie for personal gain, a shallow friendship their only connection.

In your own work, resist the urge to overexplain relationships. Everybody instinctively understands there's more than meets the eye. In every adult, there's a bit of a child. In every cop, there's a bit of a criminal. In every sadist, there's a bit of a masochist. And in every human, there's a bit of a beast—and a bit of a god. Use that knowledge to your advantage.

7. TAP INTO THE POWER OF A GRUDGE

Mythology and folklore are chock-full of motivational grudges, as is life. All of us have probably clung to a grudge against somebody for a while, fantasizing various retribution scenarios, but what kind of personality *acts* on such an impulse to the point of destructive vengeance? The sort we know too well from true-crime books and *America's Most Wanted*–type TV: a person whose self-esteem is lower than whale crap, but whose ego is as big as Kilauea. Grudge-holding characters have fueled a diverse range of popular tales, from Edgar Allan Poe's "The Cask of Amontillado" to Dan Brown's *The Da Vinci Code.*

Consider Stephen King's *Carrie.* King downplays the quality of this, his first novel, but it continues to fascinate and terrify readers. Teenaged Carrie is taunted by her classmates for being odd, dominated as she is by her warped, religious-nut mother. The other kids push her to the limit, not knowing she's developed telekinetic powers.

The story works so well because Carrie's eventual murderous rage is believable. And it's believable because in devising ways for Carrie's schoolmates to torment her, King put her into situations of intolerable shame and degradation, culminating in the pig's-blood drenching at the prom. You read that and even though you're basically a mild-mannered person, you find yourself whispering, "Kill them, Carrie—kill all those bastards!"

Your readers are going to expect any grudge you create for your characters to be *that* powerful. So do what King did: Create a character with a sensitive spirit and make him suffer injustices that would make anyone's stomach shrivel.

Then sit back and enjoy the fun.

8. DON'T OVERLOOK EVERYDAY INTERACTIONS

If you own a car and are at all like me, you can drive for hundreds of miles without reacting to the other idiots in their cars. Somebody cuts you off and you shrug or even smile indulgently. But then, one day, something is different inside you. Somebody zooms too close and your anger surges beyond all reason. You want to run him down and flatten him into the pavement. You want to bump his vehicle off a cliff. You want him to *pay.*

You don't even know his name.

Yes, a chance encounter with a stranger can be powerful enough to transform a moment, or a day, even to change your life. Just think what you can do in your fiction, with a little planning and imagination.

Similarly, acquaintanceships can bolster your characterizations. An acquaintanceship can serve to illustrate a character trait, or it can foment enormous change in a whole cast of characters. Good examples are found in Jim Thompson's noir novel *The Grifters.* In the first pages, the character Roy Dillon chisels some money out of a shopkeeper, a stranger. But the shopkeeper catches on and beats him up, setting off an entire chain of events surrounding Roy's recovery.

Let your characters approach others, glance off them, then continue on different trajectories. After all, this is what happens in real life. It's all in the relationships.

When crafting your characters' relationships, let the yin-yang symbol be your guide. You've seen this circle made of equal parts black and white, with a drop of each color in the other. No relationships are clear-cut, nor are any one-sided. Leaven the love with a little fear, or maybe even hate.

If you spend some time thinking about relationships in this way, you'll see opportunities to develop your characters further than you ever imagined. Because characters *are* people, just like us. Relationships reveal the various roles we play, the ever-changing masks we all wear, and the yearnings that expose our hearts.

ELIZABETH SIMS (elizabethsims.com) is a contributing editor for *Writer's Digest* Magazine. She's the award-winning author of seven novels and many short stories, poems, and articles.

CHAPTER 4

CREATE THE (IM)PERFECT HEROIC COUPLE

BY LEIGH MICHAELS

Romantic heroes and heroines are a bit different from the sort of people we run into every day. These main characters have their flaws, but overall they're just a little nicer, just a little brighter, just a little quicker, just a little better than real people. They're allowed their petty moments, but in important matters they take the moral high ground.

Of course, standards vary by category and type of story. The hero of a mainstream stand-alone novel can get by with things the hero of a sweet, traditional category romance wouldn't dream of doing. But even the bad-boy hero will have good aspects to his character, and the reader won't have to dig too deeply to find them. The chick-lit heroine may have some rough edges, but deep down she's not the sort to be cruel, even to people who deserve it.

How exactly do you go about uniting your hero and heroine? When creating the perfect romantic couple, consider the following.

1. USE IMPERFECTIONS TO SHOW DEPTH

To be real, your characters have to be imperfect. They must have problems, or no one will be interested in reading about them. But while heroes and heroines have almost certainly created some of their own problems, they haven't done so out of stupidity or short-sightedness, or the reader will have trouble empathizing. There is usually a good motive—sometimes even a noble one—for the action that leads them into trouble.

The problems the characters face are important to them—life-changing, in fact—but must also be important to the reader. A story about whether Susie can get Joe to improve his table manners isn't likely to keep the reader on the edge of her chair.

Main characters should grow and change during the course of a story. Since they are facing life-altering problems and situations, it makes sense that these difficulties will change their perspectives, attitudes, and outlooks on life.

The too-perfect character has no room to grow and mature as he deals with the problems he's going to face. But even in their imperfection, main characters have to remain likeable, even admirable, in order to be worthy of a story.

2. STEER CLEAR OF MEAN

Heroes and heroines are unfailingly kind to those who are less powerful than they are.

They are gentle; even if Aunt Agnes incessantly talks about her health, they don't snap at her or treat her like a nuisance. Heroes and heroines don't kick the dog no matter how angry they are. And every last one of them has an honorary degree in how to get along with a kid while raising him to be a genius.

Heroes and heroines don't gossip, and they don't generally take delight in the troubles of others, even when it's the Other Woman and she deserves it.

They're rude only to each other, and even then, they're not hateful or vicious. Wisecracks and smart remarks are acceptable; cruel taunts are another thing entirely.

Heroes and heroines don't lie, but they are allowed to be tight-fisted with the truth. The hero, in particular, can be deliberately misleading if his motive in not telling all the facts is to protect the heroine.

3. AVOID ADULTERY

Heroes and heroines don't commit adultery. They may get divorced, but they do not enter into a new relationship while there is still a legal or moral commitment to a previous partner.

This restriction is largely a matter of common sense. If a person has so little respect for a spouse that he has an affair—whether it's physical or emotional—then it's difficult to believe that he would be any more faithful to the new love.

To a lesser degree, the same rule applies to other emotional commitments. A heroine who is engaged is most likeable if the engagement is broken off as soon as she recognizes the attraction to the new partner.

Whether the previous relationship was ended by a divorce, a broken engagement, a jilting, or a partner's death, the character does not enter a new relationship until there has been adequate time to heal. Rebound relationships often don't last in real life, and they're not convincing in fiction.

The length of time needed to recover will depend on the nature of the relationship. It will take much longer to grieve the death of a partner in a solid marriage than it will to get over a steady date who suddenly decided he wanted to see other women.

4. BALANCE THE RELATIONSHIP

Main characters who are similar in style, in the amount of power they have over their situation, and in their degree of outspokenness create a nice balance in the structure of the romance. That doesn't mean they should act the same, or that they must be equal in every way—just that they should both have areas and times where they're stronger.

If the hero has the heroine completely under his thumb, where she's helpless to act or to put him in his place, then he may look more sadistic than heroic. Pairing a heroine who's an in-your-face screamer with a hero who's the silent type may make the heroine look like a verbal abuser. A hero who makes patronizing remarks about a heroine who simply absorbs the insults is annoying, but if she's able to talk back to him in the same sort of way, they're in proportion. (They may both be annoying in that case, but at least the reader can be equally annoyed.)

If one of your characters has a great deal of power over the other, look for ways to even up the competition. The romance is far more satisfying when the power between the characters is like a teeter-totter—sometimes she's on the high end, sometimes he is, but the reader doesn't know from minute to minute who's going to have the upper hand.

LEIGH MICHAELS is the author of nearly one hundred books, including eighty contemporary novels, three historical romance novels, and more than a dozen non-fiction books, including *On Writing Romance*.

DEVELOPING YOUR HERO AND HEROINE

Answer the following questions for each of your main characters. It's usually most productive to take one character at a time, but if you run into difficulty answering the questions about one, try switching over to the other for a while.

As you answer the questions, look for points of agreement and disagreement between the characters. For instance, if he's from a big family and she's from a small one, how might that create problems?

- What is this character's name?
- What is her age and birth date?
- What does she look like?
- What is her astrological sign? Does it matter to her?
- What are her parents like?
- Does she have brothers and sisters?
- How important are her family relationships?
- Where does she live? (Urban? Small town? Rural?)
- Why did she choose to live there?

- Does she live in an apartment? House? What type or style? Did she choose the residence, and why?
- Does she live by herself? With others?
- What are her important material possessions?
- What are her hobbies?
- What is her education?
- What is her job? How does she feel about her work?
- Is this a long-term career or just a job?
- What does she want to be doing in twenty years?
- If she has unexpected free time, what does she do?
- How does she feel about the opposite sex?
- What is her relationship status? Single? Divorced?
- Does she have children?
- Who is her best friend? Why?
- Who is her worst enemy? Why?
- How would a former date describe her?
- What one event has made her who she is today?
- How does that turning point in the character's life relate to the other main character in the story?
- What trait does she have that she wants to keep secret from the world?
- What does she like most about her life?
- What does she dislike most about her life?
- What would this character die to defend?
- What are her most likable and unlikable traits?
- As the story begins, what is her main problem?
- What does she do that makes this problem worse?
- Who is this person's love interest?
- What qualities in the other main character are most attractive to this person?
- What is her ideal happy ending?
- What reaction do you want readers to have to her?
- Why should the reader care about her?

Now that you know this information, you might be tempted to work it all into your story. But just because you know something about a character doesn't mean your readers need to know it. Select only those facts that best illustrate the person—the ones that have a strong impact upon the story—to share with readers, and leave the rest out.

CHAPTER 5

CHOOSING YOUR CHARACTER'S PROFESSION

BY MICHAEL J. VAUGHN

Here's the situation: You're at a party. You've just met someone. Names are exchanged—and then you face the daunting task of beginning a conversation. What are the next words out of your mouth?

"So ... what do you do?"

Why is this? Simple—a person's job provides a readily accessible, noninvasive point of inquiry that's rife with conversational possibilities. Just one tidbit can inspire common ground, follow-up questions, insights on character, avenues to humor and possibly even free advice.

Just as employment is such a big part of our lives, it's a big part of your characters' lives, as well. Even when career factors are far from the main thrust of your narrative, carefully choosing and researching occupations for your fictional heroes opens up a wealth of possibilities for enriching a story. Let's examine how some of today's best authors have done just that.

FRAMING THE POINT OF VIEW

In David Guterson's novel *East of the Mountains*, elderly widower Ben Givens discovers that he's dying of colon cancer. His reaction to this news is largely determined by the important fact that Givens is a retired heart surgeon:

> Like all physicians, he knew the truth of such a verdict; he knew full well the force of cancer and how inexorably it operated.

> He grasped that nothing could stop his death, no matter how hopeful he allowed himself to feel, no matter how deluded ... Better to end his life swiftly, cleanly, and to accept that there would be no thwarting the onslaught of the disease.

By making his protagonist a doctor, Guterson sets up the philosophical framework for his hero's quest: finding the best way to die. He also provides the opportunity for Givens to keep the disease a secret and, thereby, make his suicide look like an accident.

MAKING THE STORY WORK

In his short-story collection *Working Men*, Michael Dorris uses work not just as a point of reference, but often as the central conflict, as well. In the story "Jeopardy," drug salesman Don Banta's main task—obtaining physician signatures acknowledging their conversations—means that he spends most of his waking hours chitchatting medical receptionists. During one conversation, he talks to Dee Dee, whose son suffers from allergies:

> Lots of pollen around, huh? Hey, maybe your little boy ... That's not him in the frame on your desk? I can't believe how he's grown. No ... Maybe he could try this new inhaler. It's a miracle worker. Just remember, you don't know where you got it, right, because I could get in major trouble and it's just because we're friends, you know, and I had allergies myself as a kid.

Banta's pathetic life is brought to a devastating nadir when he learns that his father has died. Stuck in a motel room with no one to talk to, he calls Dee Dee—and learns that the inhaler he used to bribe his way into her office has saved her son from a near-fatal allergy attack.

ESTABLISHING CHARACTER

In Anne Tyler's novel *The Accidental Tourist*, Macon Leary, while trying to get over a divorce and his son's murder, also has to deal with his dog's new habit of biting people. Although dog trainer Muriel Pritchett appears in the story in a space usually reserved for a love interest, her loony verbal flights hardly seem a match for Macon, a fragile, phobic intellectual. But Muriel trains Macon's dog with a fierce competence and tells some amazing stories—like the day she was knocked down by a Doberman Pinscher:

> Come to find him standing over me, showing all his teeth. Well, I thought of what they said at Doggie, Do: Only one of you can be boss. So I tell him, 'Absolutely not.' ... and my right arm is broken so I hold out my left, hold out my palm and stare into his eyes—they can't stand for you to meet their eyes—and get to my feet real slow. And durned if that dog doesn't settle right back on his haunches.

PAINTING A CANVAS

In *The Shipping News* by Annie Proulx, Quoyle returns to his ancestral home in Newfoundland and gets a job at the local newspaper covering the harbor beat. Giving Quoyle this particular assignment allows Proulx to tap into the town's raison d'être, as well as the delicious patois of the seagoing trade, like this passage from a local boat builder:

> There's the backbone of your boat, she's scarfed now. You glance at that, somebody who knows boats, you can see the whole thing right there. But there's nobody can tell 'ow she'll fit the water, handle in the swells and lops until you try 'er out. Except poor old Uncle Les, Les Budgel. Dead now ... Built beautiful skiffs and dories, butter on a 'ot stove.

Proulx adds to this canvas by heading her chapters with diagrams and descriptions of sailors' knots.

The secret to all four of these passages is their authentic feel—as if the author himself has performed this line of work. While it's possible for writers to capture some details of a vocation through reading, firsthand experience and real-life sources are your best bet.

The following are some strategies that have worked for me.

USING WHAT DO YOU DO?

Sad to say, if you're writing fiction, you've probably got a day job. Why not use it? And don't discount the nonglamorous. A lot of your readers will have much more in common with a shipping clerk than a shipping magnate.

When I had a job soldering copper pipes for my contractor brother-in-law, I began to notice the small, poetic details of working there: the horizontal ballet of positioning the torch, the way the lead solder flashed around the joint as it melted, the pleasing hiss when I ran a damp rag over the hot pipe. I decided to give this same assignment to the poet-protagonist of my novel *Rhyming Pittsburgh*, hoping to complicate the effete intellectual stereotype with a healthy dose of blue-collar grit.

UPGRADING A HOBBY

Lots of hobbies are simply professions performed on an amateur level. Easy enough, then, to take the knowledge attained as a hobbyist and crank it up to the level of a fictional pro.

In the 1990s, I played drums for several bands. Although I never got to the professional level, I met a lot of pros, played a few clubs and got a good all-around feel for the musician's life. I've since had two drummer protagonists, made plentiful use of backstage stories and even filled out the details with specific musical passages from my playing days.

BEING A JOURNALIST

Ask questions. Be a buttinsky. People love to talk about their jobs—especially if you tell them you're working on a novel.

For my opera novel *Gabriella's Voice*, I set up an extensive research program to learn more about the profession of my singer-protagonist. I got an assignment reviewing the San Francisco Opera. I took a soprano friend out to dinner, parked a tape recorder next to her silverware, and asked three hours' worth of questions. Then I spent a full season with her company—hanging out at auditions, rehearsals, and cast parties. This was the best way to pick up great backstage stories.

The reviews I most enjoy from *Gabriella* come from singers who spent half the book laughing at inside jokes and inevitably come back to me with that priceless question, "How did you *know* all that?"

VALUING EXPERIENTIAL VENTURES

A playwright friend of mine used to say, "You gotta live before you can write." Though it's smart to use your character's occupation as an excuse to dig up firsthand experiences, the reverse is also true: You can pursue these kinds of adventures at all times, with the idea that someday later you'll use them in your writing.

It's not just a good way to approach fiction. It's a good way to approach life.

MICHAEL J. VAUGHN is the author of twelve novels, most recently *Billy Saddle*, inspired by the story of Chicago Cubs fan Steve Bartman. He is also an active poet, with more than one hundred poems published in journals.

CHAPTER 6

THREE TECHNIQUES FOR CRAFTING YOUR VILLAIN

BY HALLIE EPHRON

Today's villain is no Snidely Whiplash standing there twirling his moustache and sneering, a neon arrow blinking "BAD GUY" over his head. In a good contemporary mystery—and in a lot of other genres besides—any character who looks that nefarious is going to turn out to be innocent.

Readers are delighted when the bad guy turns out to have been hiding in plain sight, an innocuous-looking character who cleverly conceals his true self, luring trusting victims and then snaring them in a death trap. "The butler did it" won't wash in a modern mystery. Minor characters who are part of the wallpaper for the first twenty-eight chapters can't be promoted to villain status at the end just to surprise the reader. And you can't give a character a personality transplant in the final chapter. Disbelief will trump surprise unless you've left subtle clues along the way.

TAKE THE TIME TO PLAN AHEAD

Some writers know right from the get-go which character is guilty. They start with the completed puzzle and work their way backward, shaping the story pieces and fitting them together. Others happily write without knowing whodunit until the scene when the villain is actually unmasked. Then they rewrite, cleaning up the trail of red herrings and establishing the clues that make the solution work.

Which way is better? That's a question only you can answer. I personally need a plan. I have a friend, a many-times-published mystery writer, who boasts that she never plans. The identity of the villain comes as a complete surprise to her and the reader. In the next breath, she says she ended up having to dump the first two hundred pages from the draft of her latest novel. Thus having a plan up front can save a whole lot of rewriting in what should be the homestretch.

CREATE A VILLAIN WORTH PURSUING

You can't just throw all your suspects' names into a bowl and pick one to be your villain. For your novel to work, the villain must be special. Your sleuth deserves a worthy adversary—a smart, wily, dangerous creature who tests your protagonist's courage and prowess. Stupid, bumbling characters are good for comic relief, but they make lousy villains. The smarter, more invincible the villain, the harder your protagonist must work to find his vulnerability and the greater the achievement in bringing him to justice.

Must the villain be loathsome? Not at all. He can be chilling but charming, like Hannibal Lecter. Thoroughly evil? It's better when the reader can muster a little sympathy for a complex, realistic character who feels her crimes are justified.

So, in planning, try to wrap your arms around why your villain does what he does. What motivates him to kill? Consider the standard motives like greed, jealousy, or hatred. Then go a step further. Get inside your villain's head and see the crime from his perspective. What looks to law enforcement like a murder motivated by greed may, to the perpetrator, be an act in the service of a noble, even heroic cause.

Here's how a villain might justify a crime:

- Righting a prior wrong
- Revenge (the victim deserved to die)
- Vigilante justice (the justice system didn't work)
- Protecting a loved one
- Restoring order to the world.

Finally, think about what happened to make that character the way she is. Was she born bad, or did she turn sour as a result of some early experience? If your villain has a grudge against society, why? If she can't tolerate being jilted, why? You may never share your villain's life story with your reader, but to make a complex, interesting villain, *you* need to know.

By understanding how the villain justifies the crimes to himself, and what events in his life triggered these crimes, you give yourself the material you need to get past a black-hatted caricature and paint your villain in shades of gray.

INVENTING YOUR VILLAIN

1. Reread a favorite mystery novel or read Scott Turow's *Presumed Innocent* or Linda Barnes' *Deep Pockets*. Pay special attention to the villain. Think about how the author creates a bad guy who is somewhat sympathetic and three-dimensional. As you read, see how quickly you can spot the villain's motive(s), and pay special attention to the pace at which the author reveals important details about the villain. Also look for how the villain rationalizes his actions throughout the story.
2. Brainstorm your villain and jot down your ideas: family background, physical appearance, education, formative events, biggest heartbreak, greatest success, and so on. This quick character sketch will change and grow as your villain comes to life.
3. Now that you have a more detailed understanding of your villain, pick a modus operandi that matches up with your bad guy. Factor in your villain's capabilities, expertise, motivation, and personal rage factor.

MAKE THE CRIME FIT THE VILLAIN

There are many ways to kill off a character. You can have him shot, stabbed, poisoned, or pushed off a cliff. You can have him run over by a car or bashed in the head with a fireplace poker. You get the picture.

The first issue to consider is: Would your villain have the expertise and capability to commit this particular crime you've conceived for him?

Here's an example: Suppose there's a novel about a surgeon who, up to page 302, has been the soul of buttoned-down respectability. Suddenly, on page 303, he leaps from a hospital laundry bin and mows down his rival for hospital director with machine-gun fire. Never mind that up to this point in the novel the guy has done nothing more than attend board meetings, get drunk and obnoxious at a cocktail party, and perform heart surgery. Now suddenly he's The Terminator? The behavior doesn't fit the character. If he stabbed, poisoned, or pushed his rival off the hospital roof, the reader might swallow it. The author might get away (barely) with the shooting if hints were dropped earlier that this surgeon once served in military special forces.

Choose a modus operandi that your villain (and all your suspects) might plausibly adopt, and establish that your villain has the capability and expertise required. A murder by strangling, stabbing, or beating is more plausible if your villain is strong and has a history of physical violence. If your villain plants an electronically activated plastic explosive device, be prepared to show how he learned to make a sophisticated bomb and how he got access to the components. If a woman shoots her husband with a .45 automatic, be prepared to show how she learned to use firearms and that she's strong enough to handle the recoil of a .45.

The second issue to consider: Is the rage factor appropriate for the character's motivation? The more extreme the violence, the more likely the crime is to be fueled by hatred and rage. A robber shoots a victim once; an enraged husband pumps bullets into the man who raped his wife until the ammunition runs out. A villain may administer a quick-working deadly poison to a victim he wants out of the way, but a villain who loathes his victim might pick a poison that's slow and painful—and hang around to watch.

Adjust the violence quotient to match the amount of rage your villain has toward her victim.

HALLIE EPHRON is the author of more that ten books including *Writing and Selling Your Mystery Novel: How to Knock 'Em Dead With Style.*

IMAGINING THE CRIME

How would your villain kill his victim? Consider your villain's motive, strength, and expertise; consider the rage factor. Remember that the method should fit your villain's personality; otherwise it won't seem authentic to readers. Check the ones that could fit:

- Asphyxiate by smoke inhalation
- Beat to death
- Bludgeon
- Bury alive
- Drown
- Hang
- Mow down with machine-gun fire
- Poison: drug overdose
- Poison: mushrooms
- Push in front of a train
- Run down with a car
- Run over with heavy equipment
- Shoot with a pistol
- Slit throat
- Smother
- Stab multiple times
- Stab once
- Strangle

CHAPTER 7

CREATE VICIOUS VILLAINS

BY CHARLES ATKINS

It's such a disappointment to sit down with a scary novel or crime story, only to find that the killer has been portrayed one-dimensionally. Suddenly the reader finds himself rolling his eyes in annoyance instead of being struck with fear. Readers want their characters—villains or not—to be realistic and multifaceted. They want to know why a character acts the way he does, and they want it to make sense.

As a psychiatrist and author of thrillers myself, I (like many authors) have turned to specific personality disorders to flesh out a character's motivation behind criminal behavior. Most readers are familiar, for instance, with multiple personality disorder (which tends to translate to one personality being good, while the other is a crazed serial killer). Realistically, though, multiple personality disorder doesn't figure into many real-life crimes and, therefore, it would be implausible in fiction. Not only that, but not all criminals fit this mold. Here's a whirlwind review of the dark side of human nature, so you can craft believable villains and direct your reader into the mind of a madman.

NARCISSISM

Narcissism is named after the Greek god Narcissus, who fell in love with his own reflection and died pining for a love he could never have. The narcissist is a legend in his own mind; he thinks the world revolves around him. When things go well, he's highly productive and creative. Many politicians, artists, physicians, lawyers, and corporate leaders have a healthy dose of narcissism. Narcissists are self-aware; they understand themselves. In moderation, self-love and admiration aren't necessarily bad qualities; they're what give people the confidence needed to take risks. But a narcissist doesn't take criticism or rejection well. When opposed or slighted, she becomes frustrated, angry, sarcastic, even vengeful. She might steam over an insult and, if the opportunity presents itself, retaliate. If she's highly intelligent, her vengeance could be exacted in an unexpected manner, and no one will ever be able to pin the blame.

When confronted, the narcissist will lie and deny any guilt or wrongdoing, and this is where things can turn ugly—even deadly. Think about politicians who've been confronted with sexual indiscretion: They deny the whole thing, even though everyone knows all will be revealed in the end. Narcissists are natural choices for villains in novels about revenge. One famous example is Sir Arthur Conan Doyle's Professor Moriarty, whose driving motivation was to outwit and destroy his nemesis, Sherlock Holmes.

In my novel *The Cadaver's Ball*, villain Ed Tyson is a brilliant and highly narcissistic researcher who may well win the Nobel Prize. But the woman he loves rejects him for another man and is killed in a suspicious accident. When she dies, Ed fixates on the man who "stole" her from him and is out for cold-blooded revenge. Unlike the sociopath who feels no remorse, Ed has his own moral code. The wrong that was done to him, and to the woman he loved, must be corrected. If this involves the death of his rival, so be it.

A variant of the narcissist is the malignant narcissist. In addition to the previous qualities, there's an element of sadism—a taking of pleasure from another's pain. The malignant narcissist gets ahead by stomping everyone beneath him. Examples include the bullying sheriff, characters who ruthlessly climb the corporate ladder, and abusive spouses who maintain control through a mixture of oppression and brutality. Part of what makes malignant narcissists get ahead is that while they terrorize their subordinates, they kiss up to their superiors—and they do so in convincing fashion. They're wonderful yes-men to the boss, whom they secretly despise, because in their hearts they know they could do a far better job.

THE ANTISOCIAL PERSONALITY

Antisocial personality disorder (aka sociopathy) is a small hop, skip, and jump from the malignant narcissist. And this is where we find the mother lode of serious criminal behavior.

From an early age, children who become sociopaths exhibit warning signs. In my second novel, *Risk Factor*, I used several characters to show how the moral development of such a child becomes warped and distorted. This typically happens through a series of losses, traumas, and separations in the child's early life (abuse, divorce, frequent moves, etc.). Just as learning to talk and walk are important developmental milestones, learning to develop empathy also happens at a young age. If this stage is missed or seriously disrupted, a child grows to adulthood with no real concern for the well-being of others; this is the core defect in sociopaths.

Sociopaths believe they're free from the rules of society, and as such, they should be able to have what they want, when they want it, and you'd best not get in their way. Fiction (and real-life prisons) are filled with sociopaths, from Bonnie and Clyde to white-collar criminals who've plundered the retirement plans of their employees. The only time you see repentance from a sociopath is when he's caught, and the remorse isn't for the victims, it's for himself.

Sociopaths are well suited for a life of crime, as they lack the internal moral workings that lead to feelings of guilt and empathy. Because of this, they stay calm when engaged in high-risk criminal behaviors. Studies looking at heart rate, blood pressure, and other physiological indicators of stress have shown that sociopaths aren't easily flustered—a phenomenon referred to as "low arousal." This may also account for how sociopaths can often "trick" polygraph tests.

In *Risk Factor*, my villain is both sociopathic and narcissistic, a common mixture. What gives him added punch is his intelligence and ability to conceal his inner nastiness. The combination of sociopathy, high IQ and self-awareness is what creates mastermind criminals. These are the most successful sociopaths, as they know how to keep their criminal activities and lack of empathy well hidden. Some sociopaths, like John Wayne Gacy, who tortured, killed, and then buried victims in the crawl space of his house, wear the mantel of respectability. This is the killer next door—the one who leaves the neighbors stunned and commenting, "He seemed like such a nice guy."

THE BORDERLINE PERSONALITY

Unlike sociopathy, which has a definite male preponderance, borderline personality disorder affects far more women than men. Some speculate that borderline personality disorder is the female equivalent of sociopathy. In this case, instead of acting out in violent ways, the person directs the violence internally. The precipitants of the disorder are similar to what we see in sociopathy but with a high incidence of sexual abuse.

People with borderline personality disorder have chaotic lives that spin out of control in the setting of real—or imagined—rejection and abandonment. Someone with this disorder will overdose or engage in other risky behaviors to try to hold on to people in her life. "If you leave me, I'll kill myself," is a typical strategy for this group, as opposed to the malignant narcissist or sociopath, who might say, "If you leave me, I'll kill *you*."

The borderline views her world in a black-and-white way. People are either good or bad. Her boss either loves her or is an evil bitch who's out to get her. Borderlines struggle with ambiguity and can't grasp the notion that people are a mixture of qualities. These people are prone to substance abuse, self-mutilation (cutting with razor blades, burning with cigarettes), eating disorders, and brief periods of psychosis, where they lose touch with reality. Some people with borderline personality disorder will dissociate, a condition mostly linked to multiple personality disorder (aka dissociative identity disorder).

From a literary perspective, borderlines make fantastic catalysts for action because they're ruled by their emotions; they're not given over to contemplation. They act first and think later, and they have a rare talent for making a bad situation worse. In *The Cadaver's Ball*, we meet Ann, a beautiful borderline medical student who's just attempted suicide. From there, she seduces, boozes, and blackmails her way to an unhappy end.

THE PARANOID PERSONALITY

Paranoia is the unrealistic belief that people are out to get you. And because of this, it's not surprising that people with this condition can turn violent: In their minds, they're acting in self-defense. People with paranoid personality disorder view everything and everyone with suspicion. They can misread a friendly smile as a covert sign that they're about to get fired. An offhand comment or minor criticism can lead to days of obsessing over the hidden meaning and underlying motivation.

The paranoid, unlike the introspective narcissist, doesn't know he's paranoid. To him, the rest of the world has a problem. He can't understand why people conspire against him, and this makes him angry.

Those with paranoia often lead solitary lives and take jobs where they can be left alone. When a paranoid person turns violent, the anger is most often directed toward the perceived persecutor. People who spin elaborate delusional fantasies about the government are classic examples. A couple of important variants of paranoia include:

- shared paranoia, as with some religious and political cults
- drug-induced paranoia, which is common with cocaine and stimulant abuse; it's also standard with cannabis use, although it's less likely to be associated with violent behavior
- paranoid jealousy, where there's a fixed false belief that a beloved is cheating on you. Shakespeare nailed this one when he had Othello smother the virtuous Desdemona.

The truth about personality types—of which there are far more than I've outlined here—is that we all have bits and pieces of different ones. Where a character trait crosses over into something diagnosable, or potentially dangerous, is the terrain that fascinates us. Readers want to know why a twelve-year-old shows up to school with murder on his mind and what made that long-term employee shoot his boss. Understanding these killer personalities gives readers the leg up they need. When such personalities are fully fleshed out in fiction or true-crime writing, we catch a glimpse into the darker side of human nature and are able to understand the mind of the killer living next door.

CHARLES ATKINS (charlesatkins.com) is a board-certified psychiatrist and a member of the Yale Clinical Faculty.

FOCUS ON THE WRITING LIFE:

FEEDING YOUR CREATIVITY

CREATIVE LOLLYGAGGING: WORK HARDER AT WORKING LESS

BY MICHAEL J. VAUGHN

Every writer knows you can't sit down in front of a notebook or computer screen and wait for ideas to simply show up. You'd better have some ideas before you sit down, and you'd better figure out a system for harvesting those ideas.

Ironically—and happily—one of the best ways to achieve this is to do … nothing. Well, not *nothing*, exactly. Think of it as "creative lollygagging." Picture yourself as a satellite dish. The way a dish receives signals is a decidedly passive activity, but nothing comes in until the equipment is properly charged and opened to the universe. A few years ago, ensconced in one of my "brewing" modes—done with my last novel, waiting for the next to come a-knockin'—I decided to take my dish to the beach and open 'er up.

About a half mile into my walk, I noticed a friendly spark among the small rocks and found bits of frosted glass—triangular shards worn to a gem like smoothness by sand and waves. I remembered the fascination I felt as a child—that nature could take a piece of man-made litter and make it so beautiful. I walked a little farther, discovered another smattering and had the following thought: What if someone became so obsessed with frosted glass that he decided to make it his life's work? I didn't know it yet, but the satellite dish had just taken in an entire novel.

But not just that: It also took in the process for *imagining* a novel. In the following months, as I continued my beach hikes in search of frosted glass (if my character was obsessed, I had to be obsessed), I discovered an intriguing pattern. I arrived at the beach between chapters (my characters dangling in midair, awaiting their instructions); I left with pocketfuls of glass *and* my next chapter, nicely mapped out in my head.

If you subtly stimulate your other senses—in this case, tactile (the glass) and auditory (the ocean)—you can take the "edge" away from your conscious, purposive mind, return the satellite dish to a state of active passivity and open yourself to the forces of serendipity. And if you come to the beach for frosted glass, you'll also get ideas for your story, slipping in along your peripheral vision.

A CREATIVE LOLLYGAGGERS TO-DO LIST

The key to successful lollygagging is to do it creatively.

So what makes lollygagging *creative* lollygagging? Let's look at the basic elements. First, consider activity. We are *not* talking about sitting around on a couch. Just as a satellite dish needs electricity, you need some blood pumping into that brain. Next, consider low focus. The activity shouldn't be so intense that you don't have time to think (Grand Prix and ice hockey are out). Look for a mellow pursuit, surrounded by low-level distractions.

Finally, consider separation. If you don't hie thee away from the computer, the television, the bills, and the kids, you're headed for a mighty wall o' brain lock. Following are some specific types of creative lollygagging to try:

- Mobile (because it's difficult to preoccupy a moving target): biking, hiking, kayaking, rollerblading, a long road or train trip

- Idle: fly-fishing, horseshoe tossing, kite flying, a solo game of eight ball, a solo game of bowling, a session at the batting cage or driving range
- Boring jobs (for those who simply must be productive): paint the garage, rake the leaves, wash the windows, clean out the roof gutters, mow the lawn
- Dilettantism (effective only if you try something for which you have absolutely no talent): abstract painting, making up tunes on the piano, creating monsters from modeling clay, inventing a ballet to your favorite symphony, pounding on a conga drum.

THE COFFEEHOUSE RITUAL

If you'd like to take this one step further, try incorporating your lollygagging directly into your writing ritual.

The Coffeehouse Ritual is a routine I've followed for fifteen years, with excellent results (in fact, I used it to write this story).

1. Pick your place: Locate a coffeehouse that's a mile or two from your home (ideally, a thirty- to forty-five-minute walk).
2. The walk up: Head off at an easy pace (no power walking, please) and let your thoughts drift. For the first few blocks, you'll likely be occupied by small matters of the day. Don't worry—this is a necessary step, one that will clear out your mind for the work ahead. As you pass the halfway point, your thoughts should turn naturally to the project at hand.
3. Write! Buy a large beverage, find a nonjiggling table and go to it. Note: Keep your coffeehouse sacred. Be polite but not excessively friendly to baristas and regulars. If a friend drops by, tell him that you have five minutes to talk, but then you really need to get back to work. If he's not buying it, tell him you're on deadline.

4. The walk down: The hike back home is often the most rewarding part of the process. Still adrift on your creative buzz, you may find that your satellite dish is more open than ever. It's a great time to think about what you've written and to contemplate future developments.

As I continued taking my walks along the ocean, searching for inspiration and frosted glass, it began to seem, in fact, that my novel was scattered along the beach, like pirate's treasure, and all I had to do was come along and scoop it up. The real secret, however, came from my protagonist, Frosted Glass Man, as he was helping a neophyte who'd lost her "glass vision." "Let me guess," he said. "Suddenly you can't tell frosted glass from the Queen of England, and you're sort of losing your place on the sand. Feeling disoriented."

"Yeah. That about describes it."

He grinned. "You're trying too hard. When you begin to lose your sight, just rub the last piece you found, and listen to the ocean."

MICHAEL J. VAUGHN is the author of twelve novels, most recently *Billy Saddle*, inspired by the story of Chicago Cubs fan Steve Bartman. He is also an active poet, with more than one hundred poems published in journals.

PART 2:

PLOT & CONFLICT:

YOUR STORY'S ACTION & SUSPENSE

CHAPTER 8

STORY TRUMPS STRUCTURE

BY STEVEN JAMES

Imagine that I'm telling you about my day and I say, "I woke up. I ate breakfast. I left for work."

Is that a story? After all, it has a protagonist who makes choices that lead to a natural progression of events, it contains three acts and it has a beginning, a middle, and an end—and that's what makes something a story, right?

Well, actually, no.

It's not.

My description of what I did this morning—while it may meet those commonly accepted criteria—contains no crisis, no struggle, no discovery, no transformation in the life of the main character. It's a report, but it's not a story.

Over the years as I've taught at writing conferences around the world, you should see some of the looks I've gotten when I tell people to stop thinking of a story in terms of its structure. And it's easy to understand why. Spend enough time with writers or English teachers and you'll hear the dictum that a story is something that has a beginning, middle, and end. I know that the people who share this definition mean well, but it's really not a very helpful one for storytellers. After all, a description of a pickle has a beginning, a middle, and an end, but it's not a story. The sentence, "Preheat the oven to 450 degrees," has those basic elements, but it's not a story either.

So then, what is a story?

Centuries ago, Aristotle noted in his book *Poetics* that while a story does have a beginning, a middle, and an ending, the beginning is not simply the first event in a series of three, but rather the emotionally engaging originating event. The middle is the natural and causally related consequence, and the end is the inevitable conclusive event.

In other words, stories have an origination, an escalation of conflict, and a resolution.

Of course, stories also need a vulnerable character, a setting that's integral to the narrative, meaningful choices that determine the outcome of the story, and reader empathy. But at its most basic level, a story is a transformation unveiled—either the transformation of a situation or, most commonly, the transformation of a character.

Simply put, you do not have a story until something goes wrong.

At its heart, a story is about a person dealing with tension, and tension is created by unfulfilled desire. Without forces of antagonism, without setbacks, without a crisis event that initiates the action, you have no story. The secret, then, to writing a story that draws readers in and keeps them turning pages is *not* to make more and more things happen to a character, and especially not to follow some preordained plot formula or novel-writing template. Instead the key to writing better stories is to focus on creating more and more tension as your story unfolds.

Understanding the fundamentals at the heart of all good stories will help you tell your own stories better—and sell more of them, too. Imagine you're baking a cake. You mix together certain ingredients in a specific order and end up with a product that is uniquely different than any individual ingredient. In the process of mixing and then baking the cake, these ingredients are transformed into something delicious.

That's what you're trying to do when you bake up a story.

So let's look at five essential story ingredients, and then review how to mix them together to make your story so good readers will ask for seconds.

INGREDIENT #1: ORIENTATION

The beginning of a story must grab the reader's attention; orient her to the setting, mood, and tone of the story; and introduce her to a protagonist she will care about, even worry about, and emotionally invest time and attention into. If readers don't care about your protagonist, they won't care about your story, either.

So, what's the best way to introduce this all-important character? In essence, you want to set reader expectations and reveal a portrait of the main character by giving readers a glimpse of her normal life. If your protagonist is a detective, we want to see him at a crime scene. If you're writing romance, we want to see normal life for the young woman who's searching for love. Whatever portrait you draw of your character's life, keep in mind that it will also serve as a promise to your readers of the transformation that this character will undergo as the story progresses.

For example, if you introduce us to your main character, Frank, the happily married man next door, readers instinctively know that Frank's idyllic life is about to be turned upside down—most likely by the death of either his spouse or his marriage. Something will soon rock the boat, and he will be altered forever. Because when we read about harmony at the start of a story, it's a promise that discord is about to come. Readers expect this.

Please note that normal life doesn't mean pain-free life. The story might begin while your protagonist is depressed, hopeless, grieving, or trapped in a sinking submarine. Such circumstances could be what's typical for your character at this moment. When that happens, it's usually another crisis (whether internal or external) that will serve to kick-start the story. Which brings us to the second ingredient.

INGREDIENT #2: CRISIS

This crisis that tips your character's world upside down must, of course, be one that your protagonist cannot immediately solve. It's an unavoidable, irrevocable challenge that sets the movement of the story into motion.

Typically your protagonist will have the harmony of both his external world and his internal world upset by the crisis that initiates the story. One of these two imbalances might have happened before the beginning of the story, but usually at least one will occur on the page for your readers to experience with your protagonist, and the interplay of these two dynamics will drive the story forward.

Depending on the genre, the crisis that alters your character's world might be a call to adventure—a quest that leads to a new land, or a prophecy or revelation that he's destined for great things. Mythic, fantasy, and science-fiction novels often follow this pattern. In crime fiction, the crisis might be a new assignment to a seemingly unsolvable case. In romance, the crisis might be undergoing a divorce or breaking off an engagement.

In each case, though, life is changed and it will never be the same again.

George gets fired. Amber's son is kidnapped. Larry finds out his cancer is terminal. Whatever it is, the normal life of the character is forever altered, and she is forced to deal with the difficulties that this crisis brings.

There are two primary ways to introduce a crisis into your story: Either begin the story by letting your character have what he desires most and then rip it away, or deny him what he desires most and then dangle it in front of him. So he'll either lose something vital and spend the story trying to regain it, or he'll see something desirable and spend the story trying to obtain it.

Say you've imagined a character who desires love more than anything else. His deepest fear will be abandonment. You'll either want to introduce the character by showing him in a satisfying, loving relationship, and then insert a crisis that destroys it, or you'll want to show the character's initial longing for a mate, and then dangle a promising relationship just out of his reach so that he can pursue it throughout the story.

Likewise, if your character desires freedom most, then he'll try to avoid enslavement. So you might begin by showing that he's free, and then enslave him, or begin by showing that he's enslaved, and then thrust him into a freedom-pursuing adventure.

It all has to do with what the main character desires, and what he wishes to avoid.

INGREDIENT #3: ESCALATION

There are two types of characters in every story: pebble people and putty people.

If you take a pebble and throw it against a wall, it'll bounce off the wall unchanged. But if you throw a ball of putty against a wall hard enough, it will change shape.

Always in a story, your main character needs to be a putty person.

When you throw him into the crisis of the story, he is forever changed, and he will take whatever steps he can to try and solve his struggle—that is, to get back to his original shape (life before the crisis).

But he will fail.

Because he'll always be a different shape at the end of the story than he was at the beginning. If he's not, readers won't be satisfied.

Putty people are altered.

Pebble people remain the same. They're like set pieces. They appear onstage in the story, but they don't change in essential ways as the story progresses. They're the same at the ending as they were at the beginning.

And they are not very interesting.

So exactly what kind of wall are we throwing our putty person against?

First, stop thinking of plot in terms of what happens in your story. Rather, think of it as payoff for the promises you've made early in the story. Plot is the journey toward transformation.

As I mentioned earlier, typically two crisis events interweave to form the multilayered stories that today's readers expect: an external struggle that needs to be overcome and an internal struggle that needs to be resolved. As your story progresses, then, the consequences of not solving those two struggles need to become more and more intimate, personal, and devastating.

Then, as the stakes are raised, the two struggles will serve to drive the story forward and deepen reader engagement and interest.

Usually if a reader says she's bored or that "nothing's happening in the story," she doesn't necessarily mean that events aren't occurring, but rather that she doesn't see the protagonist taking natural, logical steps to try and solve his struggle.

During the escalation stage of your story, let your character take steps to try and resolve the two crises (internal and external) and get back to the way things were earlier, before his world was tipped upside down.

INGREDIENT #4: DISCOVERY

At the climax of the story, the protagonist will make a discovery that changes his life.

Typically this discovery will be made through wit (as the character cleverly pieces together clues from earlier in the story) or grit (as the character shows extraordinary perseverance or tenacity) to overcome the crisis event (or meet the calling) he's been given.

The internal discovery and the external resolution help reshape our putty person's life and circumstances forever.

The protagonist's discovery must come from a choice that she makes, not simply by chance or from a Wise Answer Giver. While mentors might guide a character toward self-discovery, the decisions and courage that determine the outcome of the story must come from the protagonist.

In one of the paradoxes of storytelling, the reader wants to predict how the story will end (or how it will get to the end), but he wants to be wrong. So the resolution of the story will be most satisfying when it ends in a way that is both *inevitable* and *unexpected.*

INGREDIENT #5: CHANGE

Think of a caterpillar entering a cocoon. Once he does so, one of two things will happen: He will either transform into a butterfly, or he will die. But no matter what else happens, he will never climb out of the cocoon as a caterpillar.

So it is with your protagonist.

As you frame your story and develop your character, ask yourself, "What is my caterpillar doing?" Your character will either be transformed into someone more mature, insightful, or at peace, or will plunge into death or despair.

Although genre can dictate the direction of this transformation—horror stories will often end with some kind of death (physical, psychological, emotional, or spiritual)—most genres are butterfly genres. Most stories end with the protagonist experiencing new life—whether that's physical renewal, psychological understanding, emotional healing, or a spiritual awakening.

This change marks the resolution of the crisis and the culmination of the story.

As a result of facing the struggle and making this new discovery, the character will move to a *new normal*. The character's actions or attitude at the story's end show us how she's changed from the story's inception. The putty has become a new shape, and if it's thrown against the wall again, the reader will understand that a brand-new story is now unfolding. The old way of life has been forever changed by the process of moving through the struggle to the discovery and into a new and different life.

LETTING STRUCTURE FOLLOW STORY

I don't have any idea how many acts my novels contain.

A great many writing instructors, classes and manuals teach that all stories should have three acts—and, honestly, that doesn't make much sense to me. After all, in theater, you'll find successful one-act, two-act, three-act, and four-act plays. And most assuredly, they are all stories.

If you're writing a novel that people won't read in one sitting (which is presumably every novel), your readers could care less about how many acts there are—in fact, they probably won't even be able to keep track of them. What readers really care about is the forward movement of the story as it escalates to its inevitable and unexpected conclusion.

While it's true that structuring techniques can be helpful tools, unfortunately, formulaic approaches frequently send stories spiraling off in the wrong direction or, just as bad, handcuff the narrative flow. Often the people who advocate funneling your story into a predetermined three-act structure will note that stories have the potential to sag or stall out during the long second act. And whenever I hear that, I think, *Then why not shorten it? Or chop it up and include more acts? Why let the story suffer just so you can follow a formula?*

I have a feeling that if you asked the people who teach three-act structure if they'd rather have a story that closely follows their format or one that intimately connects with readers, they would go with the latter. Why? Because I'm guessing that deep down, even they know that in the end, story trumps structure.

Once I was speaking with another writing instructor and he told me that the three acts form the skeleton of a story. I wasn't sure how to respond to that until I was at an aquarium with my daughter later that week and I saw an octopus. I realized that it got along pretty well without a skeleton. A storyteller's goal is to give life to a story, not to stick in bones that aren't necessary for that species of tale.

So stop thinking of a story as something that happens in three acts, or two acts, or four or seven, or as something that is driven by predetermined elements of plot. Rather think of your story as an organic whole that reveals a transformation in the life of your character. The number of acts or events should be determined by the movement of the story, not the other way around.

Because story trumps structure.

If you render a portrait of the protagonist's life in such a way that we can picture his world and also care about what happens to him, we'll be drawn into the story. If you present us with an emotionally stirring crisis or calling, we'll get hooked. If you show the stakes rising as the character struggles to solve this crisis, you'll draw us in more deeply. And if you end the story in a surprising yet logical way that reveals a transformation of the main character's life, we'll be satisfied and anxious to read your next story.

The ingredients come together, and the cake tastes good.

Always be ready to avoid formulas, discard acts, and break the "rules" for the sake of the story—which is another way of saying: Always be ready to do it for the sake of your readers.

STEVEN JAMES is a best-selling, critically acclaimed thriller author who has published more than thirty books across genres.

CHAPTER 9

MAP YOUR NOVEL WITH A REVERSE OUTLINE

BY N.M. KELBY

We can all benefit from a sense of organization. I like to think of a novel outline as the bones of a story. As a child, your bones grow to the place where they'll support who you are meant to be on this planet. If your genes determine that you're tall, your bones will form that foundation and your flesh will grow accordingly. As you grow older, you need calcium, and bones provide it to the point where they become brittle and can easily break.

This is the same with outlines. You need to create the basic framework for your story to grow on but not so much that it takes away the energy from the work.

So where do you begin? Arthur Miller once said, "If I see an ending, I can work backward." So start with the end.

KNOW YOUR ENDING BEFORE YOU START

If you start with the end of the story, the ending won't be set in concrete; it can change. But starting with what you think is the end allows you to have a firm idea of where you are going when you begin a journey with 60,000 to 80,000 words in tow. And you'll need that. Once you decide on your ending, everything in the book will be shaped to arrive there. None of your characters should be superfluous, nor should your scenes. It's all about bones.

Of course, the most difficult part of writing any story, long or short, *is* ending it.

In order to write your ending, you have to ask yourself what action you want to set forth in the start. But be careful not to create a "purse-string" ending—with all the elements brought together in a tidy bundle. At the end of your story, you don't want to give readers the sense that all there is to know is already known. You really just want to give them a whisper and a dream, and send them on their way.

Once your ending is in place, you can weave your tale. Novelist Tony Earley always says, "A story is about a thing and another thing." So it's your job to plan your story so that you give your reader the satisfaction of getting closure from one "thing," the most obvious thing, but keep the mystery of the other "thing" intact.

A good example of this can be found in Sherman Alexie's "What You Pawn I Will Redeem," the short story about a homeless Spokane Indian's circular attempts to raise $1,000 to redeem his grandmother's powwow regalia from a pawnshop. The shop owner would like to give it back, but he paid $1,000 for it himself. So he gives the homeless man $5 as seed money and twenty-four hours to raise the rest of the cash.

In the first paragraph, Alexie gives the reader notice and sets up the ending of his story:

> One day you have a home and the next you don't, but I'm not going to tell you my particular reasons for being homeless, because it's my secret story, and Indians have to work hard to keep secrets from hungry white folks.

The idea of a "secret story" is the key to the ending. While the protagonist does manage to earn money, he drinks, gambles, or gives it away. After twenty-four hours, the money has not been raised, but the pawnbroker gives him the regalia anyway. The last paragraph of the story is this:

> Outside, I wrapped myself in my grandmother's regalia and breathed her in. I stepped off the sidewalk and into the intersec-

> tion. Pedestrians stopped. Cars stopped. The city stopped. They all watched me dance with my grandmother. I was my grandmother, dancing.

Because the regalia is given back, the story does seem to tie itself up (that would be the first "thing"), but this really isn't about getting a stolen dress back. It's about the struggle to regain one's spirit—and that could be seen as the "secret" story (or the other thing) wrapped in this tall tale.

The ending that satisfies the reader, or ties things up, is never the real ending of the story. We discover that the grandmother's regalia is returned, and yet the story continued on for a moment to put the act into context. Alexie left the readers with a whisper and a dream, and sent them on their way.

OUTLINE YOUR STORY SIMPLY AND BRIEFLY

There is no set amount of pages in an outline because it all depends on how large a story you're going to tell. The story of *Harry Potter and the Order of the Phoenix* had thirty-eight chapters that spanned 870 pages. Its table of contents provides an interesting look at the bones of an outline. It begins:

> One: Dudley Demented
> Two: A Peck of Owls
> Three: The Advance Guard

If you were J.K. Rowling, and this was your outline, all you'd have to do is write a short summary paragraph after the title of each chapter. In the first chapter, you would tell us why Dudley is demented and make sure that there are bits in your description that set the action of the book in play. Then move on to the next chapter.

To build the bones of your own outline, begin by writing a short description of what happens in the last chapter, and then move to the first chapter. After that's done, divide the rest of Act 1 into as many chapters as it takes to properly introduce your protagonist and the conflict—the "who," "what," "when," and "where" of the tale.

Move on to Act 2 and, again, create as many chapters as it takes to explain the crisis, complications, and obstacles that present themselves on the protagonist's way to the climax. Make note of the emotional challenges that he faces.

Once you've written the climax, it's time to create as many chapters as you'll need to lead to the final chapter.

Try not to get too fancy with the writing. If your agent is going to pitch your outline, he's going to take fifty pages of the draft with him, so you don't need to show any style in the outline. This is all about bones.

N.M. KELBY is the author of *The Constant Art of Being a Writer*. Her story "Jubilation, Florida" was selected for NPR's "Selected Shorts."

GIVE YOUR STORY IDEA A LITMUS TEST

To see if you can turn your initial story idea into a real novel, you have to decide if it has legs or not.

Step One: Answer these questions to the best of your ability. There are no wrong answers, but there are answers that inspire you to write on ... and that's what you're looking for.

1. What about the idea draws you in? What's the most important element of it to you?
2. Who could the players be? Not just the people who inspired you to follow your idea, but the supporting characters. What types of people would be involved in the situation? Who are the friends? Who are the enemies? Try to create a quick biography of each in which you explore their relationships to one another and to the protagonist. What do they sound like when they speak? Don't forget to add physical descriptions, aspirations, and even their favorite cologne, if you know it.
3. Where and when does the story take place? Keep in mind that the details of the incident that sparked you may not be where

you choose to set your novel. Whatever you do, make the setting as concrete as possible. Every reader needs a sense of being grounded.

4. What are the possibilities for conflict? Don't just settle for what actually happened. Now that you have a chance to imagine this idea in a more fleshed-out manner, ask yourself what could happen given who the characters you've created are, in addition to where they are in this world that you've made.

Step Two: Write. This is the difficult part. Once you've decided the particulars of the story you want to tell, you need to just start writing it. Begin with what you think is the first chapter. Then write the next. Or just write a couple of chapters out of sequence. When you reach fifty pages, try to write your outline. If you can't, keep writing until you can't any more, and then try again. You're not looking for publishable pages, you're just looking to unlock the possibility of story.

CHAPTER 10

WRITE WELL-CRAFTED SCENES TO SUPPORT YOUR STORY

BY JAMES SCOTT BELL

A great story premise will not stand without solid scenes to prop it up. Colorful characters can flit across the page, but unless they are engaged in battle, the reader just won't care.

Don't let your scenes fall into cliché or monotony. Always look for ways to freshen them up. Here are five techniques to help you do that.

1. MAKE YOUR DIALOGUE FLOW

Try writing a scene in only dialogue. Let it flow. Don't think much about it. When you're finished, you can look back and figure out what the scene is really about.

I once wrote a scene between competing lawyers. Part of it went like this:

> "You think you can get away with that?"
>
> "Whatever works."
>
> "Disbarment works, too."
>
> "You want to try to prove that? Know what that'll make you look like?"
>
> "Don't presume to know what I will or will not do."
>
> "I know you better than your wife, Phil."

That last line of dialogue came out of nowhere. Why did the character say that? I could have just edited it out, of course, but it seemed far better to explore the implications. What that led to was a plot point where the one lawyer revealed he'd had an investigator on Phil for six months. And he had pictures and places and dates Phil would not want revealed to his wife.

All that just from playing with dialogue. Try it, and you'll discover undercurrents for your scene you didn't know were there.

2. CUT OR HIDE EXPOSITION

Any time the author gives information in narrative form, the immediate story is put on hold. This exposition, if you don't watch it, can bloat and choke off a good scene.

Look for exposition you don't need. If it's not crucial for the moment, delay it. If it's not crucial for the overall story, cut it. The more important information can often be "hidden" by putting it into either dialogue or a character's thoughts.

3. FLIP THE OBVIOUS

Our minds work by reaching for the most familiar choices available. For writers that usually means a cliché. So learn to flip things.

If your characters are mere types, your scenes won't engage the readers. Imagine a truck driver rumbling down the highway at midnight, holding the steering wheel in one hand and a cup of hot black coffee in the other.

Got that?

Now I'll bet the first image your mind provided was of a burly male, probably wearing a baseball cap or cowboy hat. That's a familiar image of a trucker. It's a cliché, and therefore not very interesting. But what if you flipped it around? What if the trucker was a woman?

Try it.

Now you have an image to play with. But I'll wager you still pictured a rather "tough" woman, because all truckers are tough, right?

Flip that around. Put this woman in a nice evening dress. What does that do for your image? Why is she dressed that way? Where is she going? Who is after her? You can also play this game with descriptions and dialogue.

> "It's about time we started the meeting," Johnson said. "Let's do an agenda check."
>
> "Right," Smith said. "First up is the Norwood project. Second, the P&L statement. Third, staffing."

Stop a moment and flip the obvious response:

> "It's about time we started the meeting," Johnson said. "Let's do an agenda check."
>
> "Do it yourself," Smith said.

The nice part about this exercise is that even if you decide to stick with your original dialogue, the list you come up with provides you with possible subtext or insights about your character.

Play this game, and you're guaranteed to yield fresh material for characters, scenes, and dialogue.

4. APPLY THE CLOSED-EYES TECHNIQUE

Describing a physical setting in rich detail is crucial to a vivid scene. Where do such details come from? Say your hero has just entered a house where a friend lives. Close your eyes and "see" this house. Then record what you see as if you were a reporter on the scene. Describe all of the details as they are revealed to you. Later go back and edit out what you don't need. By doing it this way, you'll give yourself plenty of good, raw material to work with.

5. KNOW WHAT YOU'RE AIMING FOR

Every scene in your novel should have that moment or exchange that is the focal point, the bull's-eye, the thing you're aiming at. If your scene doesn't have a bull's-eye, it should be cut or rewritten.

A bull's-eye can be a few lines of dialogue that turn the action around or reveal something striking. It can be as subtle as a moment of realization or as explicit as a gunshot to the heart. Many times it is found in the last paragraph or two. Identify that moment so you know what you're writing toward. Then hit the bull's-eye. You may be a little off target in the first draft, but that's what rewriting is for. You'll hit it the second or third time.

JAMES SCOTT BELL is a best-selling and award-winning suspense writer. He is the author of *Plot & Structure*, *Revision & Self-Editing*, and *The Art of War for Writers*.

CHAPTER 11

USE BRAIDING TO LAYER YOUR STORY LINE

BY HEATHER SELLERS

We start so many books. Writing for twenty, fifty, seventy pages, all high hopes and happy plan, and then stopping. Bottoming out. In the middle. Again and again.

One reason so many books-in-progress die on the vine is because there isn't enough spark, enough energy in the original design, to drive the project all the way through the middle and close the deal. The middle of a book is often compared to a lonely and vast desert the writer has to hike across. It's easy to get lost. It's easy to give up.

To get across the middle, your work must involve some element of discovery—something you have to *figure out as you write*. Otherwise your writing will feel canned, preplanned, flat. Like stale popcorn.

This is where braiding comes in.

INTRODUCE LAYERS INTO YOUR STORIES

Braided books (or articles or stories) are made up of three or four strands, or story lines. Three seems to be the ideal number (for book writing as for hairstyling). Instead of slogging through one story line and then flatlining somewhere in the middle, braids help you mix it up. You tell three stories, bit by bit. The juxtapositions lend life and surprise, tension and drama. You work in small, manageable sections, folding in new material. Things stay fresh and lively.

For example, in a braided novel about divorce and reconciliation, you would tell the story of the divorce a little at a time, interspersing the teenage daughter's first romance with the story of the live-in mother-in-law and her crazy scheme to bring fame to the town. You tell three smaller, simpler stories—one of loss, one of love, and one of generation—in small, bite-sized pieces. It is much easier to work this way: one section at a time, from each of the three "source" stories.

To braid, imagine yourself going through family photos from three different trips. The Bahamas honeymoon photos, the photos from the American Indian mounds trip when the kids were babies, and photos of your mother from the last time you visited. Take the most interesting photos from each trip or strand, and lay them out to tell a story. Start with the Bahamas kissing photo. Then choose one from the mounds trip: the one with the kids all in a heap, laughing, but Shelly is yanking Em's hair, hard. Then your mother, alone, in the doorway, the light on her face so she looks like she did when she was a child. A lot like Shelly, come to think of it.

And then you cycle through again, until you have enough images to tell a story. With three sources feeding your book, it's easier to keep things fresh and alive.

VISUALIZE EACH SEPARATE STORY LINE

For fiction or a memoir, braid with images from each of your three story lines and you come up with photolike moments: 1-2-3, 1-2-3. For other nonfiction, choose topics or approaches. A refrigerator repair manual has three kinds of information: stuff you need to observe carefully with your eyes (is the ice buildup clear or snowy?), tools and how to use them, and basic diagrams for how the fridge is put together. The manual's sections cycle through these three kinds of information. You work in little blocks.

Last year, I judged a major national essay contest. It was an interesting experience, because only about 10 percent of the pieces even remotely worked. Most fell flat because they were *about one thing,* something the writers had already decided the pieces would be about. No room to wiggle around, get lost, wonder about the deeper nature of things, wander off to the side a bit, discover the interesting, previously unnoticed thing. Those authors each had *one* thing to say, and gosh darn it, they were going to say it, come hell or high water.

Sermons, rants at teenagers, lectures for college students (especially freshmen), even love letters—these may work like that. But not art.

Art relies on surprise. In order to engage the reader (and yourself as a writer), you have to braid. You can't be confusing, but you can't spell it all out, either. The human mind, when it reads, needs something to figure out. You can't just go on and on about the refrigerator compressor, the history of the compressor, the likes and dislikes of the compressor, particular compressor models, and so on.

ENCOURAGE HAPPY ACCIDENTS

You need *more than one thing* going on at a time. And you don't need to know how everything will work out. When you braid, happy accidents occur—the image of your mother's friends in the retirement home singing off-key for her birthday, all of them crying, inspires you to write a child's unhappy birthday scene. You would never have thought of it without the prompting of the braiding activity; often these inspired surprises produce some of our best writing.

In my memoir about the neurological disorder that impairs my ability to recognize faces, I have three braids—three photo albums to draw from. Childhood. Recognition problems because of my condition. And the story of my marriage and divorce. I trust in the possibilities of how the stories will refract off one another. When I tell the story of my Florida childhood, divorce will be in some of the images. Marriage is about recognizing another person, deeply, profoundly. My braids twine in and out of one another. Coming of age, an illness, a marriage—the book *teaches me* what it is about as I write it. That's the best way to write a book: to follow a structure that allows you to discover wise insights, images, and a natural organization as you go along.

DIVIDE YOUR STORY INTO THREES

If you are concerned about organization, try dividing your book into three substories or three subthemes. You can write each one straight through. Or you can divide and conquer, working on each strand a little bit at a time. Most braiders do a little of both.

I asked my students to do a braided essay using completely unrelated topics; the only requirement was that they write things that mattered a lot to them. For Braid One, Christian chose to write about his experience in a tug-of-war ritual at our college that takes place over the Black River. For Braid Two, he excerpted journal entries from his great-great-great-great-uncle Pieter Damstra, one of the first Dutch settlers of our present-day community. For Braid Three, Christian told stories of terrible dates from his sophomore year, where he said stupid things, drove women away, or broke up for no real reason.

It's one of the best student pieces I have ever read. In class, everyone praised Christian for the subtle patterns he drew between relatives, dating, and tug-of-war. Christian smiled at us and said, "What patterns?"

He didn't see that when his ancestor talked about how his wife, Albatross, was really annoying on the boat on the way over—which came up the Black River, the very river over which Christian tugged—there was an echo, a refraction, a little mirror in the writing. He didn't see what the class could see in his piece: Love is a tug-of-war. Ancestors pull you back. Christian thought he was being lazy and cheating by using the journal excerpts because he had written less than the other students. His old Dutch relatives worried all the time that they weren't working hard enough, too. I could go on and on—and in class, we did.

BRAID YOUR STORY

Look at your book in terms of a braid structure. Have a friend or writing-group partner (since it's hard to rethink your own work on the structural level) separate three story lines. You may need to create a new line to complicate your story, or you may want to promote a line from within the existing structure to more emphatically triangulate what is already there.

Construct a new outline based on this structure and limit yourself to very small flashes or glimpses—like photographs or snapshots—for the entire length of each strand.

If this doesn't work the first time, try it again. Or try it with a different project, not the one you are working on now, just to introduce your brain to this new kind of structure. If you are one of the many people who think in terms of "the next three books I want to write," you are a good candidate for braiding.

USE BRAIDS FOR REVISION, TOO

Braiding also works as a revision strategy. Many pieces that aren't working are actually fine—they're just not complex enough. They are the Braid A, and they will not come to life, no matter what you do, until you spark-feed them with a Braid B, and then a Braid C.

This is true for articles, poems, essays, novels, nonfiction books, everything. Every episode of *Friends* is braided, for instance. Notice your conversations with your friends. Braided. Notice your favorite video games. What are the braids?

Be aware of the connections, but leave lots of room for discovery. After the draft is up and running, you can shape and bend. But braid first. And watch the sparks start flying.

Good writing has layers. It does more than one thing. It leaves room for the reader to go, *Aha!*

HEATHER SELLERS is the author of *Page After Page*, *Chapter After Chapter*, and her memoir, *You Don't Look Like Anyone I Know*.

CHAPTER 12

CRAFT AN OPENING SCENE THAT LURES READERS INTO CHAPTER TWO

BY LES EDGERTON

It's a well-known fact that a tremendous number of manuscripts never get read by agents and editors. Wait. Amend that to: A tremendous number of *possibly good and even brilliant novels and short stories and other literary forms* never get read *beyond the first few paragraphs or pages* by agents and editors. Why? Simple: The stories don't begin in the right place. When an agent or editor encounters a poor beginning, she doesn't bother to continue reading.

The opening of your story carries an awesome responsibility. Consider this: The goals of your opening scene are: (1) to successfully introduce the story-worthy problem; (2) to hook the readers; (3) to establish the rules of the story; and (4) to forecast the ending of the story. If your opening fails to accomplish any one of these elements, then guess what? Your opening will fail. To ensure that your opening doesn't have any lethal lapses, let's take a closer look at each of the opening obligations.

INTRODUCE THE PROBLEM

This is the opening's most important goal. Without a story-worthy problem, your story doesn't have much chance of success. The problem is the heart and soul of the story. The majority of the novel or story contains the protagonist's struggle to resolve this problem. You must set the stage for the story-worthy problem's eventual unveiling (which is gradually revealed) right from the get go to give the reader a compelling reason to keep turning the page. This is done via an inciting incident, which is the event that triggers the first surface problem and sets the story into motion.

It's important to note that the word *trouble* in fiction terms doesn't carry the same definition as it does in real life. A wife leaving a husband, someone losing a job, a murder next door, or even in the protagonist's own household don't, by themselves, qualify as trouble in fiction terms. Trouble, in literary terms, means the protagonist's world has been profoundly altered by some event—not altered in terms of material or surface things, such as a loss of income, the death of a loved one, or an injury but in terms of the inner psychological world of the character being significantly changed for the worse. For instance, the loss of one's job and perhaps even livelihood, while drastic in real life, isn't enough to sustain a story. If the character has tied his sense of self to his profession, however, then losing a job can easily represent an inner psychological problem and be transformed from merely a bad situation into a story-worthy problem.

Just as a story about characters who experience only good things in their lives is boring to everyone except family members and friends, a story about people to whom bad things happen—but with no effect on their inner psychological selves—is just as boring. A character with a Job-like existence isn't all that interesting, but when we find out his sorry existence is caused by a deity testing his faith and his battle to maintain it or even fight its loss, then the story becomes interesting.

HOOK THE READER

A hook is something that intrigues the reader, and it can be virtually anything that makes the reader want to continue reading. It can be a story question—will the protagonist overcome the daunting problem confronting him—or it can be the author's lovely language or any of a dozen and one other things.

Good hooks have strong inciting incidents that plunge the protagonist immediately into trouble—the trouble that's going to occupy the rest of the story. There are authors who compel the reader to invest time with solely the beauty of their prose, but you shouldn't rely on your facile command of language to draw in the reader. The surest way to involve the reader is to begin with an opening scene that changes the protagonist's world profoundly and creates a story-worthy problem.

A good hook can have other facets. Here's one hook that operates on several levels, from Jo-Anne Michiel Watts' short story "What's Not to Enjoy?":

> A few days before Thanksgiving I get a terrific recipe from the Turkey Hotline Lady while Dyna and I make love.

What a superb opening—who could possibly resist reading on? There are questions galore in this opening. First, what sort of person not only remembers getting a "terrific recipe" while making love but also places more importance on the recipe than the sexual act itself? What kind of person notices recipes she overhears on the radio while making love? Why is it important for the author to mention specifically that this happened just before Thanksgiving?

And then, the language itself draws us in. There's intelligent, understated humor in this first sentence, and that tells us that this story will likely make us at least smile—always a good feeling to have from a story's beginning. "The Turkey Hotline Lady" is just plain funny. Further, Watts employs a conversational style of language that gives us the sense that a friend is relating the tale to us.

Watts' opening is a great example of a hook that does just what hooks are meant to do: draw the reader in and make him want to read more. And the fact that the narrator/protagonist chooses to report on a recipe rather than on lovemaking tells us there's trouble ahead.

ESTABLISH STORY RULES

A novel (and short story) has certain rules—rules you, as the author, must establish and convey to readers so your story can be read intelligently. These rules can be almost anything you desire, so long as they follow one ironclad dictum: They must be consistent. You can't begin your novel by writing somberly about serious stuff, and then switch on page 30 to a black-comedy treatment of the material. You have to establish what kind of story it's going to be from the very beginning. Don't try to fool readers. They won't forgive you. However you begin the story—voice, tone, the way the story is narrated— that's the way it has to continue through the ending. Consistency is key to writing a good novel.

The beginning must be connected to the whole of the story. That may seem to be common sense, but you should never write an opening that's marginally related to the story solely to create a hook to draw the reader in.

FORECAST THE ENDING

The beginnings of the best stories often contain at least a hint of the endings. As T.S. Eliot said, "In my beginning is my end." When students approach me, stuck on how to end their stories, my first advice is always to look back at their beginning, for the answer should lie there. A good example is my own short story "It's Different," which begins:

> As a boy, he had watched his mother grow bigger with the child that would become his sister. The larger her belly grew, the more repulsed he became, shrinking from her touch, afraid to touch her skin. Two reasons: She might explode, expel the thing inside her. Her skin, the skin on her upper arms that had gotten thicker, felt cool, clammy. Skin that enveloped fatness. Now, he had one himself. A pregnant wife.

The character finds he can't relate to his wife's pregnancy, the proof of that culminating when she attempts sex with him, and he's unable to respond. When she goes to sleep, and he gets up and does a crossword puzzle, a combination of words comes up that leads him to the realization that his relationship with his mother has led to his revulsion toward his pregnant wife. It comes full circle when he remembers his own childhood and the feelings he had and what caused those feelings. The seeds of your ending can often be sown in your beginning, when it works properly. Begin with a brief hint of what's to take place at the end, and you'll create a story that comes full circle and feels complete.

WHY GOOD BEGINNINGS GO BAD

Perhaps the primary reason for beginning stories in the wrong place is a lack of trust in the reader's intelligence. This is the real key to understanding just about all of the problems that lead to the wrong beginnings. Once you begin to trust the reader's intelligence, not only poor beginnings, but many other problems that prevent stories from becoming published, begin to disappear.

Of course, it's important to note that the opening scene is developed within a vacuum. Later scenes benefit from the knowledge conveyed in previous scenes—knowledge that helps orient the reader in the scene and helps the reader understand what's going on with the characters.

Not so in the first scene. Unless the novel is part of an already established series, the reader knows nothing about the situation or the characters. Thus the writer's temptation to furnish backstory is valid, but readers don't need to know everything about your characters to fully realize the significance of what's happened when the trouble begins.

Intelligent readers understand a lot from a tiny bit of information. Give them credit for having functional brains. For instance, let's say you want to write a story about a man who has something happen that reveals to him that he needs a healthy relationship with a woman to be complete, but he's been married and divorced five times—strong evidence that he's terrible at relationships.

A writer with little trust in the reader's intelligence may feel he needs to take the reader through those five marriages to show how miserable his protagonist is at relationships. Or perhaps this writer decides not to describe all five marriages, but describes only one, maybe the last one.

This is a story that won't get read. The skillful writer, on the other hand, won't describe any of these failed marriages. He'll simply include the fact that the man's been married five times. The intelligent reader will infer that the protagonist is a guy who fails at relationships. What's ironic is that manuscripts don't get rejected because the majority of the story is good and only the beginning is flawed—they get rejected because the agent or editor never gets to the good part to begin with.

A story that begins in the wrong place won't be read past that point. If the good stuff happens later on, in all likelihood, an agent or editor will never reach it. A good, quality story beginning is a microcosm of the work entire. If you capture the right beginning, you've written a small version of the whole.

LES EDGERTON has published nine books, including *Hooked: Write Fiction That Grabs Readers at Page One and Never Lets Them Go.*

CHAPTER 13

WRITE A FIVE-STAR CHAPTER ONE

BY ELIZABETH SIMS

When you decide to go to a restaurant for a special dinner, you enjoy the anticipation. You've committed to spending sufficient time and money, and now you've arrived, and the place looks good and smells good. You smile and order an appetizer. When it comes, you enjoy it as a foretaste of the larger, more complex courses that will follow, but you also savor it for what it is: a delicious dish, complete in itself. If it's a truly great appetizer, you recognize it as an exquisite blend of flavor, texture, and temperature. And you're happy, because you know you'll be in good hands for the entire evening.

Isn't that what it's like to begin reading a terrific book?

The first chapter is the appetizer—small, yet so tremendously important. And so full of potential.

As an aspiring author, the prospect of writing Chapter One should not intimidate, but excite the hell out of you. Why? Because no other part of your book can provide you with the disproportionate payoff that an excellent first chapter can. Far more than a great query letter, a great Chapter One can attract the attention of an agent. It can keep a harried editor from yawning and hitting "delete." It can make a bookstore browser keep turning pages during the slow walk to the cash registers. And, yes, it can even keep a bleary-eyed owner of one of those electronic thingamajigs touching the screen for more, more, *more*!

Fiction, like food, is an art and a craft. Here's how to blend inspiration with technique and serve up an irresistible Chapter One.

RESIST TERROR

Let's be honest: Agents and editors like to make you quiver and sweat as you approach Chapter One. All those warnings: "Grab me from the opening sentence! Don't waste one word! If my attention flags, you've failed—you're down the toilet! In fact, don't even write Chapter One! Start your book at chapter four! Leave out all that David Copperfield crap!" From their perspective it's an acid test. They know how important Chapter One is, and if you're weak, they'll scare you into giving up before you begin. (Hey, it makes their jobs easier: one less query in the queue.)

Here's the truth: Agents and editors, all of them, are paper tigers. Every last one is a hungry kitten searching for something honest, original, and brave to admire. Now is the time to gather your guts, smile, and let it rip.

Your inner genius flees from tension, so first of all, relax. Notice that I did not say agents and editors are looking for perfect writing. Nor are they looking for careful writing. *Honest, original, and brave.* That's what they want, and that's what you'll produce if you open up room for mistakes and mediocrity. It's true! Only by doing that will you be able to tap into your wild and free core. Let out the bad with the good now, and you'll sort it out later.

Second, remember who you are and why you're writing this book. What is your book about? What purpose(s) will it serve? Write your answers down and look at them from time to time as you write. (By the way, it's okay to want to write a book simply to entertain people; the noblest art has sprung from just such a humble desire.)

And third, if you haven't yet outlined, consider doing so. Even the roughest, most rustic framework will give you a sharper eye for your beginning and, again, will serve to unfetter your mind. Your outline could be a simple list of things-that-are-gonna-happen, or it could be a detailed chronological narrative of all your plot threads and how they relate. I find that knowing where I'm headed frees my mind from everything but the writing at hand. Being prepared makes you calm and better equipped to tap into your unique voice—which is the most important ingredient in a good Chapter One.

DECIDE ON TENSE AND POINT OF VIEW

Most readers are totally unconscious of tense and POV; all they care about is the story. Is it worth reading? Fun to read? But *you* must consider your tense and POV carefully, and Chapter One is go time for these decisions. It used to be simple. You'd choose from:

a) First person: *I chased the beer wagon.*
b) Third-person limited: *Tom chased the beer wagon.*
c) Omniscient: *Tom chased the beer wagon while the villagers watched and wondered,* Would all the beer in the world be enough for this oaf?

... and you'd always use past tense.

But today, novels mix points of view and even tenses. In my Rita Farmer novels I shift viewpoints, but limit all POVs to the good guys. By contrast, John Grisham will shift out of the main character's POV to the bad guy's for a paragraph or two, then back again. (Some critics have labeled this practice innovative, while others have called it lazy; in the latter case, I'm sure Grisham is crying all the way to the bank.) It's also worth noting that studies have shown that older readers tend to prefer past tense, while younger ones dig the present. (If that isn't a statement with larger implications, I don't know what is.)

Many writing gurus tell you to keep a first novel simple by going with first person, past tense. This approach has worked for thousands of first novels (including mine, 2002's *Holy Hell*), but I say go for whatever feels right to you, simple or not. I do, however, recommend that you select present or past tense and stick with it.

Similarly, I advise against flashbacks and flash-forwards for first novels. Not that they can't work, but they seem to be off-putting to agents and editors, who will invariably ask, "Couldn't this story be told without altering the time-space continuum?"

The point is, you want your readers to feel your writing is smooth; you don't want them to see the rivets in the hull, so to speak. And the easiest way to do that is to create fewer seams.

If you're still unsure of your tense or POV choices, try these techniques:

Go to your bookshelf and take a survey of some of your favorite novels. What POVs and tenses are selected, and why do you suppose the authors chose those approaches?

Rehearse. Write a scene using first person, then third-person limited, then omniscient. What feels right?

Don't forget to consider the needs of your story. If you plan to have simultaneous action in Fresno, Vienna and Pitcairn, and you want to show it all in living color, you almost certainly need more than one POV.

And if you're still in doubt, don't freeze up—just pick an approach and start writing. Remember, you can always change it later if you need to.

CHOOSE A NATURAL STARTING POINT

When you read a good novel, it all seems to unfold so naturally, starting from the first sentence. But when you set out to write your own, you realize your choices are limitless, and this can be paralyzing. Yet your novel must flow from the first scene you select.

Let's say you've got an idea for a historical novel that takes place in 1933. There's this pair of teenagers who figure out what really happened the night the Lindbergh baby was abducted, but before they can communicate with the police, they themselves are kidnapped. Their captives take them to proto-Nazi Germany, and it turns out there's some weird relationship between Col. Lindbergh and the chancellor—or is there? Is the guy with the haircut really Lindbergh? The teens desperately wonder: *What do they want with us?*

Sounds complicated. Where should you start? A recap of the Lindbergh case? The teenagers on a date where one of them stumbles onto a clue in the remote place they go to make out? A newspaper clipping about a German defense contract that should have raised eyebrows but didn't?

Basically, write your way in.

Think about real life. Any significant episode in your own life did not spring whole from nothing; things happened beforehand that shaped it, and things happened afterward as a result of it. Think about your novel in this same way. The characters have pasts and futures (unless you plan to kill them); places, too, have pasts and futures. Therefore, *every* storyteller jumps into his story midstream. Knowing this can help you relax about picking a starting point. The Brothers Grimm did not begin by telling about the night Hansel and Gretel were conceived; they got going well into the lives of their little heroes, and they knew we wouldn't care about anything but what they're doing right now.

If you're unsure where to begin, pick a scene you know you're going to put in—you just don't know where yet—and start writing it. You might discover your Chapter One right there. And even if you don't, you'll have fodder for that scene when the time comes.

Here are a few other strategies that can help you choose a starting point:

- Write a character sketch or two. You need them anyway, and they're great warm-ups for Chapter One. Ask yourself: What will this character be doing when we first meet him? Write it. Again, you might find yourself writing Chapter One.
- Do a chapter-one-only brainstorm and see what comes out.
- The truth is, you probably can write a great story starting from any of several places. If you've narrowed it down to two or three beginnings and still can't decide, flip a coin and get going. In my hypothetical Lindbergh thriller, I'd

> probably pick the date scene, with a shocking clue revealed. Why? Action!

It's okay to be extremely loose with your first draft of your first chapter. In fact, I recommend it. The important thing at this point is to begin.

PRESENT A STRONG CHARACTER RIGHT AWAY

This step might seem obvious, but too many first-time novelists try to lure the reader into a story by holding back the main character. Having a couple of subsidiary characters talking about the protagonist can be a terrific technique for character or plot development at some point, but *not* at the beginning of your novel.

When designing your Chapter One, establish your characters' situation(s). What do they know at the beginning? What will they learn going forward? What does their world mean to them?

Who is the strongest character in your story? Watch out; that's a trick question. Consider Kazuo Ishiguro's *The Remains of the Day*. The main character, Stevens, is a weak man, yet his presence is as strong as a hero. How? Ishiguro gave him a voice that is absolutely certain, yet absolutely vacant of self-knowledge. We *know* Stevens, and because we see his limitations, we know things will be difficult for him. Don't be afraid to give all the depth you can to your main character early in your story. You'll discover much more about him later, and you can always revise if necessary.

BE SPARING OF SETTING

Another common error many aspiring novelists make is trying to set an opening scene in too much depth. You've got it all pictured in your head: the colors, sounds, flavors and feelings. You want everybody to be in the same place with the story you are. But you're too close: A cursory—but poignant!—introduction is what's needed. Readers will trust you to fill in all the necessary information later. They simply want to get a basic feel for the setting, whether it's a lunar colony or a street in Kansas City.

Pack punch into a few details. Instead of giving the history of the place and how long the character has been there and what the weather's like, consider something like this:

> He lived in a seedy neighborhood in Kansas City. When the night freight passed, the windows rattled in their frames and the dog in the flat below barked like a maniac.

Later (if you want) you'll tell all about the house, the street, the neighbors, and maybe even the dog's make and model, but for now a couple of sentences like that are all you need.

But, you object, what of great novels that opened with descriptions of place, like John Steinbeck's *The Grapes of Wrath* or Edna Ferber's *Giant*? Ah, in those books the locale has been crafted with the same care as a character and effectively used as one. Even so, the environment is presented *as the characters relate to it*: in the former case, man's mark on the land (by indiscriminate agriculture), and in the latter, man's mark on the sky (the jet plumes of modern commerce).

Another way to introduce a setting is to show how a character feels about it. In Dostoyevsky's *Crime and Punishment*, Raskolnikov seethes with resentment at the opulence around him in St. Petersburg, and this immediately puts us on the alert about him. The setting serves the character; it does not stand on its own.

GREAT CHAPTER ONES IN HISTORY

- *Don Quixote* Miguel de Cervantes (1617) Quixote is earnest, he's obsessed with chivalry, he's in love with a wench, he's crazy—and it's all there in Chapter One.
- *Jane Eyre* Charlotte Brontë (1847) How bad is Jane's life? Bad! From the first page, Jane gets trodden down again and again, until you know something's gonna give.

- *Crime and Punishment* Fyodor Dostoyevsky (1866) A young man in debt, feeling sorry for himself, already rationalizing immoral behavior.

- *Dracula* Bram Stoker (1897) After a thimbleful of history, we get frightened peasants crossing themselves, a castle, moonlight, shadows, howling wolves, and an unmistakable feeling of impending evil.

- *Little House in the Big Woods* Laura Ingalls Wilder (1932) Chapter One actually begins, "Once upon a time ..." Children love this book because it's made of stuff adults don't expect them to like—it opens with a pig slaughtering, wildcats, bears, and even deer ready for butchering hanging in trees.

- *The Violent Bear It Away* Flannery O'Connor (1960) Chapter One cuts right to the bone of what so many other authors dance around and never get to: ultimate motivations, absolute morality, and the harsh requirements of a fundamental God. Primal fury!

- *Coma* Robin Cook (1977) Deft character development plus unsettling medical detail forms a breakthrough idea—and a big what if?

- *The Remains of the Day* Kazuo Ishiguro (1988) You feel bludgeoned by Stevens' moral and emotional cluelessness; when you realize with horror that he's going to be at your side through the whole story, you cannot walk away.

- *On Chesil Beach* Ian McEwan (2007) A long Chapter One that quietly presents enormous conflict, sharpened by the fact that only one of the two characters knows it.

USE CAREFULLY CHOSEN DETAIL TO CREATE IMMEDIACY

Your Chapter One must move along smartly, but in being economical you cannot become vague. Difficult, you say? It's all in the context.

The genius of books as diverse as Miguel de Cervantes' *Don Quixote* and Robin Cook's *Coma* lies in the authors' generosity with good, authentic detail. Cervantes knew that a suit of armor kept in a junk locker for years wouldn't merely be dusty, it would be corroded to hell—and that would be a problem to overcome. Likewise, Cook, himself a doctor, knew that a patient prepped for surgery would typically be given a calming drug before the main anesthetic—and that some patients, somehow, do not find peace even under the medication, especially if they have reason not to.

If you're an expert on something, go ahead and show that you know what you're talking about. One of the reasons my novel *Damn Straight*, a story involving a professional golfer, won a Lambda Award is that I know golf, and let my years of (painful) experience inform the book. I felt I'd done a good job when reviewer after reviewer wrote, "I absolutely hate golf, but I love how Sims writes about it in this novel. ..."

Let's say your Chapter One begins with your main character getting a root canal. You could show the dentist nattering on and on as dentists tend to do, and that would be realistic, but it could kill your chapter, as in this example:

> Dr. Payne's running commentary included the history of fillings, a story about the first time he ever pulled a tooth, and a funny anecdote about how his college roommate got really drunk every weekend.

Bored yet? Me too. Does that mean there's too much detail? No. It means there's too much *extraneous* detail.

How about this:

> Dr. Payne paused in his running commentary on dental history and put down his drill. "Did you know," he remarked, "that the

> value of all the gold molars in a city this size, at this afternoon's spot price of gold, would be something on the order of half a million dollars?" He picked up his drill again. "Open."

If the detail serves the story, you can hardly have too much.

GIVE IT A MINI PLOT

It's no accident that many great novels have first chapters that were excerpted in magazines, where they essentially stood as short stories. I remember being knocked to the floor by the gorgeous completeness of Ian McEwan's first chapter of *On Chesil Beach* when it was excerpted in *The New Yorker.*

Every chapter should have its own plot, none more important than Chapter One. Use what you know about storytelling to:

- Make trouble. I side with the writing gurus who advise you to put in a lot of conflict early. Pick your trouble and make it big. If it can't be big at first, make it ominous.

- Focus on action. Years ago I got a rejection that said, "Your characters are terrific and I love the setting, but not enough happens." A simple and useful critique! Bring action forward in your story; get it going quick. This is why agents and editors tell you to start your story in the middle: They've seen too many Chapter Ones bogged down by backstory. Put your backstory in the back, not the front. Readers will stick with you if you give them something juicy right away. I make a point of opening each of my Rita Farmer novels with a violent scene, which is then revealed to be an audition, or a film shoot or a rehearsal. Right away, the reader gets complexity, layers, and a surprise shift of frame of reference.

- Be decisive. A good way to do that is to make a character take decisive action.

- Don't telegraph too much; let action develop through the chapter. It's good to end Chapter One with some closure.

Because it is Chapter One, your readers will trust that the closure will turn out to be deliciously false.

BE BOLD

The most important thing to do when writing Chapter One is put your best material out there. Do not humbly introduce your story—present it with a flourish. Don't hold back! Set your tone and own it. You're going to write a whole book using great material; have confidence that you can generate terrific ideas for action and emotion whenever you want.

If you do your job creating a fabulous appetizer in Chapter One and follow it up well, your readers will not only stay through the whole meal, they'll order dessert, coffee and maybe even a night-cap—and they won't want to leave until you have to throw them out at closing time.

ELIZABETH SIMS (elizabethsims.com) is a contributing editor for *Writer's Digest* Magazine. She's the award-winning author of seven novels and many short stories, poems, and articles.

CHAPTER 14

STRENGTHEN YOUR SCENES

BY JAMES SCOTT BELL

In the English countryside they have stone walls to keep in the sheep. Some of these walls have been around for centuries, and they're amazing architectural achievements. The flat stones are not uniform. They differ in color and shape, yet they fit together to form the whole.

The scenes of your fiction are like the stones in an English wall. You want your scenes to vary in shape and feel, but when you step back they should all fit together. You don't want any stones sticking out at odd angles or cracked through the center.

If you make each scene stand on its own and contribute to the story in an essential way, your story will be structurally solid.

But if you have weak scenes, your story may crumble.

Let's look at some simple techniques for revising scenes so your edifice will stand the test of time.

1. RELIVE YOUR SCENES, NOT REWRITE, RELIVE

Have you ever imagined yourself to be the characters? Tried to feel what they're feeling? Try it now. It's not hard. Be an actor.

Often, after I've written a scene, I'll go back and try to live the emotions. I'll act out the parts I've created. Almost always what I feel "in character" will make me add to or change the scene.

You can also imagine the scene, step by step, in your mind. Let it play like a movie. But instead of watching the movie from a seat in the theater, be in the scene. The other characters can't see you, but you can see and hear them.

Intensify the proceedings. Let things happen. Let characters improvise. If you don't like what they come up with, rewind the scene and allow them to do something else.

Look at the beginnings of your scenes. What do you do to grab the reader at the start? Have you spent too much time with description of setting? Often the better course is to start in medias res (in the middle of things) and drop in description a little later.

Examine scene endings. What have you provided that will make the reader want to read on? Some great places to stop a scene are:

- At the moment a major decision is to be made.
- Just as a terrible thing happens.
- With a portent of something bad about to happen.
- With a strong display of emotion.
- When raising a question that has no immediate answer.

Keep improving your scenes and your novel will soon develop that can't-put-it-down feel.

2. HEAT UP THE CORE

Ask yourself what the core of your scene is. What's the purpose? Why does it exist? If the core is weak or unclear, strengthen it.

3. ADJUST YOUR PACE

If you need to speed up a scene, dialogue is one way to do it. Short exchanges with few beats leave a lot of white space on the page and give a feeling of movement.

In the Lawrence Block story "A Candle for the Bag Lady," a waitress tells private investigator Matt Scudder someone was looking for him, ending her descriptions by saying he looked "underslung."

"Perfectly good word."

"I said you'd probably get here sooner or later."

"I always do. Sooner or later."

"Uh-huh. You okay, Matt?"

"The Mets lost a close one."

"I heard it was 13-4."

"That's close for them these days. Did he say what it was about?"

To slow the pace of a scene, you can add action beats, thoughts and description as well as elongated speeches. In the Block story, a killer confesses to Scudder. Scudder asks why he did it.

> "Same as the bourbon and coffee. Had to see. Had to taste it and find out what it was like." His eyes met mine. His were very large, hollow, empty. I fancied I could see right through them to the blackness at the back of his skull. "I couldn't get my mind away from murder," he said. His voice was more sober now, the mocking playful quality gone from it. "I tried. I just couldn't do it. It was on my mind all the time and I was afraid of what I might do. I couldn't function, I couldn't think, I just saw blood and death all the time. I was afraid to close my eyes for fear of what I might see. I would just stay up, days it seemed, and then I'd be tired enough to pass out the minute I closed my eyes. I stopped eating. I used to be fairly heavy and the weight just fell off of me."

4. STRETCH THE TENSION

Don't waste any good tension beats. Stretch them. Make your prose the equivalent of slow motion in a movie.

Show every beat, using all the tools at your disposal: thoughts, actions, dialogue, description. Mix these up.

In a famous early scene in *Whispers*, Dean Koontz takes 17 pages to describe the attempted rape of the lead character. Read it and learn.

AVOID MUDDY VIEWPOINTS

Each scene needs to have a clear point-of-view character. The rule is one POV per scene. No "head hopping." The exception is when you're using omniscient POV, which has its own challenges. Otherwise stick with one.

Go over your scenes and see if, within the first couple of paragraphs, the viewpoint is clear. If not, you can quickly remedy the situation. Instead of starting a scene this way:

The room was stuffy and packed with people.

Do it like this:

> Steve walked into the stuffy room and tried to get past the mass of people.

Throughout the scene, you may need to remind us whose head we're in. You can do this with little clues, such as "Steve knew that he had to ..." or "Steve felt the sweat under his arms ..."

5. CUT OR STRENGTHEN WEAK SCENES

Identify the ten weakest scenes in your work. You should have an idea of what these are. Use your gut instinct.

When you read through the manuscript, you sensed a certain letdown in some of the scenes or even outright disappointment.

To help you further, look for scenes where:

- Characters do a lot of talking to each other, without much conflict.
- The scene feels like a setup for some other scene.
- The characters' motivations seem undeveloped.
- There's too much introspection going on.
- There's not enough introspection to explain the motivations in action.
- There's little tension or conflict between characters.
- There's little tension or conflict inside the character.

Make yourself identify ten weak scenes. Even if you think only five are really weak, rate another five. List the scenes in order of their relative weakness. The weakest scene is No. 1, the next weakest No. 2, and so on.

Write these numbers on sticky notes and mark each weak scene in the manuscript. Now you're ready to work. Follow these steps:

Step 1: Cut scene 1 from the manuscript.

It's gone. It is the weakest link. Good-bye.

Step 2: Move to scene 2. Answer the three 'O' questions.

1. What's the objective in the scene and who holds it? In other words, who is the POV character and what's he after in the scene? If he's not after anything, give him something to go after, or cut the scene.

   You must be able to state the character's objective clearly and unambiguously. You must also make this objective clear to the reader at the beginning of the scene. The character must either state it or show it in action.

2. Next, what's the obstacle to his known objective? Why can't he have it? There are three primary obstacles you can use:
   - Another character who opposes him, either consciously or unconsciously.
   - The character himself is fighting an inner battle or lack of something that gets in his way.
   - A physical circumstance makes it hard or impossible for him to gain his objective.

3. Finally, what is the outcome of the scene? A character can gain his objective or not. For the greatest tension, which do you think it should be? Not. Why? Because trouble is your game, and trouble is tension for the character, and that's what

keeps readers reading. Most of the time, let the outcome be a negative—or at least an unrealized—objective.

Step 3: Repeat the above process for the other eight scenes on your list.

JAMES SCOTT BELL is a best-selling and award-winning suspense writer. He is the author of *Plot & Structure, Revision & Self-Editing* and *The Art of War for Writers*.

CHAPTER 15

RESCUE YOUR STORY FROM PLOT PITFALLS

BY LAURA WHITCOMB

We've all been there, basking in the glow of a finished manuscript only to read it over and realize something is wrong with the plot. Finding ourselves unable to identify the problem only makes matters worse. But take heart! Here are some common plot gaffes and sensible ways to revise without starting over.

1. THE PLOT ISN'T ORIGINAL ENOUGH

Go through your pages and highlight anything that you've read in another book or seen in a movie. In the margin, write where you've seen it. Then list these sections and make a note for each one about how it could differ from its look-alike. A mental patient escapes by throwing something heavy through a window. Too much like *One Flew Over the Cuckoo's Nest*? Instead the patient walks out with a visiting grandma after convincing her he's an old friend. Quick notes like these can help you detach from unintentional imitation.

2. READERS ALWAYS KNOW EXACTLY WHAT'S GOING TO HAPPEN

This may be because you've chosen a plot point that's overused or because you keep giving away the answer in advance. Readers know the villain is going to whip out a picture of the hero's son and blackmail her by pretending to have kidnapped the little boy because you showed the villain taking pictures of the child and driving away from the school yard. You could be less obvious by only showing the antagonist sitting in the car watching the boy on the playground and no more.

3. THE PLOT IS BORING

Take each page and imagine what different writers might do with the same plot. Choose extreme examples. Would a comedy writer have the cab driver and the villain coincidentally be childhood friends with unfinished business? Would the mystery writer have the taxi pass a clue on a street corner that makes a new connection for the hero? Would the horror writer have the cab driver channel a ghost? Imagine the most surprising thing that could happen in a given scene. It doesn't matter if these ideas don't fit your story. You're not going to use them. But often, after thinking of wild ideas to make the story more interesting, you begin to come up with workable ones that are just as stimulating but better suited to your book.

4. THE PLOT IS ALL ACTION AND THE FRENZIED PACE NUMBS READERS

Let them breathe. Give the readers a little downtime now and then in your action story. Look back at your favorite action novels. Notice the conversations, summarized passages, meals, introspection, and releases of emotions that are set in between the car chases, shootouts and confrontations. List them. Then give the readers a chance to breathe in your own manuscript. Find the dramatic respites that come from your characters' needs, flaws, and strengths.

5. THE PLOT IS TOO COMPLEX

Often a complex plot can be trimmed into a sleek one by cutting out some steps. Does your protagonist have to visit her father in the hospital twice—once to bring him flowers and talk about Mom, and then again to find he has taken a turn for the worse? Couldn't he take a turn for the worse while she's still there the first time? Does your villain need to have three motives for revenge? Would one or two be interesting enough? To find the messiness in your overly complex story, summarize it out loud to yourself. When a section takes too long to explain, make a note. When you find yourself saying, "Oh, wait, I forgot to mention that ..." you're probably in need of a plot trim. When deciding whether or not to simplify the plot, ask yourself over and over again, "Why does she do that? Why didn't she just do this?" Making a plot less complicated doesn't have to make it less clever.

6. THE PLOT IS TOO SHALLOW

Sometimes as writers we get caught up in the action. The symbolism. The metaphors. The witty dialogue. The great character names. The slick descriptions. Sometimes we ride these skills over the surface of the story and forget what's really important. If you or your first readers (friends, family, agent) complain that the novel feels insubstantial, step back and ask yourself these questions: Why am I bothering to write this story? Why does the outcome matter to the characters? How do the characters change? How did my favorite book affect me the first time I read it?

7. SUSPENSION OF DISBELIEF IS DESTROYED

Readers need to buy into the reality put forward by what they're reading. You may go too far with a plot point or not far enough with preparing your audience for that plot point. If something that sounded right when you outlined it is coming off as far-fetched even to you, look back at the stepping-stones that led to the event. If your murderer turns over a new leaf at the end of Act Two, make sure you've given her reason to.

SHAKE UP YOUR PLOT'S RHYTHM

Your plot has an effect on the rhythm between your scenes, summary and reflection. If for the first half of your book the protagonist is alone, there will be few dialogue scenes, lots of detailed descriptions, and probably plenty of summary and reflection. If, on the other hand, your whole novel takes place in a small boat where four people are trapped for a day, you'll probably have long scenes of dialogue.

To examine your plot's rhythm, try one of these exercises:

1. List the scenes. List all your scenes, skipping a line between each. Then write down whether there needs to be any transition between the scenes.

Can you just jump to the next scene? Then mark the scenes with a "Y" for "YES, I'm absolutely positive this part should be written as a scene," or an "M" for "MAYBE this needs to be a scene, maybe I should rethink it and turn it into a summary or a passage of reflection."

2. Compound scenes. Search your manuscript for scenes that can be combined. Here's an example: You write a scene where your protagonist argues with her husband as he's leaving for work, then you summarize her driving the kids to school, then include a scene where she gets her feelings hurt by her son as she drops him off at the curb.

Maybe you could combine the things that need to happen in the story. The other car won't start so she's got the kids and her husband squished into her car. She's arguing with the husband as she's trying to drive and can't pay attention to the children, who are trying to get her attention.

As she pulls up to the school, her son hurts her feelings on purpose as he's getting out of the car. Lots going on. Not boring. And now the argument with the husband is tied to the child hurting her feelings.

3. Scan your favorite book. Take a novel by your favorite writer, someone you would like to emulate, and flip through the first fifty pages, jotting down the length, number, and order of scenes, summaries, and passages of reflection. You might be surprised at what you learn.

8. TOO MANY SUBPLOTS MAKE THE PLOT OVERLY COMPLEX

If you start to feel weighed down by your numerous story lines, start cutting them. List the subplots (shopkeeper with a crush, neighbor's dog that tears up the garden, accountant who threatens to quit every day), and then list under each title all the ways it's necessary.

Only subplots that are so vital that you could not remove them without destroying your novel get to stick around. Be bold.

9. THE SEQUENCE IS ILLOGICAL

Sometimes the sequence set down in an outline starts to show its true colors when you're writing the chapters. If you feel the order of scenes or events in your story is off, list each scene on a separate index card and, in red ink, write a question mark on every card that doesn't feel right where it is in the story. Shuffle the cards. I'm not kidding. Mix them up completely. Lay them out again in the order you think they might work best, giving special attention to those with red question marks.

Something about these scenes tricked you the first time. This time, really look closely at the proper place for those tricky bits.

10. THE PREMISE ISN'T COMPELLING

If you fear that a mediocre premise is your holdup, take out a sheet of paper. Make a list on the left-hand side of everything that's dodgy in your present premise. Then write a list down the right-hand side about all the things that work great in the premise of a similar favorite book, play, or movie.

See where you might make the stakes higher, the characters more emotional, the setting more a part of the overall plot. Remember: The premise should make your readers curious.

11. THE CONCLUSION IS UNSATISFYING

Once again, write a list of what bothers you about your conclusion, and, next to it, a list of what worked great about the end of your favorite novel. Do you have to create more suspense before you give the readers what they've been craving? Do you need to make the answer to the mystery clearer? Does the villain need to be angrier, or perhaps show remorse? Unsatisfying conclusions are usually lacking something. Whatever that is, make your story's ending have more of it.

LAURA WHITCOMB is the author of two young adult novels and *Novel Shortcuts: Ten Techniques that Ensure a Great First Draft*.

FOCUS ON THE WRITING LIFE:

BEATING WRITER'S BLOCK

START ME UP

BY ELIZABETH SIMS

Let's get something straight. If you were a Mini Cooper and somebody drove you into a bog filled with axle-deep mud, you'd be stuck. If you were a halfback and you dodged the wrong way, you would be blocked. If you were a mountain huckleberry and somebody stewed you with pectin and countless other mountain huckleberries, then sealed you under sterile conditions and lower-than-ambient air pressure, you'd be jammed.

Luckily, you're none of those things. You're a writer of fiction. You don't get stuck, blocked, or jammed.

Yeah, right. I tell myself that, too. The truth is, the bogs and the blocks and the slow stickies get everybody at some time. But after seven novels, I've figured out ways to outwit them all—and have fun doing it.

THE RANDOM SENTENCE KICK START

If you can't get even a word on the page, try this:

1. Go to your bookshelf, close your eyes, and pick off a book at random. Fiction or not; doesn't matter.

2. Open that book to a random page.
3. Open your eyes.
4. Read the first sentence you see.
5. Put the book back.
6. Now make that sentence the basis of what you write next.

Let's say I want to begin a novel about a hot dog peddler who decides he ought to have a trophy wife.

I close my eyes at my bookshelf and pick out *The Portable Conrad.* Flip open to page 545, where my eye picks up this sentence from *Heart of Darkness*: "It was not sleep—it seemed unnatural, like a state of trance." All right, here's my beginning:

> I hadn't slept in a week, but it wasn't even that. I knew she'd come and buy a dog with mustard and a Diet Coke, no chips, on Friday. And I knew she'd drop the money in my hand and take the dog with a nervous little shake, to settle the dog better in the bun and settle the bun better in the foil. I'd been waiting for her like a schooner waits for a trade wind, like a zombie waits for a dish of brain curds. She came to buy a dog once a month, no more often, because she was a model and had to watch her weight but she loved my dogs. I saw her for two minutes on the second Friday of every month. I loved her during those two minutes and all the minutes in between.

Well, I like it. I might keep it or throw it away, but at least it gets my story going, and it's fresh. I can use my protagonist's insomnia again if I want to. He's revealed his personality and his problem, and now I can take him out for a beer and get to know him better.

SPELUNKING THE SEWER WITHIN

When your writing feels heavy and effortful, chances are your imagination is tired. Adding some nastiness can work wonders. I don't mean you should change your hero into a villain, but you must find and bring out dark nuances, which horrify and fascinate us when we see them in others—and pretend not to see in ourselves.

Think about something you did that was horrible and that you're not sorry for. That's powerful stuff.

Write about it. Now think about something you did that was horrible and that you're ashamed of. There's power there, too. Think about writing a story about that shameful thing from a *sympathetic* point of view.

Were you the school bully? Probably not. But pretend you were. Write about it. What made you mad? Whom did you hate? Why? What was your favorite way to inflict pain on your victims? Were you ever sorry? Did you ever hurt yourself?

Write answers to these questions, then go back to your fiction at hand. You'll immediately see opportunities for deepening your characters, and from that you'll see ways to add dynamic, direct action that moves your story forward.

THE CROSS-CULTURAL QUARREL

If your dialogue is falling flat, throw a couple of opposites together and make them argue. This is so much fun and will jar you out of the deepest mental rut. You can use your own characters if you're in the middle of a novel or story. I advise picking characters who may never meet: the suave drug dealer vs. the passive-aggressive university professor; the neurotic movie star vs. her long-dead idol. Why characters whose worlds don't meet? Because things you're not expecting will come out of their mouths.

Give them a setting—climbing out of their cars after colliding with each other, standing side by side in a police lineup, racing away from a mudslide, sitting down on a curbstone with a pint of Jim Beam. Start an argument. You can make one character demand something from the other, or you can make one of them nosy about the other. Here are some starter questions:

- What has just happened to you?
- What are you going to do about it?
- How do you think you can get away with that?
- Who was the last person you kissed?

If your own characters are still feeling dull, try writing an argument between someone else's characters, especially characters from vastly different books. At random: Brett Ashley vs. Hazel Motes, Zooey Glass vs. Tarzan, Count Vronsky vs. Jean Brodie (ooh!); The Wife of Bath vs. Pantagruel; Easy Rawlins vs. Aunt Polly.

As an example, I'll throw my hot dog peddler, whom I've named Rich (a little allegorical irony here), together with Jay Gatsby. Rich and Gatsby decide to take up boxing. They go to a gym, put on some gloves, and start sparring. While they jab and weave, they talk.

> Rich: So, I'm thinking I'll ask her out.
>
> Gatsby: You don't just ask her out, old sport. You have to prepare yourself. You have to do things.
>
> Rich: Well, I know. I'm going to get a haircut.
>
> Gatsby: I'm talking about everything. You can't just wave a wand and become attractive to her. Now a fellow like me—
>
> Rich: She'd never look twice at you.
>
> Gatsby: Now, look here. Do you want my advice or don't you? Your jacket is greasy, your fingernails have ketchup under them, you don't wear any cologne, and you're a high-school dropout. I'm sorry to be so honest. But a woman wants to be—
>
> Rich: I'm going to impress her by my actions.
>
> Gatsby: So, who are you going to assassinate?

How does all this feel? Disheveled and a little silly? Good! That's the point: to get your brain to a place where your inner editor gives up and leaves. When you get your writing going, keep it going. Press it. Be aggressive. When you stop, you'll feel confident about producing fresh work, because you'll have just done some.

ELIZABETH SIMS (elizabethsims.com) is a contributing editor for *Writer's Digest* Magazine. She's the award-winning author of seven novels and many short stories, poems, and articles.

PART 3:

POINT OF VIEW:

THE VOICE OF YOUR STORY

CHAPTER 16

UNDERSTANDING DIFFERENCES IN POV

BY JAMES V. SMITH JR.

There are, obviously, several different points of view available to you—and, less obviously, several advantages and disadvantages to each.

FIRST PERSON

First person POV refers to the *I, we, me, my, mine, us* narrator, often the voice of the heroic character or a constant companion of the heroic character.

> There I was, minding my own beeswax when she up and kissed me. I near passed out.

Advantages of this POV:

- It feels natural to most writers because we live in an I world.
- You have to deal with only one mind: the narrator's.
- You can create a distinctive internal voice.
- You can add an element of craft by creating a narrator who is not entirely reliable.

Disadvantages of this POV:

- You are limited to writing about what the narrator can see or sense.
- The narrator must constantly be on stage or observing the stage.
- You can't go into the minds of other characters.

SECOND PERSON

The *you* narrator, this POV is rarely successful, and even then works best in shorter books. For an example of second-person POV, check out Jay McInerney's *Bright Lights, Big City*. But know that most publishing professionals advise against using this tricky approach.

> You're just standing there. She comes along and kisses you, and you nearly faint.

Advantages of this POV:

- It gives you the power to be different, even eccentric in the way you can speak to the reader so directly.

Disadvantages of this POV:

- It begins to feel quirky, whether you're reading it or writing it.
- It can say to a publishing professional: "I'm a Jay McInerney knockoff. Reject me!"

THIRD PERSON

The *he, she, it, they, them* narrator, third person is the most common POV in fiction. It offers a variety of possibilities for limiting omniscience: information that the narrator and reader are privy to in the telling of the story.

Third Person Unlimited Omniscience

In this POV, the author enters the mind of any character to transport readers to any setting or action.

> He stood stiff as a fence post, watching her come his way. What did she want? he wondered.
>
> She had decided to kiss him, no matter what. So she did. She could see the effect of her kiss at once. He nearly fell over.

Advantages of this POV:

- It can enrich your novel with contrasting viewpoints.

- Both you and your reader can take a breath of fresh air as you shift from one character's POV to another's.
- You can broaden the scope of your story as you move between settings and from conflicting points of view.

Disadvantages of this POV:

- You can confuse yourself and the reader unless every voice is distinctive.
- You can diffuse the flow of your story by switching the POV too often. (Notice how the last passage about the kiss jolts you from one POV to the other.)
- It's easy to get lazy and begin narrating as the author instead of as one of your characters.

Third-Person Limited Omniscience

The author enters the mind of just a few characters, usually one per chapter or scene.

> He stood stiff as a fence post, watching her come his way.
>
> What did she want? he wondered, as she approached. Then he saw the determination in her face. Good crackers! She was going to kiss him, no matter what.
>
> She did, too, and he nearly fell over.

Advantages of this POV:

- It has all the advantages of third person unlimited POV.
- You can concentrate the story by keeping to major characters' (and strategic minor characters') thoughts.

Disadvantages of this POV:

- There aren't any, really; by imposing POV discipline,you minimize the downsides of unlimited omniscience.

If you want to get really complex, you can identify three or four times as many POV choices—but these are by far the most common, and will suit most any story.

JAMES V. SMITH JR. is author of five novels in the military action genre and *You Can Write a Novel, 2nd Edition* and *The Writer's Little Helper*. He is the editor, chief photographer, and writer for *Rural Montana* magazine.

DON'T LET YOUR AUTHORIAL VOICE OVERSHADOW YOUR CHARACTER'S VOICE

The most effective writing—regardless of POV—lets the reader see things through the eyes of the characters instead of the eyes of the author or omniscient narrator.

> He was tall, 6 foot 2, with a nose to match, tall, thin, and straight.

That's the author talking.

> He caught sight of his 6-foot-2 reflection in the window of a bagel shop, paused and studied his thin, straight nose, both in profile and straight on. *Straight on*, he decided, *always show your nose to her straight on. Never from the side.*

This approach provides the same facts without stopping the story as if to say, "I'm going to describe somebody now." We see the reflection through the character's eyes, not the author's keyboard. We see action, both actual and implied. Plus, we learn something about the character's personality. He's vain about the nose.

Here's another example of seeing through a character's eyes. In this brief scene only the characters do the talking.

> "You've got a stiff neck or something?" she asked.
>
> "No—why?"
>
> "You keep turning your body instead of your head when you look at me."

The characters describe the action to each other; it's entirely between quote marks. The author stays out of the picture and lets the characters react to each other and to events. You do your best writing when the people in the story make things happen. Naturally there's nothing wrong with narration. But when you reveal information this way, nobody, neither an author nor a narrator, interprets for the reader. Instead the reader interprets on her own.

Here is one final example of seeing a scene through a character's eyes:

> ... the guy staring up at the center of my face makes me wonder if my fine, straight nose is going to leave the party in the condition it crashed the party. He's a full foot shorter than me, 5 feet and change, thighs like fireplugs, a chest like a beer keg, a pony keg stacked on top for a head—no neck.

Here the first-person narrator is described by creating the image of somebody else and showing the contrast. We learn that the narrator is 6 feet tall, plus change. He wonders whether his fine, straight nose will be broken. It's the same height and nose we saw in the window, by the way. This technique shows us an image of the narrator without actually letting on that we're describing him.

CHAPTER 17

USING PERCEPTION TO ENHANCE YOUR POV

BY ALICIA RASLEY

Once you've chosen a primary POV character, you need to get to know her from the inside out. Keep in mind that readers want an experience, not just a view. They want to see the story *through that character's eyes.*

In order to create an authentic narrative voice, begin by asking yourself some key questions about your POV character: How does this person perceive the world? How does she come to understand her environment? What does she choose to notice and to ignore, and why? What does she want to do with what she learns?

In addition to defining your character's emotional and intellectual dimensions, POV reflects perceptual ability, which varies depending on a person's sensory and cognitive skills—the way we take in and use information.

PERCEPTION AND POINT OF VIEW

Most of us have one or two dominant senses. For example, I'm an auditory, not visual, person. I can see you every workday, and I can't describe you. But after a couple of phone conversations, I can recognize a voice anywhere. So as a POV character, I would not note my future love interest's looks, beyond a vague realization that he's gorgeous. But his sardonic tone, the nervous catch in his voice as he greets me, the deliberate pace of his speech—these I would take note of.

Think about your own perceptual strengths and weaknesses. Which of the five basic senses is strongest for you? Can you actually taste the difference between Pepsi and Coke? Can you distinguish the perfumes of every woman in the room? Can you tell just by the tone of a friend's voice how she's feeling? Do you love to touch different fabrics? Are you overly sensitive to color, to the point that you're unable to work in a yellow room?

Now apply the same sort of questions to a character, and you'll start to individualize her POV. Identify her dominant sense, and then think about how that will affect how she narrates a scene. A visual person will focus more on what she sees: *She was so intent on that garbage truck backing up that she missed what Judy said.* A tactile person will always be touching things and reporting on the texture: *Betty grabbed the doorknob. The brass was cool and smooth under her hand, and it wouldn't turn.* A little of this goes a long way, but even a few focused sensory references can convey how this character takes in the world around her.

THE VARIOUS MODES OF PERCEPTION

Sensual perceptivity is not the only way to "absorb" the world. There's also temperament (optimist/pessimist, emotional/rational) and personality style (problem solver, logician, competitor, and so on). Learning style also affects perception. You'll notice that schools these days tend to offer different methods of instruction because they recognize that children have different learning strengths. For example, a teacher will provide an assignment sheet but also read it aloud in class, so that both visual and auditory learners will understand it.

Visual people learn more through their eyes; they have good visual memory, are intrigued by color and motion, and will watch a video to learn how to build a bookcase. Kinesthetic learners need to participate in the lesson.

Think about how your character learned (or didn't learn) in school. And consider the character's profession, for we usually choose to do what we are naturally attuned to. Artists tend to perceive the world through their most developed sense, which will probably be the one they use in their art. An engineer will try to understand the logic, the structure, of what he's perceiving. A lawyer is a negotiator and a talker, and she'll acquire knowledge mostly through questioning and listening.

There's also a less obvious perceptive mode—a sixth sense—we call intuition. It's probably a combination of superior emotional intelligence and hypersensitivity to external stimuli, but what it means is that you can sense the emotion, intent, and fears of others. You can figure out if they're telling the truth or lying, if they're trustworthy or not. This is a wonderful "extra" sense to bestow upon certain types of characters, like cops and journalists, who have to make quick judgments. To display this sense in POV, imagine how it feels to know something instinctively, and show it that way. For example, a character's stomach might knot up, or the nerves in his arms might go on alert, when someone intends harm.

PERCEPTION AS A PARTY GAME

Now consider how these ways of perceiving will be exhibited in the narrative. Imagine a group of characters with lots of different perceptual abilities arriving at a raucous party and having to make sense of the chaos.

A problem solver sees the world as a set of problems to be solved. She will walk into a party and notice what's wrong—the music is too loud, the ice has run out, and a girl is sitting alone in the corner crying. Though the problem solver focuses on problems, she's no pessimist; rather, she's busy devising solutions—turning down the stereo, sending her boyfriend into the kitchen for more ice, and comforting the weeper.

A competitor sees life as a game. When he enters the party, he will choose a side—that weeping girl has already been cut from his team—then scout the opposition and ascertain the prize. He likes to know the rules ahead of time, and he expects a fair outcome: The swift ought to win the race, and he ought to get the most beautiful woman.

A materialist will scan the crowd and see diamonds and Rolex watches, calculating the net worth of the party and never noticing the human tragedy in the corner.

These are examples of only a few perception types. You'll come up with more on your own. Just remember, less is more. Few people are both visually and auditorily superior, and logical besides. So instead of using all five senses in a scene, consider that the more evocative viewpoint will have one dominant perception. A musical hero would close his eyes to better hear the song of his lover's sighs—and never even see the fire in her eyes.

HOW PERCEPTION CAN CHANGE A SCENE

Use your knowledge of the POV character's perspective modes to make his narration of every event unique to him. This contributes to the authenticity of the scene, strengthens a reader's investment in the story, and reveals character. Here are some examples of how perception might affect a POV character's experience of the scene and what details you choose to reveal about him.

A deliberate, judicious character will think before speaking, so you'll likely show that thinking:

> Thomas waited until they were alone. He chose his words carefully, knowing the wrong word could mean beheading. "I would not want to offend Your Grace, but his wife—it is said in the kitchens, mere rumor, perhaps, that she is spending more time with the stable boy than perhaps most ladies of her station would do."
>
> He waited for the duke's response, and when there was none except for that cold stare, Thomas realized it was not time for further revelation.

An impulsive person's thoughts will be chaotic and action oriented, and often the action will come first and the thought after:

> Thomas took the duke's arm and pulled him toward the window. "Come and see this. You'll want to see it." Well, he reflected, His

> Grace might not actually want to see it, but a cuckolded man deserved to know the truth.

He didn't see it coming, but he felt it—the duke's glove. Fist enclosed. As he went down, he thought, *Kill the messenger, why don't you?* And then he didn't think anymore.

A pessimistic person's thoughts will prophesize doom:

> Thomas watched the hard-faced duke enter and cross to the back window. Oh, woe. The duke would see his wife and the stable boy, right out there in the stable yard. There was no avoiding it. He didn't even bother to try to divert the duke's attention—what good would it do? No matter what, he would get blamed for it. It was his job around here. Whipping boy.

An optimist's POV will show an expectation of the best:

> Thomas watched the duke enter and cross to the window. That could be trouble. Then again, maybe it was for the best. Maybe the duke would see how unhappy his wife was, take pains to win her back, and give her the child she wanted so badly. Then the old castle would ring with the joyous sound of laughter and childish voices!

Same situation, same role—but a different type of character in each POV. It's not just the action that shifts with the change in character, but the very narration of that action—the word choice, the attitude, the sentence construction, the perception, the value system (the first Thomas values his position; the next values the truth; the next values his martyrdom; the final values babies and marital harmony), the analysis of what's going on, and the level of connection to reality.

ALICIA RASLEY is a Rita-award-winning author. She is the author of *The Power of Point of View: Make Your Story Come to Life*.

INDIVIDUALIZING YOUR CHARACTER'S POV

Look at your own POV character—the readers' eyes and ears in the story—and answer whichever of these questions intrigue you. (*You* in the questions refers to the character.) Freewrite the answers in the character's first-person voice:

1. How do you learn best? Observation? Participation? Trial and error? Rumination and cogitation? Consulting experts? Writing?
2. How open are you to new ideas and information? Do you change your mind frequently, based on what people have told you? Are you a traditionalist, deciding on the basis of what's always been?
3. When you walk into a party, what do you notice first? The mood? The people? The decorations? The things that need to be fixed? The background music? The food on the buffet table? Whether or not you fit in?
4. Is one sense more highly developed than another? For instance, do you tend to take in the world primarily through vision? ("I'll believe that when I see it!") Or are you more auditory? Do you determine if a person is lying by the tone of voice? What about the sixth sense—intuition? How often do you rely on your "gut" and then have your feelings confirmed?
5. Do you usually notice problems around you? What is your response? Do you write an angry letter to the editor? Shrug and move on? Analyze what's wrong and how to fix it? Take it as evidence that the world is falling apart? What about problems within yourself?
6. Would you say you are an optimist or a pessimist? Would your friends agree?
7. Are you more interested in the past, the future, or living in the now? Are you one to keep holiday traditions? If you had to move tomorrow, how long would it take you to make new friends?

8. How do you decide if you can trust someone? By experience with this person? First impressions? Intuition? Do you test the person somehow? Or are you generally disposed to trust or not to trust?

9. Are you a deliberate, careful speaker, or do you talk without thinking first? Do you use slang, or do you use the diction your old English teacher would approve of?

CHAPTER 18

POV CHARACTERS WHO OVERSTEP THEIR BOUNDS

BY KRISTEN JOHNSON INGRAM

Good writing streams from beginning to end without reminding readers of your construction. But both beginners and seasoned writers sometimes sabotage that flow when they allow in a writer's nemesis—The Viewpoint Intruder.

When you constantly reinsert the POV character into the narrative, you make readers feel as if they keep going back to the start. Read the following two examples of the same scene to see what I mean:

> Sally sits at a table in the restaurant, hoping her boyfriend, Jeremy, won't be late again. She notices the waiter looks tired. She turns to see a pair of Japanese men talking quietly in a booth near the corner. She watches as a baby in a high chair flings a spoonful of rice onto the carpet and sees the waiter sigh.
>
> Sally sits at a table in the restaurant, hoping her boyfriend, Jeremy, won't be late again. The waiter looks tired. A pair of Japanese men talk quietly in a booth near the corner. A baby in a high chair flings a spoonful of rice onto the carpet, and the waiter sighs.

When you allow viewpoint intrusion—letting Sally *see* the waiter and *notice* the baby—you haven't moved the reader into the story; you've diverted the narrative and shown the reader that someone is writing. Remember, it's understood that once you're in a character's viewpoint, you stay there until the end of the scene, and there's no need to place her in every sentence. With that in mind, here's how to find and eliminate The Viewpoint Intruder.

TAKING NOTICE

The word that opens the door to viewpoint intrusion most often is "noticed." Recently I read a student manuscript that said:

> The others were laughing and talking as they sat down at the table. As Kirk reached across the table for the bread, he noticed his hands. His fingers were long and brown, and he noticed how the light gleamed on his wedding ring.

The writer has inserted not one, but two intrusive "notices." He *noticed* his hands and *noticed* the gleam on his wedding ring. Was that the first time in his life Kirk realized he had hands? The scene would be smoother if she wrote it more like this:

> Kirk reached across the table for the bread. His fingers were long and brown, and light gleamed on his wedding ring.

The Viewpoint Intruder doesn't attack only fiction. Here's another example, this one from an essay:

> I looked over at Jenny propped up on the hospital bed. I could see her bright smile, but I knew she was in pain.

"I looked" and "I could see" are both unnecessary intrusions (and we might even include "I knew"). The POV character had been in the hospital room for some time, thinking about Jenny's circumstances. So all she needed was, "Jenny was propped up in the bed. She was smiling, but I knew she was in pain." Or even, "Jenny was propped up in the bed, smiling in spite of her pain."

SENSORY OVERLOAD

When you write about sensory impressions, the Intruder might try to take over the text. Look at this example:

> Rob opened the door. He could smell fried chicken and onions, and he heard the butter crackling in the skillet. His mouth watered from hunger.

Rob's senses are great in the narrative, but you can use them better by implying, not reminding us of, his presence until you need it:

> Rob opened the door. The aroma of fried chicken crackling in the skillet with onion made his mouth water.

This way you begin and end with Rob, but you take him out of the description.

MEMORY LANE

When writers allow their characters to remember the past, Viewpoint Intruders can run rampant. To catch them, be on the lookout for adverbial phrases. For example: "As I stopped in front of the old house, my mind reeled back to how hard it rained the day Jim shot me." That passage would be stronger as, "I stopped in front of the old house. Rain had fallen in torrents on the day Jim shot me." This passage has more zip and we don't notice the author creeping around in the bushes near the old house.

Avoid the phrase "I remember" whenever possible:

> I remember that when I was five, I used to hide from my father in the linen closet. I crawled under an old quilt on the floor, and I could hear his angry footsteps.

This passage has some good elements in it. But if you take out "I remember," you have a stronger scene:

> When I was five, I used to hide under an old quilt in the linen closet, listening to my father's angry footsteps.

We don't have to see inside her head with every move or sound.

IT DOESN'T STOP HERE

Don't assume you ever outgrow the tendency to intrude. The first draft of my twentieth book, *Beyond Words*, was full of intrusions:

> I took a break at a retreat in northern Idaho. I walked outside and sat on a log, where I watched a fat honeybee roving around a big blue pasqueflower. I could see her tasting its petals, and I heard her buzzing around the opening. As I watched, she drew back and literally hurled herself at the flower's center.

After recognizing the intrusions, I edited it down.

> During an afternoon break at a retreat in northern Idaho, I sat on a log and watched a fat honeybee roving around a big blue pasqueflower. She tasted its petals, snuffled at the opening, and then drew back and hurled herself at the flower's center.

That second version uses stronger verbs, and I've also eliminated my first-person viewpoint intrusions.

You may continue to write with Viewpoint Intruders, but with practice, you'll be able to weed them out.

KRISTEN JOHNSON INGRAM is the author of twenty-two books, including two murder mysteries and *Making Peace With a Dangerous God*. She's also an instructor for WritersOnlineWorkshops.com.

CHAPTER 19

MASTERING MULTIPLE POINTS OF VIEW

BY SIMON WOOD

Weaving multiple viewpoint characters in and out of a story is like standing trial and knowing what the judge, the prosecuting attorney and all twelve members of the jury are thinking. Each person is witnessing the same information, but his interpretation is different. But it's not like you can crack into everyone's mind simultaneously. Even if you could, it'd be impossible to comprehend what fourteen people are saying if they're all talking at the same time. Just visit your average kindergarten classroom.

Allowing multiple characters to tell your story can provide insight that a first-person POV may not be able to convey. Most stories have plenty of characters with their own tales to tell. Multiple POV characters add depth to a novel. Suddenly the story is being told from the perspective of multiple witnesses, all putting their distinctive interpretations on events. But the inclusion of multiple voices can bring with it its own problems. Those multiple points of view can get out of control and turn the story into a mess. In a novel, just like in a conversation, not everyone can speak at once. There are plenty of ways to give each character a voice without having them talk over one another.

1. USE CHAPTER AND/OR SCENE BREAKS

Scene breaks are an effective literary device. They allow you to draw a line between where one POV character leaves and another enters, which gives the reader a clear indication that something has changed. Let's say a chapter or scene is told from the perspective of one character. The reaction to this chapter or scene would have the most impact if it were told from a different character's point of view. To suddenly switch from one character's point of view to another's could jerk the reader from the story, but a chapter or scene break would be the perfect signal to the reader to let her know something has changed.

For example: With a heavy heart, POV character Molly tells David on his twenty-first birthday that she adopted him as a baby. The chapter ends on this bombshell, and the next chapter begins with David's POV and his reaction to this revelation.

2. CHANGE SPACES

As simple as it would be to break for a new chapter or scene every time you wish to switch from one character's point of view to another, it may not be convenient to do so. The story could end up as a series of short scenes and chapters, possibly making the flow of the story choppy. Additionally, a chapter and/or scene break might kill the tension you've just built. So instead of breaking for a new chapter or scene, change the scene's location for the next point of view. This can be as simple as having the characters switch to another room.

Returning to the previous example with Molly and David, instead of having a chapter break when Molly tells David that he's adopted, you could switch locations. David reacts violently to Molly's news and storms out of the house, leaving Molly behind. David is alone and in a new locale when his POV scene kicks in. Although there's been no physical break in the narrative, the reader is fully aware that the point of view has switched to David.

3. PASS THE BATON

Another way of switching points of view seamlessly is to take the relay approach, where one POV character hands over the baton to another. This is achieved by using a pivotal point in the scene as a tool to hand over the POV.

Consider a scene where two POV characters are on the phone. While the characters are speaking, keep the scene restricted to one POV character, but when the call ends, switch to the other character's POV.

Alternatively, use a setup in dialogue to pave the way for a POV change. Consider the following example. A POV character says, "What's your take on this, Bob?" This is an open invitation to switch the POV to Bob's character and take the story in a new direction.

4. MIX PERSPECTIVES

We're talking about managing multiple points of view, but which perspective do you incorporate? You aren't condemned to use multiple third-person perspectives for your POV characters. Using a mix of first, second, and/or third person makes for a clear change of POV.

Several authors have used this technique to their advantage. In Harlan Coben's *Gone for Good*, all the scenes featuring the protagonist's POV are in first person, while all the other POV characters are in third person for their scenes. It makes for a unique style and makes it impossible to confuse POV characters. The first-person narrative brings the reader closer to the protagonist, and the third-person perspective keeps the reader at arm's length from the other characters.

This same approach can also be applied to experimentation with present and past tense for POV characters, although it's risky. In Michael Gruber's *Tropic of Night*, the story is told in third person, past tense, except for a character in hiding. That character's POV scenes are told in first person, present tense, in journal fashion.

5. USE DISTINCTIVE VOICES

POV characters must possess their own distinct voices. If all the characters have the same way of describing and seeing the world, then there's a danger the reader won't be able to distinguish the differences between them. To ensure your POV characters don't all sound like the same person, you need to remember what kind of people your characters are. A teenager's view of the world is going to be much different than that of a senior citizen's. There are going to be cultural differences between someone from the United States vs. someone from Somalia. And how many books are there written about the differences between men and women?

Nick Hornby demonstrates very well how to make his POV characters sound different in *A Long Way Down*. The story is told from four first-person POV characters (potentially a reader's nightmare), but the four characters are very different people—one is an angst-ridden teenager, one is a middle-aged woman with a handicapped child, one is a disgraced TV personality, and the fourth is a failed musician now delivering pizzas. The language, belief systems, and outlooks on life of these four POV characters are so different that they never blur into one another. The reader is at no time confused about which character is speaking to him.

6. PICK THE RIGHT CHARACTER FOR THE RIGHT JOB

It's not impossible to have several POV characters from your novel end up in the same scene together. So who should tell the story of this scene—the protagonist, the antagonist, a secondary character, or all of them? You need to step warily. Switching from one character's point of view to another's throughout a scene can be annoying to read. While all POV characters might have something to say, there's a danger of creating a "too many cooks in the kitchen" scenario. You have to choose one POV character to narrate the scene—then stick to it. This doesn't have to default to the protagonist. Who at this particular juncture of the story is the best storyteller or witness? You need to choose the character that will give the reader the best report or unique perspective on the situation at hand.

Return for a moment to Molly and David. Molly's POV is used to tell David of his adoption, and the POV switches to David when he learns of the news. In this scenario, the reader first feels the mother's anguish over telling her son, then the son's shock that his mother kept this information from him for so long.

The points of view could have been reversed for totally different results. This would've put a different spin on events. Instead we'd hear from David's perspective first. It's his birthday, and he's intrigued by Molly's urgent need to talk to him. Then Molly tells him he's adopted. In the next scene, David has run off, and the perspective is Molly's. She's torn up by David's reaction and wishes she'd gone after him. The story now takes on a different complexion. It's not that either arrangement is wrong. It's up to you to decide which scenario works best for the story.

7. CREATE A HIERARCHY OF POV CHARACTERS

A key question you must decide at the outset of the story is: Who are your storytellers? If you decide there will be three, seven or a dozen POV characters, you must also decide how much page time will be apportioned to each of these characters. This may not seem important, but it is. The protagonist is the primary storyteller in any story, so it stands to reason that the majority of the POV scenes should belong to him. If not, there's a danger that the protagonist will be swallowed up by the wealth of other characters exerting their view on the story.

If you're writing a crime thriller with the investigating officer as the protagonist, the story should revolve around the officer and his investigation. The investigating officer's mark on the story might pale into insignificance if his voice is drowned out by the voices of the suspect under investigation and the other investigating officers.

So you need to allocate page time accordingly. The protagonist is the lead character and should get the lion's share, followed by the amount of time we hear from the antagonist, then the secondary characters. Minor characters are supposed to be heard from in the minority, while bit players should be seen and not heard.

When it comes to page time, you need to think of it in terms of billings. The readers will want to hear the most from the character that receives top billing. She's the star of the show, after all.

8. LIMIT THE NUMBER OF POV CHARACTERS

The key to managing multiple POV characters is selection. While it's fun to write from multiple characters' perspectives, choose wisely. You need to decide exactly how many storytellers are needed to tell the story. Don't keep creating POV characters just for the sake of it. The reader doesn't have to hear from every character. A minor player with just a glancing blow to the story doesn't need to leave his mark on the novel. You need to take an objective look at your planned POV characters, decide whether all are needed, and eliminate unnecessary voices from the story. Remember: Keep it poignant and relevant.

Managing multiple POV characters is a tough act but don't make it a juggling act. By making clear switches from one POV character to another and creating a hierarchy of key storytellers with distinctive voices, you can create a multifaceted story that no one will forget.

SIMON WOOD is an Anthony Award–winning thriller writer, including *The Fall Guy* and *Did Not Finish*.

FOCUS ON THE WRITING LIFE:
USING YOUR MUSE

MAKE YOUR OWN MUSE

BY N.M. KELBY

There's a lot of talk about this muse thing. You can take an entire weekend workshop about coaxing your muse, or flirting with your muse, or dancing with your muse, or just spending time getting to know your muse better. It's as if a muse is some sort of Chia Pet: All you have to do is water her and the next thing you know, you're Norman Mailer.

It's understandable where all this muse-centric chat comes from. There are times when you're writing and your hands type faster than your brain can even think. One moment you've just had breakfast and the next the cat is screaming for dinner. And how many times have you looked at what you've written and thought, *Who came up with that? I'm not that smart.*

If those moments make you wonder if there's some sort of otherworldly creature inhabiting your body that is smarter and more profound than you are, you're not alone. The Greek poet Hesiod (799 B.C.) was the first writer to begin this practice of muse worship and is given credit for naming them. The idea of the muse took hold in 1374 when the English poet Geoffrey Chaucer evoked them and destined all English poets to do the same forevermore.

The word muse comes from the Latin *musa,* which is derived from the Greek *mousa* and is a term given the sisterhood of goddesses born of Zeus and Mnemosyne. It's their job to inspire.

Having a muse makes sense. Fiction *is* a magical art. Writers craft paradoxical empires of logic and beauty and the reader lives within them, or at least it feels as if they do, and they do this through the simple act of interpretation—the puzzling out of an assortment of symbols on a page. Yet in their minds the characters are as real to them as that bowlegged man who walks his nervous dog past their house every evening. How is that not magic?

But waiting for a spirit to inspire you to sit down and write may not be the most prudent course; you could wait for a long time.

If you do sit down and still feel stuck, you could cruise the Internet for inspiration, but that often leads to shopping, blogging, and generalized goofing off.

If you want to catch the muse, you have to court it.

It's better to let your mind wander in a directed way. You can make yourself a set a flashcards with images you take from magazines, photographs, or postcards, or with evocative phrases like "The language they spoke was iridescent," or "He had eyes darker than any night." Or thumb through your old journals, picking up on ideas you made note of long ago. Or take a walk. Or pick up your guitar and play until the words of a song become secondary to the emotion of it.

Let the world at large be your muse. Be unafraid to walk aimlessly through a city's street at night, through unknown neighborhoods, and search for that part of yourself that is lost there. Embrace the world's sorrow. Linger in the silence of a moment. Learn the language of your own heart.

Don't wait for anything to guide your work. Dig deep inside of yourself. You are the collective memory of your culture. You hold history in your hand. Never ask for permission to write. Just take it. As Charles Simic said, "He who cannot howl will not find his pack." You have to howl until you are heard.

Embrace your muse as the spirit of life that passes through you—and there will be times that something larger than yourself will inspire you, amaze you, and overwhelm you with inspiration. But those moments are few and far between, and you must be ready for them.

You must show up for work, put in your time, always have your heart open and your hand outstretched towards the heavens.

But, whatever you do, never confuse those moments of brilliance on the page with the idea that you are brilliant. That's dangerous. It leads to destructive behavior. As does the idea that you are failed as a writer—if you've done your part to succeed, maybe your muse was just having an off day.

Elizabeth Gilbert gave a talk about the idea of genius on TED.com. Gilbert's "genius" could also be called the muse, as she defines it as a disembodied spirit that enters artists and allows them to create work that is seemingly divine.

At one point in her lecture, she spoke about the sacred dances in North Africa that went on centuries ago. People would gather in the moonlight, and the dancers, filled with a sense of ecstasy, would dance into the morning. And every now and then one of them would suddenly be filled with this sense of the otherworldly. He would become transcendent. Even though he was doing the same dance he'd done a thousand times before, time stopped, and it suddenly seemed as if he'd stepped through a portal.

"He seemed to be lit from within and lit from below and lit up on fire with divinity," she said. "And when this happened … people knew it for what it was. Allah! Allah! Allah! They would start to chant. That's God.

"… when the Moors invaded Spain they took this custom with them. However, it changed from over the centuries from Allah! Allah! Allah! to Ole! Ole! Ole!, which is still heard at bullfights."

When you write, you sit in your office and bang away hoping for brilliance, hoping that your genius, your muse, your Allah, comes to you and elevates your work. But you can't wait for it. You have to be there ready to catch it, even on days when it doesn't seem worth the effort of getting out of bed.

Never give up.

N.M. KELBY is the author of *The Constant Art of Being a Writer.* Her story "Jubilation, Florida" was selected for NPR's "Selected Shorts.

FUELING YOUR MUSE WITH COMPOST

BY HEATHER SELLERS

Compost was something I mentioned on the first day of class one year, in passing.

Now I talk about compost a lot. On the first day of a class, I have all my students write three questions for me—anything they want to know—on index cards. Then, I draw the cards at random, a few at a time for a few weeks, and I answer. They ask me about my husband, children, my mother, my dogs. They ask me how much I write, and why, and if they should be writers. They ask me which books are my favorites. And if the dress I was wearing on the first day is reversible, where I went to school, how many drafts I do, if I have done drugs. They ask me to reveal a dream.

Most often they ask: Where do you get your ideas? Writers don't so much have ideas, I tell them. Some writers have ideas. Their books are important and good—Coetzee has ideas, Gordimer has ideas, Sartre, and Murdoch, too. But really, for most of us, the writing life is more like the sex life.

It's an urge, and it has a certain dampness to it. It's a desire, a thing you look at from the side, not directly staring. The writing is gentle and fragile—nothing like an idea which is sturdy and forceful and clear.

You don't want to just stare, gaping, at a beautiful, lovely person. You try to act cool. A little not-needy. This is how the writer relates to her material. She doesn't really get ideas for writing. Writing is more of a pulse, a throb, a thrum. It feels more like desire and less like thinking.

It's something you feed, this desire.

Here's how: Finding your material is just like maintaining a compost pile.

Slowly, over years, you take your best stuff out to a secret, hidden away place in the backyard, and you dump it there. You cover the pile.

You can buy things to help digest it (therapy, self-help books, and art classes equal worms, enzymes, wood ash). But it will digest on its own, too. Without any intervention from you at all.

All my students come to me with a compost pile. If they are young, say eighteen, their compost pile might be fairly small and compact, though rich. What is vital to learn early in the writing class is this: Your best work is going to come from your compost pile. Not the neighbor's yard. Not television. Not your head, your thinking, your "idea" for a story. If you aren't working from compost, you are going to be spending a lot of time revising.

Anyone who survived childhood has a good, if small, potent compost pile. The compost pile, to be successful, as you may know, has to be kept covered—and most people have kept the lid on childhood. It has to be forgotten by the main brain, the idea-generating self. Most people have forgotten lots of childhood. Writers have to have a good "forgettery." That's part of making compost: Dump rich raw materials, build up a little heat, and neglect. Alchemy happens. Compost happens.

So many of my students want to write about *anything* but where they are from or who they are—*anything* but their own terrible, lovely, banal, fascinating lives. Say your day goes like this: It's Monday, and on Monday your neighbor leaves notes to everyone: *Please pick up after your animal!* You live in a small, ugly, boring town. You go to school or work. You obsess over your lover, and the annoying person at work. You play online chess, and eat turkey for lunch, and go to the mall, and then to a movie. You argue with your mother, and then you get ready for bed, and settle in with a good book, not doing your homework. This is your Monday. This is your life.

Instead of writing from underneath *that very life*, you turn in a story about a prostitute who likes businessmen. Or a man in World War II who lives in Chicago and writes letters to the president. Why are you writing these stories, which draw as their source television and movies and ideas for stories?

Ideas kill art.

Compost feeds it.

Compost is dark, stinky, and messy.

It's what happened to you, what *stuck* onto your soul. My main job as a teacher is to get students to write their compost; compost is where everything fascinating and good is. And it's under you. It's in the backyard of you. Stop going across town.

Stop *importing* stories that aren't really yours. If you aren't dreaming down deep into your own history, your own passions, your actual true, real, daily concerns and obsessions and the shapes of your lived life, you aren't going to be able to improve as a writer. You have to start where you are.

If you are a housewife in Cuba, you write about that (*Cuba Diaries* by Isadora Tattlin). If you are stuck in a boring town of sniping, marriage-hungry matchmakers, you write about that (all of Jane Austen). If you are brilliant and grumpy in Minsk, if you are bored and slightly drunk in Dublin, if you are from the smallest town in the Midwest, you write about that.

You gotta know what your composted material is. Start with what you have lived through. Compost—both the backyard kind and the writer kind—takes about, what, a year, three years, some say seven, to happen. To ripen and mature. You might not be able to write about things that happened last week. Most new writers have the best, most rewarding early success writing from the layers of material they've walked around with for a few years. Years.

My compost takes *seven* years. It's seven years before I can remove my own need to present myself as the Beautiful Tormented Misunderstood Star of my own drama and get at something of the truth.

Compost is how many professional writers refer to their material. How many times have your friends, the ones who know you are a writer, told you, "That is a great story. You should write that!"

Or more perversely they might say: "Well, that was horrible, that you were robbed/mugged/alone at your father's funeral, but, wow, you can write about it!"

In some way, all writers write about their family. Writers are always writing about themselves. Sarah, the nineteen-year-old student of mine from a celery farm in Rockford, Michigan, who wrote the prostitute story, is trying to find her way to her compost. I wonder if she fears her life lacks adventure, if she fears people see her as a virginal Midwestern teen, sans experience, sans life. I think she's trying to write herself a better script. My job is to nudge her into the stinky pile she's been tending. She just doesn't notice what it is that obsesses her. She just doesn't believe her life, her actual life, can teach her what she wants to know about the world.

We are a tiny cluster of human beings. We write about that tiny cluster. The best writers are able to lumber down on a stepladder into this mucky, stinky, rich, fecund place—a place where the good stuff (eggshells, coffee grounds, onionskins, and paper) transforms into the stuff that feeds, that makes growth and heat and life.

Compost is your best stuff.

Compost is the stuff of writing.

If you are fourteen years old, your compost bandwidth is probably fairly narrow, and this is a great, great thing. You don't have to dig too deep to find great stuff. Focus softly—dreaming back, and down, and in—and feel your way gently into the darkest areas, the scariest, wormiest, messiest places in your life, and just start writing there.

When you notice yourself going back up into the thinking part of your mind, what do you hear?

This isn't interesting.

Who cares?

What's the point of this?

Joey will get mad if I write this about his tattoo and his ex and the sugar cubes.

I need to sound more like a Writer.

All those sentiments are your head talking.

Forget about ideas. The critic lives in your head. When she appears, go back to your pile. Say: *I'm messing around here. Leave me alone.* Don't listen to your head. Your material is down in, a vibration just below the level of thought. If you are twenty-one, your compost pile has some pretty interesting stuff in it. At least three layers of rich, fecund material. And it's in your pile. Not in someone else's pile.

What I notice about the twenty-one-year-olds I teach is they really, really don't want to write about what they know, where they are from, how they see the world. They want to be anyone else but themselves. Because, I surmise, they fear that if they are themselves, then the chances are too good they will turn into their parents.

What's your compost?

Well, to find it, you will probably want to practice; it's like panning for gold. You write (daily, I will keep saying *daily*). Yesterday I started a new swimming routine because I want to do a triathlon. I hated the swimming. Then I did it again today. I was amazingly strong and swam for forty minutes without stopping. Delicious.

This is how the writing is. Rarely will you *want* to really sit down and do it. You'll want to want that.

To get at your compost, ignore the frenzy of fear and desire that surrounds the urge. *Call the person on the phone*, we say to wayward daters. Call the compost with your writing hand, your imagining mind. Just go do it. You won't want to. You'll hate it. It doesn't matter. Ignore all the thoughts that come up, urging you *don't go to the pile, don't get dirty, keep your clothes clean, stay inside, watch television.* Ignore all that.

Composting will not feel comfortable. Probably ever.

The hundredth time you do it, you will say to yourself, *I'm from a small suburb in the northeast, with only white people, and my father is a bore, and my mother doesn't drink enough, and she says unkind things, and my bedroom looks like I really liked* The Simpsons *way too much as a child, and I have a collection of beer cans on my bookshelves, and this is my material!*

If you don't like your compost, live differently, so that in seven years you will have other material.

HEATHER SELLERS is the author of *Page After Page, Chapter After Chapter*, and her memoir, *You Don't Look Like Anyone I Know.*

PART 4:

SETTING & BACKSTORY:

THE CONTEXT FOR YOUR STORY

CHAPTER 20

CREATING YOUR STORY'S TIME & PLACE

BY DONALD MAASS

Many novelists seem to think of setting as something outside their story. It is necessary, but it is a bother. It has to be included, yet ought to be dealt with as efficiently as possible. After all, who wants to read pages and pages of description? On the other hand, how can your story come alive in the imaginations of your readers if they can't *see* it? Readers, after all, want to be swept away somewhere else.

How, then, are we to accomplish that without being boring? In nineteenth-century novel writing, it was usual to treat the landscape as a character in the story. In the twenty-first century, we may have less patience for scenery, but we certainly expect to live in the world of the story. So what's the trick?

As our colleagues in science fiction and fantasy have shown us, building breakout time and place starts with the realization that the world of the novel is composed of much more than landscape and rooms. It is milieu, period, fashion, ideas, human outlook, historical moment, spiritual mood, and more. It is capturing not only place, but people in an environment; not only history, but people changing as the story unfolds. Description is the least of it. Bringing people alive in a place and time is the essence of it.

For example, in Jane Hamilton's 1994 novel *A Map of the World*, her first-person heroine, Alice, begins to lose her bearings when her friend's daughter drowns in a pond. In this scene, Alice goes with her husband, Howard, to a men's store to buy a suit for the funeral:

> At 6:15 the suit was finished. He paid a terrific sum, carefully writing the figures on Nellie's check, and then he went into the dressing room to put on his finery. He emerged, silent, looking down, as if he couldn't believe that anything below his neck was still his own body. I stood back marveling at him, at the handyman, who didn't care how he looked, who had little use for daily personal hygiene, and there he was ravishing in his suit. It was only June and his face was tanned to a deep brown. His teeth were blindingly white, dangerous to look at, like an eclipse. It was impossible not to admire him, hard not to want to do something to contain that kind of beauty—drink him, ingest him, sneak into his shirt and hide for the rest of one's natural life. After six years of marriage he had the power to occasionally render me weak in the knees.

You could say that what Hamilton has done in that passage is to freeze a moment in time with snapshot clarity. That's true, but I'd also say that she has brought alive the world of the story, which is to say, Alice's world. To put it differently, the key to bringing an environment alive is not to describe a location objectively, but to get inside the people who live there and let us know how they feel about what's around them.

THE PSYCHOLOGY OF PLACE

Have you ever said to yourself, *This place gives me the creeps?* If so, you have experienced the psychological influence of inert physical surroundings. We are affected by what is around us.

If you have ever stood in a room designed by Frank Lloyd Wright, you know his interiors make you relax. The high-vaulting arches of Notre Dame can lift you to a spiritual plane. A simple Shaker meeting room does both things simultaneously; it is inner peace and fervent piety captured in four walls.

Anne Rivers Siddons is good at evoking the world of the tidewater Carolinas. In her 1997 novel *Up Island*, however, she brings her heroine Molly Bell Redwine north to Martha's Vineyard to repair herself after a marital breakup. At the end of the summer season, Molly rents a small cottage on a remote up-island pond. The conjunction of house, landscape, and shattered spirit is deftly detailed:

> The house stood in full sun on the slope of the ridge that seemed to sweep directly up into the steel-blue sky. Below it, the lane I had just driven on wound through low, dense woodlands, where the Jeep had plunged in and out of dark shade. But up here there was nothing around the house except a sparse stand of wind-stunted oaks, several near-to-collapsing outbuildings, and two or three huge, freestanding boulders left, I knew, by the receding glacier that had formed this island. Above the house, the ridge beetled like a furrowed brow, matted with low-growing blueberry and huckleberry bushes. At the very top, no trees grew at all. I looked back down and caught my breath at the panorama of Chilmark Pond and the Atlantic Ocean. It was a day of strange, erratic winds and running cloud shadow, and the patch-work vista below me seemed alive, pulsing with shadow and sun, trees and ocean moving restlessly in the wind. Somehow it disquieted me so that I had to turn and face the closed door of the big, old house. I had come here seeking the shelter of the up-island wood, but this tall, blind house, alone in its ocean of space and dazzle of hard, shifting light, offered me no place to hide.

The power of this passage results from more than the objects that it describes. Molly is uniquely affected by the light and landscape around her. Another character might have seen it as bright and refreshing. Molly, in her grief, experiences it as harsh and comfortless. See the difference? That is the psychology of place.

You can deepen the psychology of place in your story by returning to a previously established setting and showing how your character's perception of it has changed. You can also give your characters an active relationship to place, which, in turn, means marking your characters' growth (or decline) through their relationships to their various surroundings. That, in turn, demands that you be writing in a strong point of view, regardless of whether your novel is first or third person.

Do you have plain vanilla description in your current manuscript? Try evoking the description the way it is experienced by a character. Feel the difference? So will your readers.

KEEPING UP WITH THE TIMES

As important in a story as a sense of place is a sense of time, both the exact historical moment and the passing hours, days, years, decades, centuries, or even millennia (if you are James A. Michener).

One of the appealing aspects of historical settings is not only discovering the charm or grittiness of a past era, but finding that folks back then felt pretty much as we do now, even to the point of longing for their own "good old days." In contemporary stories of standout caliber, a sense of the historical moment is also captured. What makes our time—this very moment in history—similar to or different from any other?

As I am sure you can anticipate, the answer once again lies in your characters' perceptions of these things. The great contemporary satirist Tom Wolfe is a master of capturing our times. His 1998 novel *A Man in Full* is a dead-on depiction of the South of the 1990s—Atlanta, in particular. All the social aspirations and insecurities of its denizens are pinned, wriggling, to the novel's hilarious pages. His portrait of our era and its follies, though, does not have a dry, documentary quality. Its dynamic colors are delivered through strong points of view.

M.M. Kaye's grand romantic epic of British Colonial India, *The Far Pavilions* (1978), is suffused throughout with details of the political and social shifts underway in that time and place. The novel tells the story of Ash, an English army officer raised as a Hindu, and of the Indian princess he loves, Anjuli, who eventually is married off to a wealthy Rana. When the Rana dies, Ash saves Juli from *suttee* (the immolation of living wives with their dead husbands) and proposes to marry her. They argue over this possibility. This minor moment is enriched with details that convey a sense of changing times:

> "They will never permit you to marry me," said Anjuli with tired conviction.
>
> "The Bhithoris? They won't dare open their mouths!"
>
> "No, your people; and mine also, who will be of the same mind."
>
> "You mean they will try to prevent it. But it's no business of theirs. This is our affair: yours and mine. Besides, didn't your own grandfather marry a princess of Hind, though he was a foreigner and not of her faith?"
>
> Anjuli sighed and shook her head again. "True. But that was in the days before your Raj had come to its full power. There was still a Mogul on the throne in Delhi and Ranjit-Singh held sway over the Punjab; and my grandfather was a great war-lord who took my grand-mother as the spoils of war without asking any man's leave, having defeated the army of my grandmother's father in battle. I have been told that she went willingly, for they loved each other greatly. But the times have changed and that could not happen now."

This is not a historical romance bashed out in six months to meet a deadline. This is not a conversation happening between contemporary Americans dressed in saris. Kaye is intimate with the details of the Raj era and lavishes them on her splendid novel. So fine is her sense of that time and place, Kaye is able to vividly locate her characters in a particular moment in the long sweep of Indian history.

Your characters live in an era, but which one? And in what stage of its life? Find the moments in the story that delineate that distinction, detail them from a prevailing point of view, and you will be on your way to enhancing your novel with a sense of the times.

WORKING WITH HISTORICAL FORCES AND SOCIAL TRENDS

A breakout setting is even more than the psychology of physical surroundings and a sense of the times. Setting can also be social context.

Social trends and political ideas influence our real actions and thinking, so why not those in our novels, too?

Anne Perry's *Slaves of Obsession* (2000) is an 1860s mystery featuring moody "agent of inquiry" William Monk and his wife, nurse Hester Latterly. In the novel's opening, conversation at a dinner party turns to the American Civil War, then just a few months old. A Union idealist, Breeland, wants the dinner's host, a British arms merchant named Alberton, to go back on his promise to sell a large quantity of state-of-the-art rifles to the South. Breeland's rigid morality is grating, but it has won over Alberton's passionately idealistic daughter, sixteen-year-old Merrit. Later, the story takes Monk and Hester to America in pursuit of Merrit, who was abducted from, or fled, London on the night of her father's murder and the theft of the guns, which Alberton had sold to the South but have been diverted to the Union. Upon their arrival, Hester observes New York:

> Hester was fascinated. It was unlike any city she had previously seen: raw, teeming with life, a multitude of tongues spoken, laughter, shouting, and already the hand of war shadowing over it, a brittleness in the air. There were recruitment posters on the walls and soldiers in a wild array of uniforms in the streets.
>
> Business seemed poor and the snatches of talk she overheard were of prize fights, food prices, local gossip and scandal, politics, and secession. She was startled to hear suggestion that even New York itself might secede from the Union, or New Jersey.

There is also debate about whether the South has the right to secede, and whether the North has the right to impose union. Later, in Washington, Monk and Hester meet up with an arms procurer for the South, Philo Trace, who wishes to help them find Merrit and Breeland. Trace's views on Northerners are those of a practical Southerner:

> "Most of them have never even seen a plantation, let alone thought about how it worked. I haven't seen many myself." He gave a harsh little laugh, jerky, as if he had caught his breath.

"Most of us in the south are small farmers, working our own land. You can go for dozens of miles and that's all you'll see. But it's the cotton and the tobacco that we live on. That's what we sell to the north and it's what they work in the factories and ship abroad."

He stopped suddenly, lowering his head and pushing his hand across his brow, forcing his hair back so hard it must have hurt. "I don't really know what this war is all about, why we have to be at each other's throats. Why can't they just leave us alone? Of course there are bad slave owners, men who beat their field slaves, and their house slaves, and nothing happens to them even if they kill them! But there's poverty in the north as well, and nobody fights about that! Some of the industrial cities are full of starving, shivering men and women—and children—with nobody to take them in or feed them. No one gives a damn! At least a plantation owner cares for his slaves, for economic reasons if not common decency."

By eschewing modern morality in her characterizations, Perry makes her people live with a realism that enlarges her fiction.

Whatever the scope of your novel, it will benefit from a depiction of the social context in which it takes place. Your characters live in society, but in which strata? At what point is their social position most keenly felt? At what moment does it change? Does your heroine's status rise or fall? How can she tell? Are your cast of characters aware of the way in which society is evolving? No? Well, why not? A wide-angle view of the civilization around your story will magnify the story in exciting ways.

GOD AT WORK IN THE WORLD

Fate or chance? Choice or predestination? What range of freedom do you feel your characters have? Do they control their own destinies, or are their actions in part futile? Do unexpected events overtake them, or do they act according to a plan? You may not think of God as part of the setting of your novel, but the actions of the universe, if any, upon your characters are an important consideration in the novel's construction.

Whatever your religion, there is a shared sense that the universe is larger than us, wouldn't you agree? Do you not feel it on dark, clear winter nights when you stare at the array of stars in the Milky Way? Have you felt the flash of understanding that death is real, perhaps after just narrowly missing a fatal accident? Have you ever been moved to tears by the self-sacrifice of a genuine heroine? Does the love of your spouse sometimes reduce you to humble gratitude? If you have experienced any of those feelings, then you know what it is to be lifted out of yourself for a moment.

If you do not have a moment of unexpected tragedy or grace in your novel, consider where you might put it in. Shatter your protagonist with a tragedy or give her an unexpected gift. These things happen in real life, and in a novel they lend an enlarged perspective, a sense that the universe is paying attention. To put it another way, if God is at work in the world of your novel, then you have a chance at giving your readers an experience that is humbling, joyful, and maybe even transforming.

How do you weave a sense of destiny at work into the setting of your story? Look for places, people, and situations that are larger than your characters. Is the couple in your romance novel going to break up? Where? In a car? Okay, then why not place that car at a rise in a highway with a mile-long traffic jam stretching in both directions? Not only is the metaphor of being stuck now made visible, but you also have available to you a dramatic exit for one of your protagonists.

Kitchens, living rooms, offices, and other commonplace settings are familiar and easy, but what resonance do they have? Usually very little. Think canyons, sports stadiums, airports, squad cars, life rafts, recovery rooms, whatever. Settings that are emptier or more crowded than usual, or that have change or inherent drama built into them, can envelop your scenes with the unfolding of other destinies.

God works in little ways as well as big ones, so look for small moments of magic as well as large ones. Have you ever felt that something that happened to you was fated? Your first meeting with your future spouse, for instance? Many people share that experience. Paths intersect in ways that are not accidents. Small coincidences lead to large changes. People repeat those special stories for years, have you noticed?

Little miracles become our personal myths. What are the little miracles that bring your characters to their moments of grand destiny? Find them. Mark them. Revisit them in retrospect, and the hand of God will show in your story.

THE SECRET INGREDIENT

The great novelists of the past and the breakout novelists of today employ many approaches to setting, but all have one element in common: detail. A setting cannot live unless it is observed in its pieces and particulars. A place is the sum of its parts. The emotions that it evokes are most effective when they are specific—better still, when they are unique.

One of the great achievements in descriptiveness of recent decades can be found in the German novel *Perfume* (1987) by Patrick Süskind (stylishly translated into English by John E. Woods). *Perfume* concerns an abominable perfumer's apprentice whose twisted pleasure is using the methods of his craft to capture the scent of young virgins at the moments of their deaths. He is a serial killer motivated by scent. The novel is set in eighteenth-century France. All its description is olfactory. No sights, sounds, touchs, or tastes are presented. Here is Süskind's opening description of this world:

> In the period of which we speak, there reigned in the cities a stench barely conceivable to us modern men and women. The streets stank of manure, the courtyards of urine, the stairwells stank of moldering wood and rat droppings, the kitchens of spoiled cabbage and mutton fat; the unaired parlors stank of stale dust, the bedrooms of greasy sheets, damp featherbeds, and the pungently sweet aroma of chamber pots. The stench of sulfur rose from the chimneys, the stench of caustic lyes from the tanneries, and from the slaughterhouses came the stench of

> congealed blood. People stank of sweat and unwashed clothes; from their mouths came the stench of rotting teeth, from their bellies that of onions, and from their bodies, if they were no longer very young, came the stench of rancid cheese and sour milk and tumorous disease. The rivers stank, the marketplaces stank, the churches stank, it stank beneath the bridges and in the palaces. ... And of course the stench was foulest in Paris, for Paris was the largest city of France.

Notice how Süskind achieves this effect: with details. Manure, urine, cabbage, mutton fat, featherbeds, sulfur, lyes, unwashed clothes, rotting teeth, rancid cheese, sour milk ... not once does he try to explain what those things smell *like*. Instead, he catalogs those awful odors, allowing his readers' memories to call up the necessary associations.

Details can also convey a character's feelings about place. George R.R. Martin's 1982 novel *Fevre Dream* is not written in the first person. Nevertheless, by writing from a strong point of view, Martin is able to let us know exactly how his characters feel. *Fevre Dream* is about steamboat captain Abner Marsh, who in 1857 dreams of setting a record for the journey down the Mississippi River to New Orleans. An icy winter has ruined his dilapidated fleet, but then a well-heeled stranger offers to build him his dream boat. Here is Marsh's first view of the finished vessel in a boatyard:

> The mists gave way for them, and there she stood, high and proud, dwarfing all the other boats around her. Her cabins and rails gleamed with fresh paint pale as snow, bright even in the gray shroud of fog. Way up on her texas roof, halfway to the stars, her pilot house seemed to glitter; a glass temple, its ornate cupola decorated all around with fancy woodwork as intricate as Irish lace. Her chimneys, twin pillars that stood just forward of the texas deck, rose up a hundred feet, black and straight and haughty. Their feathered tops bloomed like two dark metal flowers. Her hull was slender and seemed to go on forever, with her stern obscured by the fog. Like all the first-class boats, she was a side-wheeler. Set amidship, the

huge curved wheelhouses loomed gigantic, hinting at the vast power of the paddle wheels concealed within them. They seemed all the larger for want of the name that would soon be emblazoned across them.

Notice how skillfully Martin uses his detailing to suggest the pride that Marsh feels in his new steamboat: ... *gleamed* ... *bright* ... *fresh* ... *halfway to the stars* ... *seemed to glitter* ... *a glass temple* ... *black and straight and haughty* ... *like all the first-class boats.* Marshaling detail and learning the art of writing in nouns and verbs are essential to success in any type of writing. That is especially true in the breakout novel. An expansive setting is not vague. It is highly particular.

DONALD MAASS is the founder of Donald Maass Literary Agency, which sells more than 150 novels every year. He is the author of *Writing the Breakout Novel, The Fire in Fiction*, and *The Breakout Novelist*.

CHAPTER 21

REFINE YOUR SETTING SKILL SET

BY BRIAN KITELEY

What makes the location of a story vivid is what makes it human. Faulkner's Mississippi is humid, subtropical, and dark green with red dirt, but its scars of slavery and a lost war can't be described, yet can't be avoided.

The town I grew up in was a dying mill town that had a college for women in its midst. When I left for college in 1974, *The Insider's Guide to the Colleges* complained that Northampton closed shop at six in the evening, and all that stayed open after that was the Dunkin' Donuts. By 1984, that was a laughable statement. When the drinking age was briefly lowered to 18 in the early 1970s, the town began to flourish as a magnet for young people who were no longer in college (bars began to cater to Smith College students, as well as these newcomers). Now Northampton is cool, an epicenter of food, music, and the arts, with a substantial lesbian population.

Get to know your hometown—or your hometowns. Do research. Go out and interview people: friends, family and the person who was mayor ten years ago. You write best about the places you know best, but you may not know your own locales as well as you think.

Here are some exercises and prompts to get you thinking about the art of crafting a strong setting in any type of town.

USE YOUR IMAGINATION

Imagine this small town without doing any research: Biggar, Saskatchewan, is whatever you want to make of it, except for the sign outside of town on the highways leading into Biggar. Write a fragment of fiction about this place. Populate it with whomever you'd like. Most of these people will be Canadians, but other than that you're free to do whatever you wish. This is an exercise to challenge you to take a real place and fictionalize it, based on nothing more than your own sense of what it might be like and what you want it to be. This is also an exercise in imagining your way into the life of a very small town. If you're a city person, or someone who grew up in a town of even 30,000 (as I did), you may have difficulty imagining the world of a village with 432 souls, for example (I'm not saying Biggar is that big or small). Aim for about 750 words.

WRITE AN INTERNATIONAL LOVE STORY

Write a fragment of fiction about high school sweethearts who live in two towns very close to each other but separated by the U.S.–Canada border, say Oroville, Washington, and Osoyoos, British Columbia, both of which are on Osoyoos Lake; or Vanceboro, Maine, and St. Croix, New Brunswick. They might be children of prominent citizens of these very small towns. They watch the same TV shows, listen to the same radio stations, read the same newspapers (sometimes), and they've grown up in very similar surroundings. But one is Canadian and one is American. Explore the differences between these two cultures. Do some research. Write 500 words.

COMBINE PAST AND PRESENT

Choose a setting and present both a relatively modern version (though it may be slightly historical, like 1952 Biloxi or 1985 Oshkosh) and a version of the same place one hundred years before. Write about one historical moment for two paragraphs, then about a modern moment for two paragraphs. For the last sentences of the piece, alternate sentence by sentence between the modern and older versions, making sure the reader can reasonably understand this alternation. This exercise should be seven paragraphs and about 750 words long.

MASTER METONYMY

Write a biography of a real country. This will have to be ridiculously condensed. Or you may choose a few exemplary tiny stories to stand for this country. Keep this one at 250 words.

Metonymy is crucial for this type of writing (an example of metonymy is the crown standing for the queen). We see something and we're desperate to make it mean something else or some much larger thing. We create narrative where it does not exist, because we're narrative minded. We create metonymy in the same way. Think of a traveler's perspective. Travelers often see the worlds they visit in ways no local could possibly see them—travelers have the keys to the local myths, but they can't communicate these myths to the locals. That's your job here. Find a handful of metonymic images or symbols that stand for a whole country.

CREATE A LOST SETTING

Write about a town that has disappeared. It could be a Palestinian village on a hillside in what is now Israel, forcibly evacuated and then "erased" from maps and view (though there are remains of the town that show its outlines from the air). It could be a ghost town in the American West—a gold rush boomtown that remains but is empty of people. It could be an African town erased by the encroaching Sahara. There are also new ghost towns on the Great Plains in Kansas, Nebraska, and the Dakotas that are slowly (or sometimes quickly) depopulating. Or it could be a village sunk under the Quabbin Reservoir, which was made in the 1930s in Massachusetts.

Write about it at three different times: in the present; at the moment of its last human habitation; and at its most vibrant, lively apex. In other words, write the history of this town backwards. Write 500 words.

PORTRAY A NAKED CITY

"There are 8 million stories in the Naked City. This has been one of them." Those were the closing lines of the voice-over narration of the police drama *Naked City*, which ran from 1958–1963. The show broke new ground for TV dramas—no neat resolutions and trials for every episode, like *Dragnet*, which was on the air around the same time. The show also introduced the novelty of location shoots, many in the south Bronx near where the series was produced, and New York City became its biggest star. The series was inspired by a 1948 film of the same name by Jules Dassin, one of the prototypical film noirs of that period.

For this exercise, write an examination of a big city: Chicago, Los Angeles, Mexico City, Tokyo, Cairo, New York, or any place you know well. Populate the city with brief brushstroke portraits of its inhabitants. Aim for 500 words.

MYTHOLOGIZE HOME

Write a short fragment of nonfiction prose in which you venerate your own home state. Do some research first. Find out the state bird, the state lizard, the biggest cash crop, the last politician to commit suicide while in office. Write as if you are writing an official report, in advertising or chamber of commerce language. Include your own life story around the edges of this fake pamphlet. The target length: 750 words.

BRIAN KITELEY is the author of three novels and *The 3 A.M.. Epiphany* and *The 4 A.M. Breakthrough.*

CHAPTER 22

WHY BACKSTORY IS ESSENTIAL

BY LARRY BROOKS

In the fall of 2009, a football player at the University of Oregon made national news—and YouTube—by punching a Boise State University player after losing the opening game of the season. It was an immediate hit (pun intended) on the Boise State University stadium's JumboTron, then on the news as it was dissected every which way by sportscasters, and finally in the court of public opinion. None of it pretty.

The player was suspended for the season. Massive approval ensued in the press and among the general public. The school saved its waning reputation. The new coach saved his job. The critics saved face. And in the process the player lost his dream and possibly a shot at an NFL career.

Great story, eh? Know what makes it even better? Something called the *backstory*. The events and dynamics that preceded the event itself but continue to exert influence on the players in this little athletic soap opera.

There was a lot that went into the dynamics of that dark moment—just as there is a lot that goes into the dynamics of the key moments in *your* stories.

The loss of that player's cool was his third dimension of character—his true character—exposing itself. As were the decisions that were made *after* the fact, by the coach and by the player. The reasons behind it all, though—the backstory—were second-dimension issues of characterization. And while they didn't get that much play in the press, they would be essential if this true story were part of your novel.

In the heated moment it went down, the punch was a combination of both superficial and deep-seated issues driving the player's decisions and actions. The way the player danced and backpedaled with a recycled Mike Tyson shuffle after the cheap shot was thrown was a first-dimension, or surface-level, character quirk. It meant nothing ... unless you *think* it did. And that's the point. But the punch itself was all third dimension, an expression of character that had nothing at all to do with impressing anyone—it was all about who that guy was at his core.

Which, interestingly enough, was precisely the opposite of what critics of the decision to suspend, and later the coach himself, cited as a counterpoint. That view held that the moment did not represent the true character of the young athlete at all, that he was merely caught up in the moment. Which raises the question—if that were true, would every player on the Oregon roster have done the same thing?

USING BACKSTORY TO ADD DEPTH TO CHARACTERS

In our fiction, it's our job to give our characters such moments to react to. The decisions and actions they take in those moments are absolutely expressions of their true character, arising from the third dimension of character depth. Throwing a punch isn't a first-dimension affectation. The second-dimension background of the young man is what it is, and in the moment when it counted, he reverted to his truer nature.

Here's the backstory of this example: First of all, the offending player had come from a culture of conflict—the mean streets of the inner city—with childhood, scholastic, and domestic backgrounds that positioned football as his ticket out. His *hope*. Prior to the incident he was a budding star, a tale of triumph over adversity. The next day he was done.

Remember nothing fuels a story quite like *hope*.

Then there was the hype leading up to the game itself, in which the player boasted to the press about how Oregon would "whoop on" this opponent (all this being first-dimension trash talk), leading toward what he hoped would be revenge against a loss to these same guys the previous year.

Then the coach wrote it all off as part of football being an aggressive game played by aggressive young men, all but sanctioning the trash talk, and thus fueling the bad blood between the two teams and schools. At this point nobody on the Oregon side was being accused of having high character, and nobody on the Boise State University side was saying anything at all.

Show enough backstory to allow the reader to glean and make assumptions about what remains behind the curtain of time, yet continues to influence the character's worldview, attitudes, decisions and actions.

Then there was the kid who received the cheap shot to the jaw, a defensive tackle the size of a small bus, who after his team pummeled Oregon in convincing fashion, confronted the guilty player with taunting words and an unfriendly tap on the shoulder pads. One can almost write *that* dialogue from where you sit. He reportedly had a history—a backstory—of mouthing off and would be receiving a *talking-to* for his role. Also a first-dimension issue of characterization, leading to third-dimension consequences. All of this is *backstory*. What went down before, and behind, the actual event.

From there it gets worse. The Oregon coach had second thoughts about the season suspension of his star running back and decided to bring the offending player back to the team, albeit with certain academic and citizenship criteria and conditions, which were never disclosed. This apparent change of heart was in direct contradiction to his proud and prompt disciplinary action the day after the incident, for which he had accepted gracious praise. Enough human psychology to fuel a season of soap operas with a bubbling stew of first-, second- and third-dimension characterization.

Backstory is the stuff of second-dimension characterization. It can explain and rationalize both first-dimension affectations and third-dimension choices and behaviors, and it can stand in contrast to either, in which case it adds an interesting layer of complexity to it all. Either way, great stories always cover this base.

FINDING THE RIGHT BALANCE OF BACKSTORY

Your characters' actions need to have psychological validity and, at the very least, a visible connection to some behavioral explanation (second dimension) with roots in the past. Backstory is how you make that happen.

Some writers actually write out a backstory for their major characters, often at great length. The objective of this exercise is to create a linkage between their actions within the story and the psychological roots that fueled them. There is, however, a risk if you choose to craft a detailed backstory ahead of time. By writing out and investing a lot of energy in a backstory, you'll be tempted to use *too much* of it.

If you're writing your story on the fly, you'll have to retrofit a backstory that makes sense in a subsequent draft. But just like everything else about storytelling, you can choose to play this element in detail, and with proper context. If you don't get it right, you'll find yourself with a one-dimensional hero.

The trick is to show just enough backstory that the reader can intuit where the character is coming from. Flashback scenes solely for the purpose of explaining backstory are rarely a good idea. You should be artful and subtle in delivering backstory as part of the narrative flow, rather than spelling it out.

Then again, if backstory is a major element of the story—as it is, for example, in Dennis Lehane's novels *Mystic River* and

Shutter Island—you can certainly weave it into the narrative as you see fit.

Here's the primary guideline, called the "iceberg principle": Show about only 10 percent of your character's backstory. Literally. A glimpse, leading to an ongoing context. Show enough to allow the reader to glean and make assumptions about what remains behind the curtain of time, yet continues to influence the character's worldview, attitudes, decisions, and actions.

RECOGNIZING THE POWERFUL EFFECTS OF BACKSTORY

As it is with many elements of storytelling, the best way to get a feel for execution is to look for and acknowledge it when you see it in other stories. Pretty much every novel you read and movie you see will have a strategic backstory in play. Your job as a writer-in-progress, or even a crusty old pro, is to notice how it's done and reflect what you've learned in your own manuscript.

In the TV drama *Castle*, the backstory involves the occupation of the hero and his playboy ways. He's a famous novelist with a talent for womanizing and an aversion to commitment. That explains his role and his attitude as he works alongside a gorgeous police detective doing her best to remain immune to his undeniable charms, not to mention his investigative sensibilities.

In the hit show *House*, the lead character brings a backstory of drug addiction (to quell the pain of a major leg problem) and relationship failure to every episode. This licenses his continued pill popping and interpersonal abuse, which juxtaposes his diagnostic genius to create a complex and fascinating hero who does his best to masquerade as an antihero. Each episode offers delicious subtext as the characters openly discuss their efforts to mess with one another—a tasty stew of first-, second- and third-dimension characterization that has become a perennial Emmy nominee.

In the movie *Avatar*, the hero's backstory is visible: He's disabled from his military service, and he's the brother of a highly trained guinea pig about to participate in a massively technical scientific experience. Unforeseen events result in the hero taking his brother's place, and his lack of experience—direct from the backstory—becomes the primary catalyst in his relationships and his experiences.

These are just a few examples of the many ways that with a deft touch and an understanding that backstory is a contextual tool, rather than part of the real-time storytelling sequence, you can infuse characters with believability and accessibility, both of which are essential to reader empathy.

LARRY BROOKS is the author of five critically acclaimed thrillers and *Story Engineering: Mastering the 6 Core Competencies of Successful Writing.*

CRAFTING BACKSTORY FOR A SERIES

If you're writing a series, backstory is even more critical. In fact, the influence of backstory is the primary thing—in addition to the character and her ongoing growth—that carries over from book to book. Each novel should stand alone in terms of a book-specific plot, with full resolution delivered. But the backstory-inspired story line remains unsolved, though each entry should move that level of the story forward concurrent with the complete resolution of the more immediate plotline.

Harry Potter is a great example of this. Harry's past is the driving force of the ongoing tension in the series, as Harry gets ever closer to finding a way to thwart the plans of the dark wizard who murdered his parents and as, once discovered, Harry maneuvers himself into position to exact revenge in the name of justice.

The first book in a series is where the backstory naturally gets the most play and focus. What you establish there—which may comprise the book-specific plotline in this first volume—becomes a less-direct focus in subsequent books, though enough revisiting is required to acquaint new readers with the driving context that continues to exert a powerful influence.

We see this everywhere on television, where we are used to watching episodic series. In the old classic *The Fugitive*, backstory permeated every scene, yet each episode found Dr. Richard Kimble presented with a new adventure and a new problem to solve.

Novelists can learn much from television with regard to how to connect episodes of a series, and the focus of that learning curve is always backstory.

CHAPTER 23

SIX WAYS TO LAYER IN BACKSTORY

BY HALLIE EPHRON

Suppose you're writing a novel that starts with a brutal rape and murder. In the opening scene, Renata Ruiz, a medical examiner, inspects the body. The reader doesn't know that Renata grew up dirt poor on a farm in central California, put herself through college, modeled for the *Playboy* college issue to make ends meet and, most important, was the victim of a brutal rapist who also raped and murdered her roommate and best friend. Yet you want to convey all these aspects of her background because, by the end of the novel, you want Renata to triumph on two levels—first, putting this sexual pervert in jail, and second, coming to terms with her own "survivor's guilt."

So when do you reveal Renata's backstory?

Tell it a little at a time. Too much backstory in the beginning can bog down your novel before you get it off the ground. Initially your reader may need to know only that Renata is an experienced medical examiner. Then, once you're airborne, slip in more at opportune moments.

The really dramatic information that resonates with this investigation—that Renata was herself a rape victim and her best friend was murdered by the rapist—is best revealed in layers as part of the unfolding drama. You might slip in, early on, that Renata was a crime victim. Later, that she was raped. Later still, that her best friend was raped and murdered. At a major turning point in the novel, perhaps when Renata is about to confront the villain, you might write a vivid flashback that dramatizes the rape or her dead friend's funeral.

The stronger and more compelling your front story, the more backstory it can hold. Here are three rules of thumb to keep in mind:

- Hold the backstory until your novel is launched.
- Gradually layer in backstory wherever it resonates with your main story, letting the past drama reinforce the drama in the present.
- Reveal the backstory in a variety of ways.

So when it comes time to add backstory, what's the best way to do it? Here are six strategies.

FIRST-PERSON NARRATION

A first-person narrator can break the "fourth wall"—that imaginary barrier between the characters and the audience—and tell the reader about his past. In this example from Kathy Reichs's *Monday Mourning*, Temperance Brennan enters a courtroom. As she walks up the center aisle, she talks to the reader:

> I have testified many times. I have faced men and women accused of monstrous crimes. Murder. Rape. Torture. Dismemberment. I am always underwhelmed by the accused.

Voilà. For the reader who hasn't read the earlier Temperance Brennan novels, this is a snapshot of her background as an expert witness. Talking directly to the reader like this is an easy and economical way to convey a first-person narrator's background. It's an efficient device for conveying facts or downplaying some information that will become important later on. On the downside, it can also be emotionally flat and lack dramatic impact.

THIRD-PERSON EXPLANATION

Another simple, straightforward way to reveal backstory is to have a third-person narrator tell the reader. Here's an example from Gary Braver's *Elixir*:

> Chris had been as good as his vow. For six years only one other person at Darby Pharms knew of his research. They had worked on the sly—nights and weekends—isolating, purifying, synthesizing, then testing the flower extract. And Chris got away with it because as senior researcher he had complete autonomy in the lab and could mask requisitions for material and animals.

The backstory continues for several pages, explaining the main character's research to find an antiaging drug. This information is delivered in the third chapter, after Braver has set up and launched his story.

Having a third-person narrator give the reader backstory is effective and efficient, though not dramatic; it's a good approach to use in small doses after your story is launched.

REVELATORY DIALOGUE

An equally simple, somewhat more artful way of layering in backstory is through dialogue. In this example from *Mansions of the Dead*, Sarah Stewart Taylor uses dialogue to let her readers know that the protagonist is an expert on mourning jewelry:

> "Sweeney?" Mrs. Pitman's hesitant voice came over the phone. "This is kind of strange, but the Cambridge police just called. A Detective Quinn. They need to talk to someone who knows about mourning jewelry. I thought of you of course and they said they want to talk to you as soon as possible."

Done well, dialogue that delivers information like this slides by easily. Done clumsily, it sounds stagy and artificial, as in this passage that I made up to demonstrate the point:

> "Here's something right up your alley, Digby," Prothero said, jabbing his finger at a newspaper article. "You know all about poisons. Wasn't your brother killed eating poisonous mushrooms? I heard that's why you became an expert and wrote that definitive pamphlet for the Poison Control Center."
>
> Digby scanned the story. "Dr. Willem Banks. Died of strychnine poisoning. Isn't he that old codger who lives in that huge mansion I wanted to buy a few years back? Maybe one of my three sisters knew him."

Yes, we get tons of backstory. There it is, in all its glory, wedged into wooden dialogue. Never force words into characters' mouths like this. Use dialogue to convey backstory only when it feels natural and works dramatically.

The stronger and more compelling your front story, the more backstory it can hold.

DOCUMENTATION

Another way to deliver backstory is through documents you dream up to serve a role in your story—wills, newspaper articles, photographs, letters, school yearbooks, and so on. You can reproduce the "document" or have one of the characters summarize what's in it.

For example, your main character might receive a letter from an old friend, reminiscing about when they were in school together, asking after the main character's family, and reminding the character that the friend once saved his life. Now the friend is cashing in his chips and asking a favor. The letter effectively moves the story along while delivering information about the main character's past.

BACKSTORY CHECKLIST

Each time you layer in some backstory, remember that the stronger and more compelling your front story, the more backstory it can tolerate. Always remember to:

- Be sure this is the dramatically appropriate spot to deliver this layer of backstory.

- Choose the most appropriate method to deliver the backstory.
- When using memories, trigger them with something in the present.
- When employing flashbacks, orient the reader to the time and place shift, shift verb tense, and then segue back to the main story at the end.

MEMORIES

One of the more dramatic ways to convey backstory is as a memory. In this example from Luiz Alfredo Garcia-Roza's *A Window in Copacabana,* Inspector Espinosa remembers his grandmother:

> He dedicated the following two hours to examining a book that, along with a few hundred others, he'd inherited from his grandmother. Every once in a while his grandmother had felt the need to purge some of the thousands of books piled in two rooms of her apartment, and these were destined for her grandson, who also inherited her habit of stockpiling books. Their styles were different: Hers were anarchic piles, his orderly stacks against the wall. They shared a disdain for shelving.

Looking at a book triggers a memory of Espinosa's grandmother. This memory is not essential to the plot but gives the reader insight into Espinosa's character, revealing a contemplative, literate side to this tough police inspector. The "orderly stacks" suggest an orderly mind, and a "disdain for shelving" suggests a man who lives alone and feels no need to conform to conventions.

Here are some examples of what might trigger a memory:

- What a character says: He sounded just like Red, my mentor at the police academy who ...
- How a character looks: She had that same look on her face as my first wife, right before she slapped me with divorce papers.
- A dream: I dreamed I was back in elementary school, fourth grade, Mrs. Joffey standing there, glaring at me bug-eyed, like I had the IQ of a frog ...

- An object: Whenever I saw that photograph, I thought of Joe and the day we …
- A song: That was our song. I remember the first time …

In this way, snippets of memory conveyed in a sentence or a few paragraphs, strategically sprinkled throughout your novel, can prove a wonderful and organic way to reveal layer after layer of your characters' backstories.

EXTENDED FLASHBACKS

Another strategy for delivering backstory is to insert an extended flashback. An extended flashback can be a clever way of showing why a character's past experience compels him to behave the way he does in the present. It can also build understanding of how a situation got to be the way it is now.

Here's how William G. Tapply starts a four-page flashback in the second chapter of *Bitch Creek*:

> An hour before sunup on a June morning almost exactly five years earlier, Calhoun had been creeping along the muddy bank of a little tidal creek that emptied into Casco Bay just north of Portland. A blush of pink had begun to bleed into the pewter sky toward the east. The tide was about halfway out, and the water against the banks lay as flat and dark as a mug of camp coffee. A blanket of fog hung …

A tricky part of writing a flashback is handling the time and space shift. Notice Tapply does it simply. The time shift: *almost exactly five years earlier*. The space shift: *along the muddy bank of a little tidal creek*.

A second tricky part is handling verb tense. If the main part of your novel is written in the present tense (he pulls the trigger …), a flashback is written in the past tense (he once killed a man …). That's easy. But what if the body of your novel is written in the past tense? Logic dictates that the flashback would be written in the past perfect (he once had killed a man …). Notice that the flashback in the example from *Bitch Creek* begins that way, in the past-perfect tense: *Calhoun had been creeping ... a blush of pink had begun to bleed ...*

Had, had, had. Past perfect quickly gets cumbersome, but the good news is once you've launched your flashback and oriented the reader by using past perfect a few times, you can revert to the regular past tense, as Tapply does in writing, *The tide was about halfway out ...*

At the end of a flashback, once again you need to cue the reader to come back to the present. To show the transition, insert the past perfect a time or two at the end of the flashback; when you're out of the flashback and back in the main story, revert to past tense. Here's an example that signals a transition back:

> She had never called him. At the time, he had thought it was odd. Now he wasn't so sure. He got up and headed ...

While an extended flashback is a dramatic way to tell the reader about past events, keep in mind that it also interrupts the narrative flow of your main story. Delivered at the wrong time, a flashback can derail the current action and waste any momentum you've gathered. But delivered at the right dramatic moment, a flashback, like backstory itself, enhances and deepens your story. Use a balance of these six strategies at the right times, and your subtle backstory will be at its most powerful.

HALLIE EPHRON is the author of more that ten books including *Writing and Selling Your Mystery Novel: How to Knock 'Em Dead With Style.*

CHAPTER 24

WEAVE IN BACKSTORY TO REVEAL CHARACTER

BY RACHEL BALLON

Creating characters' backstories is crucial because you'll want to determine each one's past experiences and the repercussions these experiences will have on your story before you begin. All characters come to your story with a problematic past and unresolved personal conflicts, so you should have a full understanding of what these problems are right from the start—even if readers don't see the connections until later.

The most common methods you can use to give the audience this important background information include dialogue, narration, internal dialogue, and flashbacks. This information must be presented in a natural progression and as an integral part of the story; otherwise it will seem forced and unnatural.

DIALOGUE

If two people are giving vital information about a character's backstory in a factual conversation, it's likely to be dull and uninteresting to the audience. However, if you show the same two characters having a heated discussion or argument, then the information is revealed through conflict, and it's likely to be more exciting for readers.

Let's say, for example, that a couple is having a conversation in a restaurant. This is rather uninteresting, unless what they are discussing is highly secret. The situation becomes even more suspenseful if they're unaware a man is listening to what they're saying. The audience is aware of the intruder but the couple isn't, and this creates tension. By constantly making the stakes higher and the conflict greater, you'll be able to reveal information and backstory while simultaneously building suspense and keeping the action moving.

Tennessee Williams does an excellent job of providing backstory through dialogue in *A Streetcar Named Desire*. When Blanche DuBois comes to visit her sister, Stella, and Stella's husband, Stanley Kowalski, at their rundown apartment, she comes with a suitcase full of secrets. Plus, Stanley hates Blanche because he knows she feels superior to him, and as a consequence, he lashes out at Blanche and Stella:

> "Who do you think you are? A pair of queens? Now just remember what Huey Long said—that every man's a king—and I'm the king around here, and don't you forget it!"

Again, Stanley wants to undermine Blanche to Stella when he reminds her of the good times the two had before Blanche arrived:

> "Listen, baby, when we first met—you and me—you thought I was common. Well, how right you was! I was common as dirt. You showed me a snapshot of the place with them columns, and I pulled you down off them columns, and you loved it, having them colored lights goin'! And wasn't we happy together? Wasn't it all OK? Till she showed up here. Hoity-toity, describin' me like an ape."

What colorful, rich dialogue Stanley uses to express his present conflict, while at the same time giving information about his happier past without Blanche.

NARRATION

Although it's not done much in modern plays, playwrights used to develop characters who walked directly out of the set or stood in front of the curtain to provide revealing information about the characters to the audience. In Thornton Wilder's Pulitzer Prize-winning *Our Town*, the character of the Stage Manager functions as the narrator when he relates to the audience:

> This is the way we were in our growing-up and in our marrying and in our doctoring and in our living and in our dying.

INNER DIALOGUE

Thoughts or interior dialogue can also be valuable tools for revealing a character's backstory and psychology. Take a look at this example from Judith Guest's novel *Ordinary People*. Here, we see the central character, Conrad Jarrett, interacting with his swim coach. Notice Conrad's internal thoughts in italics, which ultimately provide readers with more insight into what the boy's truly feeling and thinking:

> "Jarrett, you got to be kidding me. I don't get it. I excuse you from practice twice a week so you can see some shrink. ... What the hell more am I supposed to be doing for you?"
>
> "Nothing." Shrink. *Hate that word coarse ignorant just like the kind of word you'd expect from stupid bastard like Salan will not get mad control is all just someday come down here tell him what he can do with his goddamn ignorant opinions.*

FLASHBACKS

When you interject a scene from the past into the present plot, you're using flashback. Flashbacks are done either visually, as in film, or by using a character's interior thoughts or interior monologue, as in prose. The flashback gives information or an explanation about a specific character or event that is important for the audience to know. Be careful, however, not to use a flashback if it has no relationship to the present scene; doing so will create confusion. Flashbacks can often slow down a story or interrupt the flow, and you'll want to make sure you weave them in smoothly.

Toward the end of F. Scott Fitzgerald's *The Great Gatsby*, the narrator of the novel, Nick Carraway, relates through summary Gatsby's last night with Daisy before Gatsby goes off to war:

> On the last afternoon before he went abroad, he sat with Daisy in his arms for a long, silent time. It was a cold fall day, with fire in the room and her cheeks flushed. Now and then she moved and he changed his arm a little, and once he kissed her dark shining hair. The afternoon had made them tranquil for a while, as if to give them a deep memory for the long parting the next promised. They had never been closer in their month of love, nor communicated more profoundly one with another, than when she brushed silent lips against his coat's shoulder or when he touched the end of her fingers, gently, as though she were asleep.

This flashback provides readers with a glimpse of the relationship Gatsby and Daisy once shared, and adds emphasis to angst now felt by Gatsby as he watches Daisy with her husband, Tom.

Remember that you want a flashback to enhance your present story and allow the audience to learn secrets from the past, so they'll understand what's happening. But don't rely on flashbacks to structure your story, and make sure you use them sparingly.

RACHEL BALLON is a is a licensed psychotherapist, script consultant, and author of *Breathing Life into your Characters: How to Give Your Characters Emotional & Psychological Depth*.

CHAPTER 25

HOW TO BUILD SUSPENSE WITH BACKSTORY

BY LEIGH MICHAELS

To keep the readers' attention through the long midsection of your book, you'll need to continually develop the conflict and advance the plot in logical steps without making the story predictable. What keeps readers turning pages is suspense, which you can create using a variety of techniques, including tension, pacing, and foreshadowing.

The suspense we're discussing here doesn't necessarily involve the characters being in peril; it's created whenever there's something the reader wants to know. Will Joe kiss Brenda? Will Sally give in to Brad's demand that she work for him? Will Jared answer Katherine's question or dodge it?

Whenever you cause readers to be curious about what comes next, you're creating suspense. Suspense arises naturally from good writing—it's not a spice to be added separately.

Putting too much backstory early in the book to divulge information about your characters can bore your readers and destroy any suspense you may have established.

In fiction, you create suspense by withholding information, and the best type of information to withhold is often the backstory. You, as the author, can create suspense in three main ways:

BY WITHHOLDING INFORMATION FROM READERS. As the author, you know the entire hidden story behind the plot and characters: the backstory and the plot twists that are yet to come. You might be tempted to spill out the backstory and hidden story right away, but most stories are improved when at least some of that information is held back—sometimes up to the very end.

BY WITHHOLDING INFORMATION FROM THE MAIN CHARACTERS. This is the Hitchcock effect—so called because Alfred Hitchcock was a master of it in his films. By reading between the lines and applying common sense and experience, the readers (like Hitchcock's movie audience) can draw conclusions about what's likely to be coming up. But, like the movie audience, the readers are powerless to prevent a character from stepping into a yawning trap that only readers can foresee.

BY HAVING THE CHARACTERS WITHHOLD INFORMATION FROM THE READERS—AND FROM ONE ANOTHER. Just because a character knows something doesn't mean he has to share it (even if he's a POV character). And even hidden motives will affect how a character acts, cluing in alert readers to what's really going on.

When you're writing scenes in which suspense is crucial, you also need to know what to avoid. Keep in mind that putting too much backstory early in the book, or using too much introspection to divulge information about your characters, is a great way to bore the readers and destroy any suspense you may have established.

There are, however, five simple steps you can take to increase the level of suspense in your scenes.

- Keep the action intense. If significant amounts of time go by without suspenseful action—which is often most powerfully motivated by backstory—the story loses momentum and readers lose interest.
- Make the danger feel real. If the hero and heroine stop in the middle of a chase to share a passionate interlude while trusting dumb luck to keep them from being discovered, it's going to be hard to convince readers that they have reason to be fearful. If readers are to believe the danger, then the characters must act as if they're threatened. Even if the danger

isn't physical, keep pressure on the characters. Don't stop for backstory; weave it in.

- Keep the emotion high. Even if the story doesn't involve physical danger for the characters, their lifelong happiness is at stake. Keeping emotions at the core of the story reminds readers how important the situation is.
- Repeat an action, phrase, or event. The first use of the action or line of dialogue may be almost casual, doing little more than getting the readers' attention. The second use makes it clear that this bit of information is important (though readers may not quite see why) and foreshadows the important action to come. The third use is the most emphatic: The stakes have grown enormous since the backstory first laid the groundwork, and the readers, having been properly prepared, are on the edge of their seats waiting to see what will happen.
- Hide what characters are thinking. If the heroine assesses the hero's clenched jaw and assumes he's mad at her, and then you show him thinking about his aching molar, the heroine doesn't know she's wrong, but readers do—and all the suspense is gone from the scene. In this example from Claire Cross's novel *Double Trouble*, we see the heroine drawing conclusions about the hero based on his backstory, but we have no idea whether or not she's correct:

> I never could figure out why he married my sister. Unless a wife and kids were necessary accessories for the lawyer-destined-for-Great-Things—and she was as good a choice as any. They never seemed to have much in common, but maybe it was something basic between them. Like lust. Marcia used to be quite a looker, and I say that with the undue modesty of an identical twin.
>
> Tonight, James looked surprisingly haggard and annoyed for a man made of granite, and as I mentioned, that expression didn't improve when he saw me.
>
> "What the hell are you doing here?"

> Oooh, a vulgarity. Of course, the strumpet sister had invaded the last bastion of propriety in the Free World. That, at least, conformed to our usual script. His job was to make sure I didn't feel welcome enough to hang around too long and taint the precious boys. I knew my lines by heart.
>
> Too bad I hadn't worn something really skimpy, just to tick him off. I slouched harder, knowing that perfect posture was a household holy grail. "You should be more gracious to the one doing your dirty work."
>
> The man glowered at me. "What are you talking about?"
>
> "Your kids called me from the pool when no one picked them up."
>
> James flicked a glance up the stairs, some parental part of him clearly reassured by the ruckus coming from the bathroom. "Where's Marcia?"
>
> "Where were you? Takes two for the fun part. Why should one be left with all the work after that?"

What's going on with James? We don't know why he's haggard and annoyed. We know what conclusions the heroine has drawn—but is she correct? Why does the heroine have a reputation as the strumpet sister? Why are these two in so much conflict that they have a "usual script" for their interactions?

We will have to turn the page and go on if we want to find out.

LEIGH MICHAELS is the author of nearly one hundred books, including eighty contemporary novels, three historical romance novels, and more than a dozen non-fiction books, including *On Writing Romance*.

FLASHBACKS VS. BACKSTORY

A flashback is a sudden, brief relocation to a previous time and then, just as suddenly, a return to the present story. Flashbacks can hint at backstories, but they aren't backstories themselves. A backstory is a longer trip (in fact, sometimes backstories make up most of a story or even a novel).

In a flashback, a character is usually reminded of something or someone from his past. The smell of cabbage cooking might cause him to see a kitchen that he hasn't actually seen in years. Or you might have a character who looks over at his wife of fifty years and, in just the right light of a nice afternoon, sees her as the teenager he married.

Flashbacks come in handy when you need to infuse a clue or two into a mystery or when some character trait needs to be enhanced or explained. Let's say you have a fellow in your story who doesn't like dogs. Your reader wants to know why, so you lead her along for a while and then give her a nice little flashback, in which the man recalls being bitten by a dog as a child.

Flashbacks are quick. Backstories, because they drag in the baggage of a character or a situation, are longer.

Backstory, when layered effectively, can be a good way to establish setting and provide description. Diverting your readers' attention away from the here and now allows you to focus on times and places that give deeper insight into a character or a situation.

RON ROZELLE is the author of five books, including *Write Great Fiction: Description & Setting.*

FOCUS ON THE WRITING LIFE:

BALANCING WRITING WITH THE REST OF LIFE

MARRY YOUR LIFE TO YOUR WRITING

BY SHEILA BENDER

Like many aspiring writers, for years I buried my desire to write under the activities of a busy life. I taught English and reading at a junior high school while I studied for my graduate degree, went on to direct a day care center and started a family. I assumed life would not allow me the time to write.

But at the libraries and bookstores my kids and I visited, volumes by contemporary poets began falling into my hands, and I'd jot down lines of verse that came to me. I finally decided to apply to a poetry writing workshop at the University of Washington. I knew I could arrange my work schedule around the class times, but I still wasn't sure I could find time to "really" write. Once class started, though, something miraculous happened: Writing began making its own space in my life. Somehow, like the leaves of pioneering weeds that collect soil for more weeds to grow, my small bits of writing attracted more time to write. Eventually I found I'd written enough poems to apply to graduate school, and so I did.

For two years, I wrote in my car before class started. I wrote at public parks on the way to pick up my kids at day care. I learned how much I could accomplish in ten or twenty minutes.

When I finished my degree and began teaching at community colleges, I made a life-changing decision: I'd incorporate my teaching life into my writing. My instructional writing would be as much "my writing" as what others call "my *own* writing." Pivotal in my decision not to make a distinction were lines from Robert Hass' poems in *Praise.*

In "Heroic Simile," he writes:

> The young man is thinking he would be rich if he were already rich and had a mule.

And in "The Beginning of September," he writes:

> No one really likes the odor of geraniums, not the woman who dreams of sunlight and is always late for work nor the man who would be happy in altered circumstances.

I would not yearn for altered circumstances to write or shirk my responsibilities in hopes of dreaming about sunlight. I would find patches of writing light while performing daily tasks. I would not fantasize about how I would be rich and famous if only I had time to go on prestigious writers' retreats. I would create a writing life from available resources.

You can make this commitment to your writing, too—and you can start just like I did, by advancing your relationship with your work in four simple steps: First, seize every opportunity to write, even if only in ten-minute snatches of time; second, take classes and participate in writing groups; third, read, read, read writing that resembles what you're writing; fourth, join other writers in organizing community readings and editing literary journals. When I did this—and stopped making the distinction that one kind of writing was "real" and the other less important—I wrote more, and the resulting pieces, whether for educational publications or literary journals, informed one another.

Marrying your life to your writing means agreeing "to have and to hold from this day forward" all parts of yourself so neither your life *nor* your writing suffers unrequited love. Here are ways to say "I do" every day, and to cherish and nurture your writing as you cherish and nurture the rest of your life activities.

USE CREATIVE STRATEGIES TO SPEND TIME WITH YOUR WRITING

At home or at work, you *really can* push everything aside for ten minutes to write ideas for the larger work you are creating, to write passages you might use in that work, or to do a writing exercise to develop something new.

You can find prompts for your writing everywhere. Point to a word or a sentence in any text and write for ten minutes about whatever you (or your character) associate to. Turn an iPod or radio on and off and use the few words you hear as a jumping-off place for inventive writing. You can make a habit of creating your own inspiration and have faith that the words will begin flowing more freely as a result.

You can pay close attention to and write down what you (or characters would) touch, smell, hear, taste, and see wherever you are sitting.

You can do all of this writing for ten minutes before leaving for lunch or in your car by arriving ten minutes early for work. You can park a few blocks from home at the end of the day, and stop and write. You can learn to use it to your advantage when you have to stop midway through a piece of writing. This way, you already have a place to start and can be more productive the next time you sit down to write. You can keep a book of writing exercises with you to provide prompts when a dry spell sets in. Failing pen and paper, with nothing but a cell phone, you can take voice notes. Many associations will arise from this writing; you'll be surprised at how deep you can go.

SURROUND YOURSELF WITH THOSE WHO SUPPORT YOUR RELATIONSHIP

Sign up for something social to do with writing—critique groups or workshops (online or off), for example—for "evenings out" with this cherished partner. The deadlines these groups supply will help prompt you to notice more places in your life for doing your writing.

If the idea of networking with new people doesn't appeal to you, think of your current connections. There's a good chance you already have a writing buddy or two with whom you can form a small group. E-mail one another drafts and let group members know which of their words and phrases are memorable, and what feelings you have as you read their writing. Give feedback on what propels you forward and what gives you pause. Share what you'd like to know more about in the writing. It doesn't take long to respond this way; giving and gathering this kind of response is as exhilarating a break from chores and work as a movie or TV show.

You might also find you can form a writing group at work and do freewriting exercises together, perhaps meeting for breakfast or lunch once a week. Having support in your regular commitment to your writing can help you keep it.

And the successful results of such group efforts often are quantifiable. Take essayist Brenda Miller, who tentatively formed a writing group with two women she'd met in a service-learning program. Their shared goal was simple: to make more time for their writing. Miller's essay "Swerve," which was published in the online literary magazine *Brevity*, resulted from a group prompt experience that she describes this way: "I had to let my intuition guide me to that dangerous place, knowing I'd be safe in the company of newfound friends."

LOVE THE ONE YOU HAVE

Decide to enjoy whatever kind of writing you're already doing, even if it's all work-related. If you write frequent e-mails to co-workers or clients, pay attention to the details, tone, and succinct way you find to say something. If you're writing fiction, maybe your characters can write e-mails like you do. Maybe they can write them like a co-worker writes them. Jot down your ideas for how a character's e-mails would sound. Have the character e-mail you frequently, even daily. You can learn a lot about a character this way.

If you write reports, realize that editing for clarity and the use of precise language is an exercise in revision that is helpful in all types of writing. Realize, too, that you can use forms of writing you already know in order to develop your characters. Let them write reports on events in their lives; you'll learn more about them. You also can use the tone of your reports for personal essays or articles by taking a lesson from Russell Baker's entertaining essay "The Plot Against People," in which the author adopts the persona of a professor lecturing on the ambitions of inanimate objects. Baker begins:

> Inanimate objects are classified into three major categories—those that don't work, those that break down and those that get lost.

The goal of all inanimate objects is to resist man and ultimately to defeat him, and the three major classifications are based on the method each object uses to achieve its purpose. As a general rule, any object capable of breaking down at the moment when it is most needed will do so. The automobile is typical of the category.

By applying an instructional tone to a relatable topic, Baker effectively created a piece that strikes a chord with readers about the frustrations we all face with the things in our lives.

Think you can't apply your own work-related writing skills to your creative writing in a similar way? You can. A special-education teacher I know felt the only writing she knew how to do was for Individualized Education Plans (IEPs). She wanted to do some personal writing but felt she knew nothing of the craft. So, I suggested she write herself an IEP. The result was brilliant: Her IEP for how she would manage and flourish in her coming retirement had a roomful of people laughing at the way she described herself and the ways her family could support her life change.

You can find a way to do this no matter what you do. If you're an expert in a process or product you've learned on the job, you might write (and perhaps even sell) an instructional article on the topic for laypeople. If you're a waitress, use the order pad you have to write about your life. What would you order up for your day?

If the writing you're doing is making up stories for your children or grandchildren, or blogging about a topic you find interesting, you may not even realize you're creating writing that can become fodder for pieces you might submit to magazines and other markets. Nurse Kate Bracy started a free blog on Open Salon (opensalon.com) as a way of writing personal essays to self-imposed deadlines. Soon, one of her essays earned the "Editors' pick" designation, and an agent approached her to write a book proposal, which she did.

As Bracy says, "Of course, the movie *Julie & Julia* is also based on [a Salon] blog. But the lesson isn't to blog on *Salon*. The lesson is to write." Even if you write only e-mails most of the time, think about how they might be reinvented. They're a well you can draw from to write about your life and knowledge.

Think of *all* the writing you do as skills building, format providing, and information gathering. Don't waste time wishing for altered circumstances. You support your family, your community and yourself with your work and your activities; you can support your writing, too.

By considering everything you write your "own writing" and starting from the forms you're most practiced in, you'll learn to get into a writing mind-set quickly and without resistance while you fill your box of craft tools.

SHEILA BENDER'S most recent book is *A New Theology: Turning to Poetry in a Time of Grief.* She publishes an online magazine at writingitreal.com.

THE WRITE-AT-HOME MOM

BY CHRISTINA KATZ

The challenges of raising kids and a career under one roof are impossible to enumerate. So it's a good thing so many parents are experts at finding rhythms and routines that work best for everyone in the family. The questions that are good for the kids are good for the mama (and papa), too: What would simplify your morning routine? When do you feel most productive? What shortcuts would help you set aside more time to write?

The answers to these questions are a start, but—as you well know—family life can be a tad unpredictable, and those "routines" can fly out the window before the ink dries on your well-meaning to-do list. So I've put together some concrete ideas for plucking spare moments to write between child duties/activities. Morning, noon, or night, the time is there—you just have to know where to look.

For starters, break your weekly tasks down in advance, based on what you think you can accomplish in the amount of time your kids will be occupied. (Sunday night is a good time to do this.) For example: A beginning writer might plan to write one article per week during the times her kids watch *Sesame Street*. As the week unfolds, keep in mind the following breakdown of potential writing moments.

MORNINGS: RISE AND WRITE

GET UP EARLIER: I know, I know—this has never been a very popular suggestion. But it doesn't have to be painful. Perhaps you and your spouse could trade off night and morning duties, so you can get to bed earlier on some nights. In other words, your spouse oversees the bedtime routine, and you oversee the morning routine—*after* you get in an hour of early-morning writing.

SKIP THE BUSY WORK: If morning is your most mentally productive time of day, don't waste your energy on things that could just as easily be done later: folding laundry, talking on the phone, making grocery lists.

PRE-PREP MEALS: Prepare lunches, set the table for breakfast, set up the coffee machine and put out the nonperishable foods the night before. Making this a habit will better prepare you to meet your day while giving you precious extra time during the hectic morning hours.

TAILOR TO FIT: Create morning routines to suit each family member's personality so they'll be self-directed and leave you to your writing. For example, your six-year-old may love to pick out her clothes the night before and lay them out for the next day, but your teenager may view this as a major violation of his rights. No need to micromanage; just help each child find a system that works. The operative word here is works.

TURN ON THE TV: Of course, moderation is the key, but you can use television, VCRs, and DVDs as part of a regular routine to carve out writing time. Remind everyone involved that watching television is a special treat. Let the kids know you'll be working while they watch but that you're available if they really, *really* need you. Explain that you expect them to behave and give them a preview of what's coming next. For example: After *Arthur*, we'll take a walk to the park (or have a play date, or color, etc.).

MULTITASK: Don't forget morning activities that give you a little time here and there. Can you get a few notes written in the waiting room at a doctor's appointment or during children's classes or activities? Some groups require your participation, but others, especially after toddler age, don't. I recently roughed out several pages while my daughter was in a morning dance class, and those pages came faster and more easily than anything I wrote in my office that day.

AFTERNOONS: EVERYBODY RECHARGE

LET 'EM EAT SLOWLY: At lunchtime, toddlers can be notoriously slow. If you're blessed with a pokey or picky one, make use of the time you spend sitting at the kitchen table. Keep a notepad handy and pull it out after you serve lunch for brainstorming ideas while the kids eat.

GET A HEAD START: If you have kids of various ages at home, lunchtime probably isn't going to yield any literary breakthroughs. If you spend your time wisely at lunch, however, you can earn time before or after dinner when backup (your spouse or older children) arrives. So go ahead and set the table for dinner after lunch, get the recipes and ingredients out for dinner and, if possible, get a jump-start on preparation while everyone's still finishing their lunches.

DECLARE QUIET TIME: If you're really lucky, your child's naps afford you valuable extra work time. But even if you don't have a napper, you can declare an hour or so of quiet time in the afternoon. During quiet time, all children must go to their rooms, play quietly and leave mommy alone (unless it's urgent, of course).

REST UP: Alternately, you can go ahead and take a nap yourself during quiet time so you'll have more energy to write in the evening. Just crash with your kids or find a resting spot within earshot of their stirring. You'll be more energized in the evenings even if you don't actually fall asleep.

EVENINGS: WRING OUT EVERY SECOND

HOMEWORK FOR EVERYONE: If you have older kids, they likely have homework. While they work, you can work. Or they may have practices, Girl Scouts, or other activities that allow you some quiet time. And if you have very young children, chances are they go to bed fairly early, which can open up your evening hours.

STRETCH IT OUT: After dinner, you may want to just get to your desk and get straight to work—but a fifteen-minute power walk around the block, a quick dance, or a big stretch will help you revitalize yourself so you can work more efficiently.

EASE IN: Once you sit down, set a timer for twenty minutes and do something easy or fun right off the bat. Type up a funny anecdote from your day. Or rough out an inspirational article. Go in a direction that feels easiest for you or that you associate with warming up. Then, when the timer rings, you'll be ready to ring out some nitty-gritty research for an article or edit the draft of your personal essay for the zillionth time.

STAY IN THE ZONE: When the sitcom laughter from another room starts to lure you away from work, grab your timer again, but this time for the tough stuff. Here's how it works: Respond to e-mails—twenty minutes—go! Draft article—twenty minutes—go! Proofread yesterday's draft, plan for next week—you can get a lot done in short bursts if you practice working that way.

LATE NIGHT: THE LAST REFUGE

Writer Heather Sharfeddin awoke in the middle of the night with the idea for her first published novel, *Blackbelly*. Fortunately she'd been dealing with insomnia long enough to already be in the habit of shuffling to her computer, where she'd write until sleep beckoned her back to bed. For some mamas, late-night hours are the best you can get. But hey, you can still make it work. Just be sure to get the rest you need to function the next morning.

CHRISTINA KATZ has written over two hundred articles for magazines, newspapers, and online publications. She is the author of *Writer Mama, Get Known Before the Book Deal*, and *The Writer's Workout*.

PART 5:

DIALOGUE:

WHAT YOUR CHARACTERS SAY TO EACH OTHER

CHAPTER 26

AMP UP DIALOGUE WITH EMOTIONAL BEATS

BY TODD A. STONE

Dialogue benefits from variety. To maintain your reader's interest, insert a variety of beats into your dialogue. Beats are descriptions of physical action—minor or major—that fall between lines of speech. Try these techniques to punch up your dialogue.

USE FACIAL EXPRESSIONS

When a character raises an eyebrow or furrows his brow, this action, or beat, interrupts the dialogue and telegraphs a change in the character's emotional state. As an exchange progresses and the emotional intensity rises—as the character's dissatisfaction grows into anger, for instance—he might set his jaw, bite his lip, or narrow his gaze. His eyes may darken, his face may redden, his nostrils may flare, and so on. These are all conventional and commonly understood signs of anger. You can read a dozen clinical texts on which facial expressions most strongly signal which emotion, or you can watch a few good dramatic films or TV shows with the sound off. It won't take you long to see how the actors use facial expressions to signal emotion.

MAKE THEM TALK WITH THEIR HANDS

Characters can point, steeple their fingers, clench their hands into fists, pound tables, hold their hands up to surrender, cross their arms in front of their chests, throw up their hands in resignation or despair (though this gesture is much overused), or twiddle their thumbs (does anyone actually do that?). In the following example from the best-selling novel *Wonder Boys*, notice how author Michael Chabon instills movement and tension into the dialogue simply by focusing on what college student James Leer is holding:

> "It's a fake," said James Leer, holding out his hand to me, palm upward. Upon it lay a tiny silver pistol, a "ladies' model" with a pearl handle, no bigger than a deck of cards. "Hello, Professor Tripp."
>
> "Hello, James," I said. "I didn't know what you were doing out here."
>
> "It's my mother's," he said. "She won it in a penny arcade in Baltimore, in one of those machines with the claw. When she was in Catholic school. It used to shoot these little paper caps, but you can't find the right kind anymore."
>
> "Why do you carry it around?" I said, reaching for it.
>
> "I don't know." His fingers closed around the little gun and he slipped it back into the pocket of his overcoat. "I found it in a drawer at home and I just started carrying it around. For good luck, I guess."

ADD MOVEMENT

Your characters can cross the room or push back from a desk or table to get physical and emotional distance from a heated conversation, an intimate moment, or even another character. They can move in closer to become more threatening or more intimate, or to drive a point home. If a character puts a piece of furniture or some other object between himself and someone else, that's a clear signal that he's blocking the other character—emotionally, physically, or intellectually, depending upon the nature of your scene. Use movement to support and enhance your dialogue, and your readers will pick up on all this and more.

It's not hard to spot the building hostility in this exchange from Khaled Hosseini's novel *The Kite Runner.*

> "Amir agha and I are friends," Hassan said. He looked flushed.
>
> "Friends?" Assef said, laughing. "You pathetic fool! Someday you'll wake up from your little fantasy and learn just how good of a friend he is. Now, bas! Enough of this. Give us that kite."
>
> Hassan stooped and picked up a rock.
>
> Assef flinched. He began to take a step back, stopped. "Last chance, Hazara."
>
> Hassan's answer was to cock the arm that held the rock.
>
> "Whatever you wish." Assef unbuttoned his winter coat, took it off, folded it slowly and deliberately. He placed it against the wall.

DON'T FORGET THE BIG STUFF

If it's within your character's personality, don't be afraid to have him take big actions—throw a fit, throw a plate, or throw a punch. And don't hesitate to skip the buildup if a character's personality demands it. If your character has a hair-trigger temper, bypass any eyebrow raising and go straight to breaking the furniture.

Make sure the actions you choose are consistent with your character's traits. Every action should be a reflection of the character's objectives and emotions, and of the scene. If your character seldom shows emotion, focus on small details that show his true feelings leaking out: a tightening around his eyes, a deliberate forcefulness in each step as he walks across the room, a tense grip on a pen.

Beats like these make it easier for your reader to see and feel the emotion in your dialogue. Render your characters' words with care—and then do everything you can to make them shine.

TODD A. STONE award-winning screenwriter and author of *Novelist's Bootcamp*. He's the head writer for the interactive mystery website Crime Scene www.crimescene.com.

EDITING YOUR DIALOGUE

If dialogue stops or delays your novel's progress toward resolving the conflict, it must be cut, pared down, or rewritten. Your characters don't want to wait through an unnecessary conversation, and neither do your readers. Look for these areas in your manuscript.

Opening Niceties

In real speech, we open most conversations with introductions and small talk. In fiction, these introductions and small talk do nothing but get in the way:

> "Good morning, Sam."
>
> "Morning, Wally."
>
> "How are you?"
>
> "Fine. Nice looking day today, isn't it?"

Sam and Wally may soon reveal their needs in conflict, but why wait? Cut the niceties and get to it:

> "Good morning, Sam."
>
> "It would be, if I didn't have to look at your backstabbing face so early."

There's no waiting and no doubt at all what the conflict is here.

Pauses to Think

In real speech, we use filler words or sounds to buy time to think about what to say next.

In dialogue, words like *well*, *ahem*, *ah*, and *uh* dilute the conflict and get in the way of its progression. If your character needs to stall for time, have her do something that signals her need to stall or her reluctance to answer:

> "What's the status of the Corbin Project?" said Al.
>
> Linda bit her lip and looked down at the floor. An eternity of tense seconds passed.
>
> "There are serious problems."
>
> "Unsatisfactory. I told you I wanted that project straightened out by now."

Here the conflict is intense, the action moves fast, and we know Linda is in hot water.

Echoes

In real speech we use echoes to ensure understanding, to buy time to form a reply, or to continue a conversation.

> Pat said, "I went to see Fred today."
>
> "You saw Fred, did you?" said Lois.
>
> "Yes, I saw Fred. We talked about the Jackson case."
>
> "You discussed the Jackson case? What for?"

Rewriting to delete the echoes and to foreground the conflict yields a much more intense passage.

> "I saw Fred today," Pat said. "We talked about the Jackson case."
>
> "You had no right to do that," said Lois.

Give your readers what they want and give it to them fast. Use echoes, fillers and niceties in your draft if you must to prime your writing, but make sure you take them out later, before they drag down your reader.

CHAPTER 27

WEAVE ACTION, NARRATIVE, & DIALOGUE

BY GLORIA KEMPTON

Most of the time, we want to balance our scenes using three elements of fiction: dialogue, action, and narrative. This is one reason you want to put your character in a scene with other characters as often as possible. Scenes that weave together these three elements engage the reader at an emotional level much more effectively than scenes that are only dialogue, only narrative, or only action.

The following is an example of a well-woven scene from Sue Monk Kidd's *The Secret Life of Bees*. In this scene, Kidd seems to want to talk to us about the risk of getting "stung" if we want to be true beekeepers. If we want to make a difference in the world, we must take risks, and loving something is enough reason to do it. Rather than "preach" to us through narrative alone, the author blends the scene using dialogue, action, and narrative, pulling the reader in.

> Rescuing bees took us the entire morning. Driving back into remote corners of the woods where there were barely roads, we would come upon 25 beehives up on slats like a little lost city tucked back in there. We lifted the covers and filled the feeders with sugar water. Earlier we'd spooned dry sugar into our pockets, and now, just as a bonus, we sprinkled it on the feeding rims.
>
> I managed to get stung on my wrist while replacing a lid onto a hive box. August scraped out the stinger.
>
> "I was sending them love," I said, feeling betrayed.

> August said, "Hot weather makes the bees out of sorts, I don't care how much love you send them." She pulled a small bottle of olive oil and bee pollen from her free pocket and rubbed my skin—her patented remedy. It was something I'd hoped never to test out.
>
> "Count yourself initiated," she said. "You can't be a true beekeeper without getting stung."
>
> A true beekeeper. The words caused a fullness in me, and right at that moment an explosion of blackbirds lifted off the ground in a clearing a short distance away and filled up the whole sky. I said to myself, Will wonders never cease? I would add that to my list of careers. A writer, an English teacher and a beekeeper.
>
> "Do you think I could keep bees one day?" I asked.
>
> August said, "Didn't you tell me this past week one of the things you loved was bees and honey? Now, if that's so, you'll be a fine beekeeper. Actually, you can be bad at something, Lily, but if you love doing it, that will be enough."
>
> The sting shot pain all the way to my elbow, causing me to marvel at how much punishment a minuscule creature can inflict. I'm prideful enough to say I didn't complain. After you get stung, you can't get unstung no matter how much you whine about it. I just dived back into the riptide of saving bees.

How did Kidd know when and where to put what? This is largely an intuitive process, and I'm guessing she didn't do a lot of thinking about how she was weaving the elements of fiction as she was writing her first draft. You have to move inside of your characters in order to do this. You can't be thinking about how to do it, at least not while writing the first draft. During the revision process, when reading back through the story, you can see better when a scene is top-heavy with dialogue, narrative, or action. The perfectly balanced scene has a rhythm to it; you'll learn to recognize it when it's there.

KEEPING TALK IN THE FOREGROUND

Having said all that, knowing when to only focus on one element is as important as learning to weave them all together. Is it ever a good thing to create a scene with only dialogue? Only narrative? Only action?

If you want to highlight a particular character trait in your viewpoint character or focus on something specific that the characters are talking about, you don't want the scene cluttered, the reader distracted, or the pace slowed by action or narrative. You know how sometimes when someone is telling you a story, the setting, the other people around you, everything just kind of fades away, and you're intent only on what the other person is saying? This is what it's like when you cut away action and narrative and leave only your characters' spoken words.

Check out this scene in *The Feast of Love* by Charles Baxter. The viewpoint character, Bradley, works at a coffee shop called Jitters. His co-worker, Chloe, asks him what's the worst thing that ever happened to him. Up until that time, the author had woven dialogue, narrative, and action into a nicely balanced scene, but it was time to speed things up. Bradley starts to tell Chloe about how he and some buddies were in the cathedral at Notre Dame in Paris. The story's getting long and Chloe tells him to hurry it up. What the author wants to highlight here is that Bradley actually thinks the worst thing he's ever done in his life is knock over a bunch of candles in a cathedral. The dialogue focuses on this alone:

> "Let me finish this story ... and because my hand was shaking, I reached down to the holder, this freestanding holder or candelabra or whatever of votive candles, and somehow, I don't know how this happened, my hand caused this holder of candles, all these small flames, all these souls, to fall over, and when it fell over, all the candles, lit for the sake of a soul somewhere, there must have been a hundred of them, all of them fell to the floor, because of me, and all of them went out. And you know what the nun did, Chloe, the nun who was standing there?"

"She spoke French?"

"No. She could have, but she didn't. No, what she did was, she screamed."

"Wow."

"Yeah, the nun screamed in my face. I felt like ..."

"You felt like pretty bad, Mr. S., I can believe it. But you know, Mr. S, those were just candles. They weren't really souls. That's all superstition, that soul stuff."

"Oh, I know."

"No kidding, Mr. S., you shouldn't be so totally morbid. I thought when you were telling me about the worst thing you ever did, it'd be, like, beating up a blind guy and stealing his car."

"No, I never did that."

"Oscar did, once. You should get him to tell you about it."

"Okay."

"He was drunk, though." She prettily touches her perfect hair. "And the guy wasn't really blind. He just said he was, to take advantage of people. It was, like, a scam. Oscar saw through all that. It's nine o'clock now, Boss. We should open up."

"Right." And I unlock the curtain, and touch a switch, and slowly the curtain rises on the working day. The candles are nothing to Chloe; they're just candles. I feel instantly better. Bless her.

The scene wouldn't have had the same impact if the author had woven action and narrative throughout the dialogue. This is a neurotic character, and this fast-paced scene of dialogue shows the extent of his neurosis, especially compared to Chloe's explanation of the candles being just candles. Because this part of the scene is only dialogue, we get the full impact of his neurosis and how it expresses itself in his life. When you isolate a character's dialogue, if the reader is paying attention, he'll become privy to the character's personality and motives in a way that's not possible in the woven scene just because there's too much going on.

It can take the protagonist pages to *tell* us something in narrative, whereas a scene of dialogue can quickly *show* us through that character's own words said out loud. Narrative explains, and dialogue blurts out.

PACING YOUR SCENES

Pacing is probably the most common fiction element to pay attention to when considering when and when not to weave dialogue, narrative, and action. If you're creating a fast-paced conflict scene between two or more people, you might do well to consider only dialogue, at least for parts of it. In Wally Lamb's *She's Come Undone*, the young viewpoint character, Dolores, is fed up with her mother, who has been grieving over the loss of her baby for more than four years and has acquired all kinds of obsessive-compulsive disorders, the most recent being an obsession with her new parakeet, Petey. Dolores has already been narrating a lot of this, but now it's time for her to act out her feelings. In a scene of dialogue, the author quickly shows what Dolores has taken pages to tell us:

> I hated Petey—fantasized about his flying accidentally out a window or into the electric fan so that his spell over Ma would be broken. My not kissing Ma anymore was a conscious decision reached one night at bedtime with the purpose of hurting her.
>
> "Well, you're stingy tonight," she said when I turned my face away from her goodnight kiss.
>
> "I'm not kissing you anymore, period," I told her. "All day long you kiss that bird right on its filthy beak."
>
> "I do not."
>
> "You do so. Maybe you want to catch bird diseases, but I don't."
>
> "Petey's mouth is probably cleaner than my mouth and yours put together, Dolores," was her argument.
>
> "That's a laugh."

"Well, it's true. I read it in my bird book."

"Next thing you know, you'll be French-kissing it."

"Never mind French-kissing. What do you know about that kind of stuff? You watch that mouth of yours, young lady."

"That's exactly what I'm doing," I said. I clamped my hand over my mouth and stuffed my whole face into the pillow.

As you can see, this passage is very effective without a bunch of narrative bogging down the moment. The dialogue here shows Dolores' true attitude toward Petey, but more important, it demonstrates her feelings toward her mother. This is dialogue at its most powerful. It can take the protagonist pages to *tell* us something in narrative, whereas a scene of dialogue can quickly *show* us through that character's own words said out loud. Narrative explains, and dialogue blurts out.

Similar reasoning applies when writing scenes with only narrative or only action. You want to focus on something in your character's mind or describe something that would only sound contrived in dialogue, so you use straight narrative. Or the action needs to drive the scene forward because it's intense and emotional, and your characters just wouldn't be talking during this time.

Sometimes, as in real life, there's just nothing to say at the moment. Always, always, always let your characters lead you.

STRIKING A BALANCE

There are no hard-and-fast rules about when and when not to blend dialogue, action, and narrative. To weave them together well is to find your story's rhythm. But there *are* a few questions you can ask yourself about your story, especially in the rewrite stage, that can help you know which elements are most effective for a particular scene, and which might be better used elsewhere.

Ask yourself:

- Is the story moving a little too slowly, and do I need to speed things up? (Use dialogue.)

- Is it time to give the reader some background on the characters so they're more sympathetic? (Use narrative, dialogue, or a combination of the two.)
- Do I have too many dialogue scenes in a row? (Use action or narrative.)
- Are my characters constantly confiding in others about things they should only be pondering in their minds? (Use narrative.)
- Likewise, are my characters alone in their heads when my characters in conversation would be more effective and lively? (Use dialogue.)
- Is my story top-heavy in any way at all—too much dialogue, too much narrative, or too much action? (Insert more of the elements that are missing.)
- Are my characters providing too many background details as they're talking to each other? (Use narrative.)

Whether we're using dialogue, action, or narrative to move the story forward, any or all three of these elements are doing double duty by revealing our characters' motives. Your story's dialogue can reveal motive in a way that's natural and authentic, because whether we're aware of it or not, we reveal our own motives all the time in our everyday lives.

And to understand a character's motive is to understand the character.

GLORIA KEMPTON is the author of ten books, including *Write Great Fiction: Dialogue*.

CREATING THREE-DIMENSIONAL SCENES

Choose a scene from your own work or one you want to add to your story. Practice writing the same scene over and over. Use all dialogue the first time. Then use all narrative. Then all action. Finally, weave all three fiction elements for a three-dimensional effect.

Pull a troublesome scene from your own story. Which element does it have too much of? Too little of? Consider how you might weave all three elements to make it more three-dimensional.

Take a look at some of your woven scenes and see if you can speed them up by taking out all of the narrative and using only dialogue. Or slow them down by taking out the dialogue and using only narrative. Maybe a scene should be focused on the action alone, for the sake of moving the external plot forward. Remember that not every scene needs to be woven to be effective.

CHAPTER 28

AVOID WRITING SAME-OLD, SAME-OLD CONVERSATIONS

BY MICHAEL LEVIN

1. KEEP YOUR CHARACTERS IGNORANT

Casting director Michael Shurtleff makes a fascinating point in his book *Audition* that applies equally to actors and to writers. He says that actors sometimes play a scene as if they know the scene's ending before it happens.

For instance, at the climax of one particular scene in a Tennessee Williams' play, an insane person puts out a cigarette in the palm of the hand of the nurse who's trying to help her. But the nurse, according to Shurtleff, wrongly played the whole scene as if she didn't like the patient.

Shurtleff told the actress playing the nurse, "If you treat the patient really nicely and kindly throughout the scene, and you show the audience you like her and you're trying to help her, it's a thousand times more powerful if she then turns around and puts that cigarette out in your palm."

And that makes sense. Even though you know how the scene will end before you start to write it, don't let your characters act or speak as if they know where it's going. Preserve surprise and the scene will be a thousand times more powerful.

2. BECOME THE CHARACTER

Amy Tan says that when she writes dialogue, she stares at her shoes until suddenly she becomes the character. Her dialogue is superb. So try to find a pair of Amy Tan's shoes on eBay, and you'll be published almost instantly.

3. IT'S NOT A TRANSCRIPT

Excellent dialogue sometimes just happens, but most of the time, we have to sit there for a while until we get exactly the right words we want. So take it slowly when you're writing dialogue. Remember that you're not a court stenographer, charged with getting down every single word the characters might say. Instead you just have to report, or include, the dialogue that's most important to the story.

4. MAKE EVERY WORD COUNT

The first page of Amy Tan's *The Joy Luck Club* contains the following lines of dialogue:

> [Mother:] "Auntie Lin cooked red bean soup for Joy Luck. I'm going to cook black sesame-seed soup."
>
> [Daughter:] "Don't show off."

Do you see what the daughter's three little words did? (1) They tell us that the mother is obviously showing off her cooking skills by one-upping Auntie Lin; (2) They tell us that the relationship between the mother and daughter is combative; (3) They show us the nature of the daughter: She's hard sometimes. She isn't always nice. All that information about character in three little words. Fantastic. The mother then comes back with the third and last line of dialogue in the scene:

> "It's not showoff."

Clearly, the mother feels hurt. And the running together of the two words (*show off* becomes *showoff*) demonstrates that the mother isn't a native English speaker. Through this short exchange, Tan shows the reader a lot about her characters. The author provides the evidence through dialogue and the reader draws the conclusions.

5. REALISTIC DIALOGUE INVOLVES RISING CONFLICT

In Lajos Egri's book *The Art of Dramatic Writing*, the author describes three kinds of conflict:

1. **STATIC.** Nothing happens. The story is no further along at the end of the scene than it was at the beginning. It's blah.
2. **JUMPING.** We leap from setup to resolution without the intervening steps. This gives the reader mental whiplash.
3. **RISING CONFLICT.** (The kind you want.) The confrontation heats up little by little to an inexorable conclusion.

You want rising conflict in every scene. And you get it by notching up the tension, or the comedy, with each successive line of dialogue. It sounds hard in theory, but it isn't. Think about the last argument you had with someone. Chances are it started with a tense moment, grew and grew in intensity, and then *whammo*— big-time conflict. If you think of writing good dialogue as being as easy as getting into an argument with someone, you're all set.

6. MORE ON WHY LESS IS MORE

When you watch any film, or read any story, notice that there's about as much dialogue in it as there is in any dream you have. This is why I strongly advocate going back to a movie you liked within a few days, just to see how it worked. One of the discoveries I always make is that the scenes are much shorter—and the dialogue less wordy—than I remembered.

7. WRITING DIALOGUE IS A MULTIDRAFT THING

In the first draft, just get the basic words down. In the second draft, make it sound exactly the way the character would speak.

8. YES, YOU CAN USE ADVERBS—JUDICIOUSLY

Remember at all times that the reader isn't "reading" your story or novel. She's using it as a script in which she's playing the part of the main character—and every other character. So be sure that she understands exactly how to give the right reading to every line.

Most of the time, the reader should be able to tell how to read a line of dialogue just from the dialogue. But if it's not exactly clear, then, by all means, use an adverb.

9. AVOID REPEATING WHAT THE READER ALREADY KNOWS

For example:

> "Why do you think Ellen killed him?" Margaret asked.
>
> John summarized what the policeman had just told him. "It looks like Ellen's our woman," he concluded.

Obviously the scene that preceded this one was between John and the policeman. So we don't need John repeating everything to us that we just saw and heard.

10. STICK TO PEOPLE YOU KNOW

Make sure that your Southerners, mobsters, or foreigners sound real. You wouldn't forgive an author who made his characters sound foolish or stereotypical. So don't expect your reader to stand for it, either.

Agatha Christie, in her autobiography, wrote that in a hundred or more novels she never once described three workmen sitting in a pub, because she never sat with three workmen in a pub and she didn't know what they talked about. If it's okay for Agatha Christie to stick to her knitting, it's okay for you to stick to yours.

11. WHEN REWRITING DIALOGUE ...

Read the scene aloud or, better still, into a tape recorder. Fiction writers may tell themselves that they'll "get around" to rewriting the dialogue, yet sometimes they never do. The best advice I ever got about rewriting dialogue came from Bob Asahina, my former editor at Simon & Schuster. Asahina had me read an entire novel draft into a tape recorder, so that I'd have to speak aloud every single line of dialogue in the manuscript.

When you have to speak your own dialogue, you suddenly know which lines need attention and which lines are fine. Stilted dialogue is a deal killer in the minds of most agents and publishers.

12. IF IT AIN'T BROKE, DON'T FIX IT

Sometimes you write a great line of dialogue and say to yourself, "Boy, that's good." The second time you look at it, you smile. The third time, you stare at it. The fourth time, you change it.

Did the line get less good? No, it just got more familiar to you. If you write a great line, resist the urge to "improve" on it. Trust your taste.

MICHAEL LEVIN has co-written, edited, or created more than ninety books. He is a New York Times Bestseller and runs www.businessghost.com.

FOCUS ON THE WRITING LIFE:

MAXIMIZING YOUR PRODUCTIVITY

REINVENTING YOUR RELATIONSHIP WITH TIME

BY SAGE COHEN

The universal chorus of complaint from writers of all stripes seems to be: not enough time. Let's investigate how our relationship with time is moving us forward and holding us back.

We all get the same twenty-four hours in a day. What you do with yours is up to you. You may believe that you have "no time," but the fact is, you have just as much time as anyone else. What varies for every writer is our unique mix of work and family responsibilities, financial commitments, sleep requirements, physical and emotional space for writing, and perhaps most importantly, our ability and willingness to prioritize writing in this mix.

Writers make time for writing. And everyone does it her own way. Your job is to find your way.

BE CONSCIOUS OF YOUR TIME

The best way to get a handle on how much authority you actually have over your time is to start becoming aware of how you are spending your time.

Pay attention to how you're investing your time today, and you'll develop a clear picture of the mix of mandatory and voluntary activities that shape your days. Once you become conscious that your relationship with time is not something that happens *to you* but a dynamic orchestrated *by you* through dozens of large and small choices you make every day, you can evaluate whether you would like to choose to continue the pattern you are in or to create a new one.

HONOR YOUR RHYTHMS

Honor your biorhythms by planning your writing time for the part of the day you're most capable of doing it. For example, my friend Chloe De Segonzac just wrote to say that she's learned that waking up at 6:00 A.M. to write an important sex scene is not the way to go for her. It's hard to feel *steamy* when she's overwhelmed with *sleepy*.

I'm restless in the mornings and do my most focused work later in the day. Because I am fortunate to work for myself, from home, I have the flexibility to shape my time in a way that works for me. My schedule is always fluxing to accommodate changing workflow and family needs, but these days it generally looks something like this:

I'm with my young son until the late morning or midday, at which point someone else in the house cares for him. Once I put on my work hat, I'll participate in any client calls or meetings, business development opportunities, and such during the early hours of the work day. When I'm teaching, I find that I am able to focus and respond to student work very well at any time of the day. Nonfiction books and poetry and essays and everything that is being generated from the depths of my being and written onto the page generally happen in the evenings after my son is asleep.

Having transitioned from college directly to a series of office jobs, I had no idea what my biorhythms for different kinds of work were until I attended graduate school, where I had the flexibility to experiment with the various elements of my schedule. Chances are good that you've been in whatever life rhythm you're currently in for a good long while. This means you may not have any idea what might work best for you. Get ready to find out!

Define Your Prime Time

This is your invitation to start experimenting with your own sense of prime writing time. Right now. Does your cup overflow with imagery with that first coffee on the drive into work, or are you tapping the revelation vein at two in the morning when you can prowl in the shadows? Or maybe you're an "anytime is fine for me" kind of writer.

Do you need a six-hour chunk of uninterrupted time to really hit your stride, or can you make good progress during lunch break, standing in line at the post office, and waiting for your dentist appointment? How can you create more of the time-of-day and time-to-work intervals suited to your writing rhythms? No one can answer these questions but you, and even you may not have an informed answer yet. But soon, if you commit to finding out, you will.

Work With What You Have

I have just implored you to define your ideal writing times and patterns. And I meant it. But now, with equal emphasis, I would like to insist that you dig deep to define the scope of what's possible right this very minute.

Today I am able to shape my workdays. But for many years, I was not. Despite the fact that it was not optimal for me to have my butt-in-chair in the morning (and it absolutely withered my soul to be in an office), there I was doing exactly that—sitting at a desk from 8:30 A.M. until at least 6:00 P.M. So I made the best of it and worked with the margins I had. I carried a notebook when walking my dog in the mornings. I went to live music cafés in the evenings, in my pajamas, and while the people around me drank beer and sloshed about in time to the music, I filled pages with music coming through me in words.

In short, I refused to let a meaningless, demanding job deplete my creative stores. I insisted that my heart stay open to poetry and wrote myself awake every time my muse started to wander off looking for someone more reliable to haunt. I made writing my "everything else" around work, blended it with eating and entertainment and social time and care of my animals, and felt integrated, inspired, whole.

What are you doing right now to make the most of the time you do have, even if it's not your prime time? Start there, and experiment with how you might do a little more of it, and then a little more.

YOU HAVE THE REST OF YOUR LIFE

My computer monitor looks like a root system for sticky notes; it has become host to the layers and layers of pastel-posted ideas and to-dos that I scribble and stick as they flit through my mind while working. The accumulation of such notes creates a feeling of clutter, but more uncomfortably a sinking feeling that there will simply not be enough hours in my life to accomplish everything I want to do. But I know better.

Several years ago, I took a workshop called "Falling Awake" with Dave Ellis. One of the preliminary assignments we were asked to do to prepare for the class was to chart out our major life goals for each area of our life in five-year segments. I defined my major areas as: health, finances, family, work, spirituality, and writing. And I brainstormed a mighty comprehensive list in each area.

I was thirty-four years old and single at the time. Based on longevity of my family members, I estimated that I'd be alive with my thinking cap on until at least age eighty-five. This gave me ten, five-year sets of time.

I dove into this exercise and was intently focused on plotting out conservatively realistic deadlines for my overwhelming list of goals throughout a fifty-year time spread when suddenly I came up empty-handed. Having arrived at age seventy I had run out of goals. Everything I could possibly imagine that I might want to do in my life was accomplished. Imagine that! And I still had fifteen years to work with, give or take the unpredictable bargain of mortality.

What would life be like if you felt assured that there was plenty of time for every writing goal (and every life goal) on your dance card? What would you write (or not write) with fifteen gift years?

Make a "Rest-of-My-Life Plan" and Plot Your Possibilities

The common wisdom is, "Live like you're going to die tomorrow." My variation on this theme for writers is, "Write like you have the rest of your life ahead of you." And make your own rest-of-my-life plan to help you conceive the general shape and scope of what is possible.

With this big picture of your future sprawling out before you in measurable increments, you'll know far better whether you're aiming too high or leaving a purposeless decade or two dangling.

Don't worry, this plan isn't fixed in stone. So much happens in life that we can neither predict nor control. This is simply a way to estimate your capacity to inhabit the time you are given with the intentions you have chosen. It's just another way of reassuring yourself that you have all day.

PROCRASTINATE PRODUCTIVELY

So you don't feel like writing. Or you're stuck on something and can't go any further right now. Or you're too tired or broke or can't find your pink slipper. Okay. You are excused. I don't do that stern schoolteacher, butt-in-chair guilt trip. In fact, I've sworn off guilt trips altogether. So how, you may wonder, is this woman going to convince me to keep up all of that good, earnest writing work? She's not.

What I have come to trust from more than a decade of firsthand experience is that when we feel backed into a corner, we will rebel. So the more we try to force ourselves to write, the more we will resist, the less we will write, and the more frustrated and despairing we will become.

I would like to propose an alternative to this cat-and-mouse loop: Waste time well. If you do things that need doing—that you're actually in the mood to do—even procrastination can be productive. One of the things you'll start to learn over time is your rhythm for settling down to make stuff happen and the times when you need to rearrange your bulletin board and eat lots of cookies.

Build Wasted Time Into Your Schedule

You probably know yourself pretty well by now. If you were the kid who had your term paper finished two weeks early, you're likely to be delivering ahead of your deadlines today. And if you needed the adrenaline rush of the all-nighter to crank out an entire thingamajig the night before it was due, chances are good that you possess a very high-end coffee machine to help you keep up the good work.

I happen to be a "waste time while fearing that I can't do it" type. Always have been. No matter how many thousands of times in my life I have proven this fear incontrovertibly wrong, it persists with its own independent logic and food supply. What I have learned to do is simply accept that this is going to be part of my process, not take it so seriously, and simply build the freak-out into my making-it-happen schedule.

When I signed my first book contract, I planned for a month of floundering, and I executed this step in the schedule fabulously well. I spent that month freaking out about not being smart enough, capable enough, worthy enough to write a book, while gobbling up multiple episodes of *Six Feet Under* on DVD every night. Suffice it to say that within about six weeks or so, I was stuffed uncomfortably full of death and dysfunction, and felt ready to shift gears.

Do you put obstacles in your own way when it comes to writing? How might you plan to accommodate your own resistance in a way that lets it think it is winning while burning out its fuse?

TOP TEN TIME-WASTING STRATEGIES

When you're not in a go-get-'em writing mode, the most important thing to do is keep your creative engine warm and running. The following list of possibilities is designed to help you keep your head in the game by doing things that indirectly benefit your writing life and can quickly create a feeling of either relaxation or reward.

1. **WRITE A BLOG POST.** Reinforce your expertise while doing a little fun, informal writing.

2. **VISIT YOUR ONLINE COMMUNITY.** Take a five-minute coffee break with other writers on Facebook and Twitter. Let their good news, struggles, and insights percolate through you; chime in here and there. Notice any seeds of new ideas or projects taking shape in your peripheral vision.

3. **MAKE ORDER.** Sort and purge your in-box. Vacuum or do dishes or fold laundry. You can improve beauty and order around you while resetting whatever brain pretzel you may be locked in.

4. **STAND UP AND STRETCH.** It's far easier to keep butt-in-chair if blood is flowing to it!

5. **DO YOUR DUE DILIGENCE.** Enter your business expense data into QuickBooks or pay bills.

6. **GET PREPARED.** Update your to-do list.

7. **EMPTY YOUR MIND.** A three-minute meditation can settle your stirred waters so you can see clearly again.

8. **MANAGE YOUR CONTACTS.** Add business cards and other contact information you've collected recently into your contact database, sorting and categorizing appropriately by type of audience.

9. **SHARE THE WEALTH.** Visit a few favorite blogs or websites, and tweet about your findings.

10. **CALL YOUR MOTHER.** (But don't open the mail while you talk; she won't like that.)

TAKE A TIME-OUT

I believe in signs. That's why, when my ten-month-old son pulled the book *Sabbath: Restoring the Sacred Rhythm of Rest* by Wayne Muller off the shelf for the third time, I decided it was time to read it.

Lo and behold, on that fateful Saturday, I took a day off from my computer. When my son Theo napped, I napped. Our family took a leisurely trip to the pool. My husband and I cooked a meal together. I felt like a human *being* instead of a human *doing*.

Muller credits Brother David Steindl-Rast for reminding us that the Chinese pictograph for *busy* is composed of two characters: heart and killing. This stopped me in my tracks. I, like almost everyone I know, am chronically, overwhelmingly busy. Muller proposes that a day of rest gives us the replenishment we need to live our lives well. To solve our problems creatively. To nourish our hearts—and in our case, dear reader, our writing.

That day of Sabbath was such a success that my husband and I committed to a family Sabbath every Saturday in which all work comes to a halt and the family simply relaxes, enjoys each other, and follows the threads of curiosity and delight wherever they might lead us.

The good news for all of us overachievers is that slowing down actually produces more: work, joy, equilibrium, love. I wonder if rest may be all we need to replenish our creative wells when they run dry.

HONOR YOUR TIME, SO THAT OTHERS CAN

Let's do some expectation setting here: No one in your family or community of friends is likely to have any idea what your writing life is all about. It's not that they won't want to support you; it's just that they won't know how.

Years ago, when I was employed as a writer on a marketing team for a company, the woman whose job it was to track and ship inventory reported me to my boss. According to her, I was "just sitting at my desk, staring out the window and doing nothing all day." The reality was that I was producing newsletters, articles, and brochures at an unprecedented rate and speed. People who don't write don't necessarily understand that there is often reading, thinking, and rumination involved in the writing process—and this may not look like much to the casual observer.

People who don't write may not be able to imagine that you really and truly want to be in the closet with the door shut for three hours without talking to anyone. When you leave for that desperately anticipated writing retreat, don't take it personally when everyone you know wants to "come on vacation" with you.

The good news is that everyone who loves you can and will learn about your writing life if you are willing to teach them—and hold the line for yourself. All you need to worry about is being clear about the time you need and asking the people close to you for support in respecting that time.

SAGE COHEN is the author of *The Productive Writer: Tips & Tools to Help You Write More, Stress Less & Create Success*; *Writing the Life Poetic: An Invitation to Read and Write Poetry*; and the poetry collection *Like the Heart, the World*.

PART 6:

DESCRIPTION & WORD CHOICE:

WHAT YOU TELL READERS

CHAPTER 29

BALANCING DESCRIPTION & SUMMARY

BY RON ROZELLE

Showing versus telling is a constantly waged war in creative writing. You might expect the absolute rule to be: Show, Never Tell! Always and forever. No exceptions.

The trouble is that for a writer there aren't as many absolute rules as one might think. There are certainly a few, like run-on sentences never being acceptable, and subjects having to agree with verbs (though even that one can be broken when writing dialect). But this matter of showing and telling refuses to be governed so strictly.

First, let's determine the distinction between the two. Then we'll look at a few ways you can sharpen your skills, when tackling description and setting, at combining showing and telling.

UNDERSTAND THE DIFFERENCE BETWEEN SHOWING AND TELLING

Think about *To Kill a Mockingbird*. Never on any page in that novel does Scout, the narrator, tell us that Atticus Finch, her father, is a good man. But throughout the novel, we know it; at the end, one of the strongest images is his goodness. The author, Harper Lee, carefully gives us scene after scene in which Atticus' actions speak for themselves. She shows us his goodness constantly, and tells it never.

Now consider this statement:

> A good time was had by all.

Now, spend a moment with this paragraph from Toni Morrison's novel *Sula*:

> Old people were dancing with little children. Young boys with their sisters, and the church women who frowned on any bodily expression of joy (except when the hand of God commanded it) tapped their feet. Somebody (the groom's father, everybody said) had poured a whole pint jar of cane liquor into the punch, so even the men who did not sneak out the back door to have a shot, as well as the women who let nothing stronger than Black Draught enter their blood, were tipsy. A small boy stood at the Victrola turning its handle and smiling at the sound of Bert Williams' "Save a Little Dram for Me."

A question: Which of the two descriptions does more for you as a reader? I'll bet you chose the longer one, unless you're one of those people who likes to be different just for the heck of it—one of those go-against-the-grain sorts.

But the point is this: In terms of what we end up knowing about this celebration, they both do the same thing. We end up, both times, realizing that a good time was had by all.

So why should we opt for the longer one when the snippet fills the bill?

Because brevity doesn't usually fill the bill for a writer or—much more to the point—for a reader. The big difference between these two examples isn't that one is considerably longer. It's that the most essential image, a sense of universal enjoyment, is not specifically mentioned at all in the longer one. The first version is telling; the second is showing. We know that all of the participants in Morrison's paragraph are enjoying themselves because we watch them doing it.

Showing rather than telling is part of the magic that you have to work as a writer; in fact, it's one of the most vital parts. Your reader has to make his way through your story or novel—and then finally come away from it—with a sense of the characters and the settings and the situations that must have seemed to occur naturally. To use a sewing metaphor: You have to stitch your images together so meticulously that the seams are invisible.

LET READERS SHARE IN YOUR CHARACTERS' EXPERIENCES

One of the most effective ways to pull that off is to let your reader experience things rather than be told about them, to *feel* them rather than have them reported to him.

In *Black Rain*, Masuji Ibuse's novel about the dropping of the atomic bomb on Hiroshima, Japan, this sentence does not appear:

> The city suffered significant damage in the blast.

But this paragraph does:

> Among the ruins, the reflection of the sun on the pieces of broken glass on the road was so strong that it was difficult to hold your head up as you walked. The smell of death was a little fainter than the day before, but the places where houses had collapsed into tile-covered heaps stank vilely and were covered with great, black swarms of flies. The relief squads clearing the ruins seemed to have been joined by reinforcements, since I saw some men whose clothes, though bleached with frequent washing, were not soiled with sweat and grime as yet.

Again, as in the previous example, we get the pertinent information in the first version. But we see and hear and touch and taste and smell the experience in the second. The difference between the two accounts is something like the difference between an accident report that a patrolman would write and the sensation of being in the accident itself. If you've ever been in one, you know that the curt, factual summary is worlds away from the reality of experiencing it.

"The city suffered significant damage in the blast" is too cold, too distant and too all-inclusive. So what Ibuse does is drive home the image in small details, one after the other, throughout the novel. Pay attention to the delicate pictures here, almost like miniatures arranged on a wall: the reflection of the sun on the pieces of broken glass, the collapsed houses, the smell of death. The swarms of flies. All bits and pieces of wordsmithing that add up to an inevitable conclusion: The city suffered significantly in the blast.

In short, the second piece is considerably better. And it's better because it brings the reader more fully in.

Now, this is important—so heads up, please. The longer version is not better because it is all showing and no telling. It's better because it is *both* showing and telling. Your fiction has to be a balanced blend of both approaches.

USE DESCRIPTIVE DETAILS TO SHOW YOUR STORY

In her novel *The Book of Mercy*, Kathleen Cambor could have written this:

> In addition to the potential risk and the possibility of notoriety, one reason he chose to become a fireman was that he liked the uniform, which his mother also admired. But his father was against the whole idea.

It would have gotten the point across. But not nearly so effectively as what she did write:

> He liked everything about the idea of being a fireman. The excitement, the danger, the chance to be a hero or a prince. The dress-blue uniform, dark serge, a knifelike crease down the center of each pants leg, patent-leather visor on the cap, in which a man could see himself reflected. "Very fancy," said his mother. His father's eyes were wells of rage and disappointment. He spit onto the floor.

The short one tells us pretty much what we need to know to understand this part of the story. But the longer one—the real one that Cambor actually did compose—does far more than that. It takes us into the attitude of the character, into his sense of values. Rather than telling us, it shows us how he feels about becoming a fireman. And there is more drama and description in those last two sentences, about his father's reaction to it, than the author could have conveyed in a page or more of explanation.

Look a little farther along at a bit more about how the character feels about his new job:

> He learned to smell the smoke from blocks away, he watched for the sky to begin to lighten, as if from the tip of a rising sun. Each time, he felt his heart pound, his own heart filled his chest, it echoed in his ears until they made the final turn into the red-hot stunning light.

Here again the writer could have told us what we needed to know in fewer words. "His job was exciting" might suffice. Or, if you want a little more detail: "His heart rate elevated when his truck approached a fire." But the point is that your reader wants, in fact demands, a lot more detail, not just a little.

Your characters, their situations, the basic logistics of your plot—how characters move from Point A to Point B and the chronological order of their actions—are all important to your story, essential, in fact. What brings the story to life and makes it all as real as seeing it happen for the reader, is your description. Showing these things, as opposed to simply reporting them, will be what finally makes the whole thing work.

Dig back into that last example. Note the strong images of the lightening sky and the pounding of the fireman's heart. That's fine stuff that drives home to the reader exactly how this fellow is feeling at that moment, in that place. Because the reader has probably felt that way, too.

In your story, you need to plug your reader into images like that—to situations and emotions he can relate to. That's difficult, maybe impossible, to do when you are telling the thing. But your images can ring soundly and true when you are showing.

RON ROZELLE is the author of five books, including *Write Great Fiction: Description & Setting*.

PRACTICE DESCRIBING COMMON ACTIONS

Make a list of several common action verbs that are generic in their meanings—words like *walk, talk* and *hit*. Then take a few moments and write down as many verbs or phrases you can think of that are more specific. Your goal is not to create a catalog of more precise descriptions; instead, practice refining an action down to its clearest description.

Use a thesaurus. Many of its offerings will be what you're looking for. Some won't. And others will help you come up with some of your own.

CHAPTER 30

FOLLOW THE RULES FOR STRONGER WRITING

BY NANCY LAMB

Strong prose is a matter of practice and discipline and conscious awareness of the words you put on the page. There are rules for effective writing, and you can save yourself a lot of unnecessary grief if you take the time to incorporate them into your writing psyche.

These rules can't make a good writer a brilliant one. But they can make an average writer a good writer, and a good writer better. They can turn a mediocre story into a memorable one. And they're a great guide for revising your work.

1. NEVER LET THE TRUTH GET IN THE WAY OF YOUR STORY

Creative writing is just that: creative. If the truth prevents you from telling your fictional story effectively, get rid of the facts and invent something that makes the story work.

2. NEVER USE TWO WORDS WHEN ONE WILL DO

Less is more. Usually one powerful word will do the same job as two weaker ones. Instead of:

> Andrea stared at the horrible, slithering mass of snakes.

Write:

> Andrea stared at the writhing mass of snakes.

3. USE THE ACTIVE VOICE

The difference between adequate prose and good prose is the difference between passive and active voice. Make certain that active verbs drive your prose. Instead of:

> There were many dead bodies on the ground.

Write:

> Dead bodies littered the ground.

4. USE PARALLEL CONSTRUCTION

Parallel construction allows you to write in the most interesting, economical fashion by aligning your verb tenses and uniting phrases with a common construction. Instead of:

> The vampire bared his teeth and then, raising his claws to sharpen them, he started licking his chops. "Gotcha!" he said with a grin.

Write:

> The vampire bared his teeth, sharpened his claws, and licked his chops. "Gotcha!" he said with a grin.

5. KEEP RELATED WORDS TOGETHER

Linguistic studies have shown that most of us have a natural instinct for the placement of adjectives. We don't say, "I have a blue shiny car." Instead we say, "I have a shiny blue car." The same principle should be applied to sentences you write. Instead of:

> Frankenstein noticed a large bloodstain in the rug that was in the middle.

Write:

> Frankenstein noticed a large bloodstain in the middle of the rug.

6. REPLACE ADJECTIVES AND ADVERBS WITH VIVID NOUNS AND ACTIVE VERBS

Cultivate the use of strong verbs and concrete nouns. They are the most powerful tools in a writer's arsenal. Instead of:

> Since the day Barbara met the werewolf, she felt very scared and frightened.

Write:

> Since the day she met the werewolf, terror haunted Barbara's heart.

There is no surer way to weaken your prose than to pepper it with adverbs. There are, of course, times when the adverb is appropriate and necessary. Choose those times carefully.

> She looked longingly and lovingly at the chocolate.

Or:

> She looked at the chocolate with longing and love.

Or better:

> Her eyes consumed the chocolate.

7. DON'T OVEREXPLAIN

Give your reader the benefit of the doubt and allow him to intuit the meaning of the dialogue, rather than read about it. Instead of:

> "I'm sorry," Peter said consolingly.

Write:

> "I'm sorry," Peter said.

8. WRITE CINEMATICALLY

When you write, think visually. Language holds endless possibilities for a creative approach to expressing an idea.

Eddy Peters exemplified this when he wrote, "Not only does the English Language borrow words from other languages, it sometimes chases them down dark alleys, hits them over the head and goes through their pockets."

9. VARY YOUR SENTENCE STRUCTURE

Using nothing but noun-verb declarative sentences makes for dull reading. Break up the monotony. Instead of:

> John walked to the closet. He opened the door. He took one look inside and he screamed.

Write:

> John walked to the closet and opened the door. Taking one look inside, he screamed.

10. CREATE INTEREST BY MIXING IDEAS

Mixing alien ideas and drawing unlikely parallels will make the writing fresh.

> She was the kind of girl who collected men like she collected speeding tickets. They both happened when she wasn't paying attention.

11. LISTEN TO THE MUSIC OF THE WORDS

The best prose has a rhythm to it. Honor that rhythm. There have been days when I've spent half an hour searching the thesaurus for a word that has three syllables instead of two. Sometimes the difference is subtle, but it can make the reading experience more satisfying. Instead of:

> Some writers catch on to the rhythm and they delight in the sound of the music as soon as they learn to write.

Write:

> Some writers feel the rhythm and hear the music from the moment they learn to write.

12. AVOID WORD REPETITION

There's nothing more tiresome for a reader than seeing the same tiresome words over and over in the same paragraph. This creates the overall impression that the reader is reading the same repetitive, tiresome prose over again and it tires out the reader. Note: The exception to this rule—the critical exception—is when you repeat a word for emphasis.

13. BEWARE OF *IT*

Grammarians call it an "obscure pronominal reference." That's when *it* is left dangling in a sentence without a clear reference to whom or what it refers. Double-check for dangling *it*s. Where you find:

> Kathy couldn't believe it was happening.

Clarify:

> Kathy couldn't believe her sister was finally accepting the blame.

NANCY LAMB is the author of fiction and nonfiction books for adults and children, including *The Art and Craft of Storytelling* and *The Writer's Guide to Crafting Stories for Children.*

CHAPTER 31

KEEP YOUR STORY LEAN

BY NANCY KRESS

Besides a careful blend of elements in your writing, successful fiction also requires a strategic approach to what you leave out of the story. Needless reiteration and superfluous detail can bog down your tale—but prose that's lean and mean in a "less is more" approach draws readers in with its effectiveness.

Specifically, a story can often be much improved by avoiding our things: expository openings, descriptive repetition, explanatory dialogue and Aesopian moralizing.

NIX THE EXPOSITION

Especially if you write commercial fiction, you'll find that readers like to be propelled right into the middle of some interesting event, and they want to see that event as it unfolds. This means starting your story with a dramatized scene. There should be characters onstage immediately, talking and interacting. Leave out explanations of how they got there—you can explain it later, if necessary.

Which of these two openings is more satisfying?

> Five years ago, John Meadows married Linda Carrington. Although both had grown up in Brooklyn and didn't want to leave, John had accepted a job in Montana and moved his young family west. He found he liked the mountains and open sky, but Linda was frustrated and unhappy. This all became clear the night they attended a party at their neighbors' house.

> "I told you I didn't want to go to this," Linda said as she stood beside John on their neighbors' steps. "It's just going to be as lame as every other party we've been to since we got here."
>
> "You used to love parties," John said, avoiding eye contact.
>
> "Yeah, well, that was back in Brooklyn. But Montana isn't Brooklyn."
>
> "No." He looked at the mountains colored flame by the setting sun, the sky he had come to love. Then he looked at Linda, glowering even before they went inside. In five years of marriage, she had changed so much. They both had.
>
> He pressed the doorbell.

In the second passage, the exposition has been left out— but not neglected. Instead each expository point is shown through thoughts, dialogue, and actions.

LET THE IMAGE SPEAK FOR ITSELF

Descriptive repetition occurs when an author tells us what's already been shown. For example, consider the following paragraph:

> Walking her dog through the park, Tessa abruptly stopped in the middle of the rose path. She turned slowly, sniffing in all directions, nose wrinkling in disgust. Something here smelled very bad. At the same moment, Duke started barking frantically and straining at his leash. Tessa could barely hold him as he nosed under a rose bush.
>
> He'd smelled the odor, too. What, Tessa wondered, could it be? She peered under the bush.

Can you spot the three superfluous sentences? They are:

- The third sentence: We already know that Tessa smells something bad, so we don't need to be told.
- The sixth sentence: It's already very clear that Duke, too, has smelled the odor.
- The seventh sentence: Tessa's curiosity is made obvious by her sniffing and peering.

Repetition dilutes your effect. As readers, we want to experience the story along with the character, not have it narrated for us from the outside. Reiteration also increases word count and slows pace, while uncluttered prose delivers more punch, faster.

Ironically most writers tell after they show not because they mistrust the reader's intelligence to "get" the point, but rather because they lack faith in their own prose. The unnecessary recurrence of telling after showing will drive away sophisticated readers. If, on the other hand, your writing hasn't made events and motive clear enough, then you can strengthen it through additional action.

CUT EXPLANATORY DIALOGUE

Purge your fiction of lengthy dialogue explanations that wear down readers. This often involves one character clarifying the meaning of events for another character, as in this example:

> Martin lit a cigarette. "Do you really want to know why I didn't double-cross John?"
>
> "Yes," Kara said.
>
> "I could have, at several points. First, you remember, there was that time he practically goaded me into telling the others about what he did."
>
> "I remember."
>
> "Then, after he pulled those other stunts ..."

Martin will go on to explain his reasoning and code of ethics, but we'll be asleep by then. If the story has done its job of dramatization, we already know all the times Martin behaved well, plus the reason he did so. Let the story dramatize the meaning of its events, instead of the characters expounding on them.

AVOID "AESOP ENDINGS"

Closely related to explanatory dialogue, but even worse, is narrative moralizing at the end of a story. This is when the author—not the character—tells us "what it all means." This worked very well for Aesop in ancient Greece, but his purpose was to illustrate life lessons, not to create a dramatic story with believable characters doing interesting things.

This is not, of course, to say that modern fiction doesn't illustrate lessons. It's possible to interpret Lady Brett's actions in *The Sun Also Rises* as "It's better to give than receive," and *Moby-Dick*'s Captain Ahab is a clear symbol of "Pride goeth before a fall." But these are characters, not merely symbols, with fully developed pasts, problems, angers, loves, and regrets. More important, the morals that their stories demonstrate are implied by the story's action, not stated outright by their authors. Create strong characters in dramatic situations, and the outcome of those situations will guide our interpretations.

Each of these avoidable story aspects follows the same principle: Leave out whatever you can that's not pertinent in a particular scene. If you don't naturally write like this, print out your first draft and edit ruthlessly. By leaving out all you can, your story will gain immeasurably.

NANCY KRESS is the author of twenty-eight books, including *Write Great Fiction: Characters, Emotion & Viewpoint*. Her work has garnered her four Nebula Awards and two Hugo Awards.

CHAPTER 32

MAKE YOUR TONE PITCH-PERFECT

BY ADAIR LARA

Do you obsess about the tone of your writing as you revise? You should. Tone is one of the most overlooked elements of writing. It can create interest or kill it.

It's no wonder that so many of the countless conversations I've had with writing students and colleagues have been about problems related to tone. A friend submitting a novel says the editors "don't like the main character." A nonfiction book on balancing a family and a career skirts the edge of whining. An agent turns down a query because she feels "too much distance from the heart of the story." I scan the latest work of a journalist friend who's coming to dinner and find it meticulously sourced and well written, but grim in outlook.

And of course any publication you want to write for will have its own tone, which it would be smart for you to try to match. Notice how quietly all *New Yorker* profile pieces begin, while *Utne Reader* favors unconventional and unexpected viewpoints that challenge the status quo.

What exactly do I mean by *tone*? That's a good question, as there are many terms—mood, style, voice, cadence, inflection—used to mean much the same thing. For now let's agree that tone is the author's attitude toward his subject: grave, amused, scientific, intimate, aggrieved, authoritative, whatever.

If you were a photographer, tone would be the way you light your subject. For dramatic shadows, the subject would be lit from the side. For a scary effect, from above. For romance, lit with candles. In a movie, tone is often conveyed with music—think of the ominous score accompanying the girl swimming in shark-infested waters in *Jaws*.

A writer doesn't have a soundtrack or a strobe light to build the effect she wants. She has conflict, surprise, imagery, details, the words she chooses, and the way she arranges them in sentences. Like the tone you use when you talk to somebody, tone in writing determines how a reader responds. If the piece sounds angry, he gets nervous. If it's wry and knowing, he settles in for an enjoyable read. If it's dull, he leaves it on the train, half read.

Thus the wrong tone can derail an otherwise good piece. I'm surprised how seldom writing students note this during our workshop discussions, as if it's impolite to admit that they're made uncomfortable by how much the narrator seems to hate her mother or to say that their thoughts drifted elsewhere by the second page of the overly abstract piece about mindfulness in the workplace.

You can detect tone problems in your own work simply by noting where your attention wanders as you reread it. Or, better, by reading it aloud. When you're ready to revise a piece, read it to someone else or ask someone to read it to you. You won't have to search for awkward or boring or whiny parts—you'll hear them.

Some problems with tone are small and can be easily fixed during revision. Others might require a new approach to the piece as a whole. Let's look at a few of the easiest and most effective ways to improve the tone of your writing.

1. AVOID A PREDICTABLE TREATMENT OF YOUR SUBJECT

In the first draft you write what people expect you to write—what you expect yourself to write. "I wanted a car." The tone becomes predictable. Now, during your revision, go deeper. Seek out the harder truths. It's in the second, third, fourth draft that you say something we don't expect you to say, something even you didn't expect you to say. When you get tired of being nice. "I wanted a car so I could drive out of my marriage." Surprise yourself, and you will surprise your reader.

Similarly you'll want to avoid taking an overly emotional approach to an overly emotional subject. Think of the dry, reserved tone in which Joan Didion recalls the anguish of losing her husband in *The Year of Magical Thinking*. What if she had wailed about her loss? There would be nothing for us readers to do, even if the emotions being reported to us were very sad. (Note: If you're having a hard time distancing yourself from the raw emotion of a personal subject, this may be a sign that you need to let time do its magic work. Frank McCourt said it took him years before he could detach from his anger toward his feckless father enough to give *Angela's Ashes* its nonjudgmental tone. When something bad happens, of course we feel upset, even as if life has treated us unfairly—but that's not a great place to write from. Let the experience ripen in your memory until you've achieved the distance you need.)

If your subject is inherently serious, try taking a lighter approach. *What's Your Poo Telling You?* came to Chronicle Books as a serious examination of—well, you know. In that form, it might have sold a few thousand copies. The lighter treatment led to sales of *hundreds* of thousands of copies. There's no denying that titles with tone sell books: Consider *My Miserable, Lonely Lesbian Pregnancy* or *Skinny Bitch*.

2. KEEP TONE CONSISTENT FROM START TO FINISH

Make sure your very first sentence establishes the tone you want. Look at the opening line of "The Lesson" by Toni Cade Bambara:

> Back in the days when everyone was old and stupid or young and foolish and me and Sugar were the only ones just right, this lady moved on our block with nappy hair and proper speech and no makeup.

In one sentence, you know who everybody is. Not only do you want to read on, but you want to know what else she's written so you can get that, too.

You will choose different tones for different subjects, of course, just as you would dress differently for a date than for an interview. But stay away from changing tones within a piece. One minute you're riffing comically on Uncle Frank's parade of girlfriends, and the next, the reader is caught chortling when you shift to Uncle Frank's abuse of his daughter. Or the thriller shifts from a slumped body in an alley to the detective's girlfriend shopping for bridal gowns, and suddenly we're in a romance. (Notice, by the way, how many genres actually have tone in their names: *thriller, romance, mystery, horror.*)

Read your work looking for places where the tone fades or shifts. Focus your revision there.

3. CUT RUTHLESSLY

If you reread a piece and decide that nothing works until the second page, why not simply start it there?

The delete key is your friend. The novelist Carolyn Chute told *Writers Ask*: "I write a lot of junk. On and on and on, all this junk. But every now and then this dramatic moment happens, so I lift that out and put that aside. And then I write all this junk: They're brushing their teeth, they're sitting there, they're looking around—you know. Then something will happen and I'll pull that out. Because those are the only strong things."

Read your work looking for places where your engagement wanes. Boring is bad. Careful is right next to it. When it comes to tone, don't try to fix the boring parts—toss them. You can't fix boring. Other places where the delete key comes in handy:

- Off-topic tangents. You start out writing about the president's pooch and by the homestretch you're discoursing disdainfully on the state of our economy and what a boob the president is—as if people are lining up to hear your thoughts on that. Stick to the subject at hand.

- Overemphasis on themes. Don't hit readers over the head with your own interpretation of the meaning of it all. You provide the right detail—say, the wooden coffin—and they'll supply the mortality of man. Resist the urge to overtly explain—it's condescending and redundant.

4. LET TENSION SUSTAIN TONE

Your piece, whatever it is, should be rife with conflict. It's not enough to write an essay about how much you like to spend the day in bed. If nothing is stopping you from lazing around under the sheets, then you have no problem, and thus the piece has no tension—an essential element in sustaining any tone for the long haul. If you find you've committed this mistake, whether in a fictional story or a true one, bring in someone with the opposite point of view (mothers are always good for this!). That's why columnists so often reference their mates—to be the foil, the reasonable one, so the author isn't ranting in a vacuum.

5. USE YOUR VOICE

Are you one of the many writers who blog? Unless you know tomorrow's stock prices or are telling readers how to relight a furnace on a freezing day, it will be your voice, not the content, that draws them in. So you must sound like somebody. This is true with other forms of personal writing, as well. Resist the urge to come off as uncomplicated, reasonable, or polite. If you're expressing opinions, express them! (Note that this is a format where opinion is the point, not a tiresome add-on.) Don't say that whether or not someone likes a particular film "seems to me a matter of sensibility and perspective." We know that! Be in a mood. Take a position. "Anyone who doesn't like *The Ruling Class* should be cast into hell for all eternity." Look for opportunities to bring a human voice into your work.

There's more sense of someone behind the words "I had a breast cut off" (Molly Ivins) than "I had a mastectomy."

THREE TIPS FOR CONSISTENT TONE

1. Find a paragraph that sounds exactly the way you want to sound and tape it to your computer so that it's always in front of you.
2. Each time you're about to return to the piece, spend twenty minutes reading the work of an author who writes in the tone you're after. We're natural mimics. You might try taking this a step further by more closely examining the sentence rhythms and word choices and looking for ways to make them your own. John Lukacs once said, "Style begins the way fashion begins: Somebody admires how the other man dresses and adapts it for himself."
3. Starts and finishes are especially important to tone. When revising your work, try moving some of your best sentences, the ones with the right energy and tone, up to the top of your document. Could the piece begin this way? Experiment with moving equally strong sentences to the conclusion of your piece, for a cohesive ending.

6. CONVEY TONE THROUGH DETAILS AND DESCRIPTIONS

Consider the difference between "in October" and "under an October sky." A description of scenery, however luscious, can tire the reader if that's all it is. Use the imagery to show us your character's mood: A sad character will notice rotting houses and untended yards; a contented one will see picturesque shacks and gardens in a profuse state of nature.

When adding details to enrich your writing, tone comes from being as specific as possible. Change "My husband committed suicide" to "My husband gassed himself in our Passat in the Austrian Alps."

I once taught a travel-writing class aboard a cruise up the Amazon and sent passengers ashore to a remote village with notebooks. One student, surprised and amused by the satellite dishes towering over the small huts, dubbed them "the flowers of the Amazon" in her resulting piece. Another, having overheard the song "The Air That I Breathe" on an antiquated village speaker, wrote, "The fact is you can hear the whole planet breathing while you're here. As one Brazilian told me, it's the lung of the world." Tone in travel writing comes from such acute observations.

In memoir or fiction, it comes also from offbeat character details, like this one from the memoir *The Glass Castle* by Jeannette Walls:

> Dad was so sure a posse of federal investigators was on our trail that he smoked his unfiltered cigarettes from the wrong end. That way, he explained, he burned up the brand name, and if the people who were tracking us looked in his ashtray, they'd find unidentifiable butts instead of Pall Malls that could be traced to him.

The narrator here, it is safe to say, is not admiring the cunning of her father; the tone suggests she is old enough to worry about the folly of her parents.

7. LEARN TO RECOGNIZE BUILT-IN PROBLEMS WITH TONE.

Everybody who's ever been fired has sat down to write a book about it. But harping on the wrong that's been done to you can make your readers uneasy. If they were seated next to you on a plane, they'd be desperately longing to change seats. Lawsuits, controversial issues, other people's behavior, how overwhelmed you were by the flood of wedding gifts and what a chore it was to write all those thank-you notes: all such topics force you to work hard to overcome the reader's unease at smelling an agenda, or anger, or bragging.

In these instances, to fix the tone, you have to fix the way you think about a given subject. You have to back off, calm down, see other points of view, maybe even take some responsibility for whatever happened. When writing about such delicate subjects, you must not let a negative tone take over by ascribing motives to people: You just tell what they did, and let the reader read motive into it. You must write with forgiveness, understanding, and humor. In some ways, this can be a payoff to examining your tone as you write: You change the writing, and the writing changes you. But if you find this is not possible with your subject, don't be afraid to scrap a project that you discover has inherent problems with tone. You'll be a better writer for it.

ADAIR LARA is the author of numerous columns and books, including *Naked, Drunk, and Writing.*

CHAPTER 33

UNDERSTANDING GENDER DIFFERENCES

BY LEIGH ANNE JASHEWAY

Men and women are different. There, I said it.

Now let me go even further out on a limb. Chances are, if you're female, you write like a girl, and if you're male, you write like a guy. Not that there's anything wrong with that ... unless, that is, you'd like your writing to be read by members of another gender, or you're trying to create characters of the opposite sex. If so, it might just help to have a better understanding about how the other half thinks, acts, reads, and writes.

Linguists, sociologists, behavior specialists and functional brain researchers have documented gender's effect on almost everything, so it's natural that it plays a role in how we write and what we're attracted to as readers.

The ability to use language that has appeal outside your own gender can boost your success as an author; take the U.K. bestseller *Holly's Inbox*, which has often been compared to Helen Fielding's runaway hit *Bridget Jones's Diary*. The name on the cover of the book? Holly Denham. Its real author? Bill Surie, who wrote for his female audience so convincingly that readers had no problem believing the story had been written by a woman.

And then there's J.K. Rowling, who is so good at transcending gender (and age) that her books are devoured by girls and boys (and women and men) by the millions.

If you haven't considered the impact of your own gender on your writing, it's time to start. By educating yourself about how men and women differ, you'll be able to better understand your audience, broaden your writing's appeal, and make educated choices when it comes to language, story, and style—no matter what you're writing or who you're writing it for.

TALK THE TALK

If you're writing a romance novel, you know your audience is primarily female; if you're working on an exposé about steroid use in baseball, you can assume you'll have mostly male readers.

But when most of us sit down to write, we're really just thinking that what we have to say will grab any reader who finds our topic interesting. We don't usually pay enough attention to how something as simple as choosing our words can attract or turn off prospective readers.

At a recent writing workshop, I critiqued a manuscript on mind mapping. The topic usually fascinates me—but this piece used decidedly masculine language, from the chapter titles to the metaphors, complete with references to NASCAR, rocket launchers, and drill sergeants. Because I didn't relate to these examples, I wasn't drawn into the manuscript. In fact, I felt almost excluded.

Gender-specific terms aren't always immediately obvious; there are plenty of seemingly ordinary words and phrases that are much more likely to be uttered by one sex or the other. A woman is three times more likely to use the word *gorgeous*, for example. And when men do use it, it's typically only to describe a woman—not a baby, a pair of shoes, or a piece of chocolate cake.

So let's start with some basic guidelines. No matter what you're writing, if your intended audience is female, make sure to include plenty of personal pronouns—*I*, *you*, and *we*—and descriptive terms. If your intended audience is male, on the other hand, trade in pronouns for articles—such as *a*, *the*, and *that*—choose active verbs, limit adjectives, and include concrete figures, like numbers. Observe the stylistic differences between these two statements: "I'm sorry we're late; we had a flat tire on our way here," and, "The tire blew when we hit seventy on the freeway." Chances are you can tell right away which sex is talking in each one.

When you want to appeal to a mixed audience, review your writing with an eye for instances in which the language skews toward your own gender. When you find them, make revisions to include a balance of wording that caters to the other sex as well. Pay special attention to your analogies; if you're writing an article on choosing energy-efficient appliances, for example, and you compare a refrigerator to a sports car, counter later in the piece by mentioning that the dishwasher purrs like a kitten. Or opt for gender-neutral analogies, such as this one from Wendy and Larry Maltz's *The Porn Trap: The Essential Guide to Overcoming Problems Caused by Pornography*: "Don't think of [the six steps] like stepping stones across a creek, but rather sections of a bridge ..."

WALK THE WALK

No matter what you write, one of the earliest decisions you'll make is how to approach your topic. Gender should definitely play a role here. Whether they're watching a movie, reading a novel, or consulting a self-help article, men generally prefer to see something accomplished—a battle won, a dog trained, a disease conquered. Women often favor a focus on the relationships and emotions behind the story—what happens to the family left at home while the spouse is off fighting the war, what it's like for the dog to learn to sit and stay, how to handle the strain of caring for an ailing family member. This helps explain why recent surveys show that women read approximately 80 percent of all literary fiction and most self-help books, while men are more likely to read history, science fiction, and political tomes.

At a writing workshop I recently taught, I asked my students to write a paragraph about what it would be like to be an astronaut during liftoff. Once they were finished, I asked them to write another paragraph from the perspective of someone from the opposite gender. Both the males and the females writing from a male perspective emphasized the thrill of the ride ("I felt like I was straddling a 200-ton bucking bronco headed into the cosmos!") and the sense of accomplishment of being chosen for the mission. The women and men writing from the female perspective focused on being separated from family and friends ("Will the kids remember to feed that cat?") and having doubts about the whole decision to go into space.

Here's an example from an exercise in a college English class in which students were paired up and asked to craft a story together by taking turns writing alternating paragraphs. With one particular team, the gender differences became glaringly (and amusingly) obvious:

> At first, Laurie couldn't decide which kind of tea she wanted. The chamomile, which used to be her favorite for lazy evenings at home, now reminded her too much of Carl ...
>
> Meanwhile, Advance Sgt. Carl Harris, leader of the attack squadron now in orbit over Skylon 4, had more important things to think about than the neuroses of an airheaded bimbo named Laurie with whom he had spent one sweaty night over a year ago ...
>
> He bumped his head and died almost immediately, but not before he felt one last pang of regret for psychologically brutalizing the one woman who had ever had feelings for him ...
>
> Little did she know, but she had less than 10 seconds to live ...

The female writer focused on the emotional issues she felt were vital to her heroine—even when to do so, she had to kill off Advance Sergeant Harris. The male writer, on the other hand, did everything he could to move the action along and cut out "extraneous" details.

The lessons are clear if you're writing for a single gender, but what's a writer to do to be more inclusive of both men and women? Where there is yin, balance it with yang. Janet Evanovich does this exceptionally well. Her most popular novels feature Stephanie Plum, a bail bondswoman who works in a male-dominated industry but does her job with a characteristically feminine style (relying on friends, trying to be a good daughter, taking care of her hamster, mulling over her intimate relationships, etc.). Employ Evanovich's method: If you choose a female approach to a topic, bring balance by incorporating more masculine elements, and vice versa.

DRESS THE PART

Sociologists suggest that the female focus on nurturing relationships and the male compulsion to get the job done not only affect what we're interested in, but the way we use language—and, naturally, the style that appeals to us on a page. Take these recent reviews of two movies meant to speak to very different audiences. For *Motherhood*: "If you are a mother, if you know a mother, if you have a mother, this is the movie for you"; "The best comedy about being a mother in modern America today. And a must-see for every father, too"; and, "Sweet, charming and frantically funny." Notice how the language conjures up images of not just motherhood, but also friendship ("if you know a mother"), daughterhood ("if you have a mother") and fatherhood. The adjectives let us know the movie will focus on someone women can relate to: an overworked mother trying to keep her sanity in today's fast-paced world. Contrast this with reviews for *Law Abiding Citizen*: "A taut thriller"; "A breathtaking thrill ride"; and, "This is one fight to the finish you won't want to miss." The language here is sparse, action-packed, and absent of real detail. What is the movie about? We're not sure, but we know there will be car crashes and things blowing up.

Style differences are especially important to understand if you're writing dialogue. One of the most difficult undertakings we face as writers is putting the right words into our characters' mouths. Recognizing differences in the way the genders communicate can help you create more believable, engaging characters that will ring true for your readers. Linguistic research has found that women are more likely to state preferences rather than demands ("I would like a glass of wine"), start a sentence with a question ("What do you think about ... ?"), and use apologetic language even when being decisive ("I'm so sorry, but I'm going to have to lay you off"). Men, on the other hand, use more commanding and aggressive language ("Grab me a beer") and are more likely to pepper everyday conversation with less accommodating phrasing (which can include things like sarcasm, put-downs, or references to *taboo* body parts). Studies have also shown that men don't divulge much personal information in everyday conversation, while women frequently do.

To help illustrate these differences, let's look at two real-life writing samples, both on the topic of exercise. The first is from Amy Gallo's "Whittle While You Work," which appears in *Self* online: "This is our kind of on-the-job training! Daniel Loigerot, a Pilates instructor in New York City, designed these moves to help you tone all over in about 10 minutes using a resistance band and chair." The second is from "Gut Check," an unattributed piece on the *Men's Fitness* website: "If you fail both tests, you need more core work. Simply perform the tests as exercises, three to four times a week—doing one to two sets for 50 percent of your max time for each—before you do any other lifts. Hartman also advises that you not use more than 20 percent of your body weight on any lift until you achieve a passing score. That may seem drastic, but your core will get up to speed quickly, and you'll immediately be able to lift heavier."

First, compare the style of the titles: "Whittle While You Work" to "Gut Check." As you might guess, in the first piece, the style is soft and sounds helpful. In the *Men's Fitness* article, can you feel the author goading the reader to be competitive? The reader may have already failed some tests; he needs to "achieve a passing score" so he can achieve his goal to "lift heavier."

If you're writing for a single gender—whether you're penning an instructional piece or working on your novel-in-progress—don't shy away from integrating these style differences into your work. They may seem subtle, but you'll be surprised at how much careful attention to these preferences can boost your writing's appeal to your audience.

Of course, we're not all the same in our differences—I'd be willing to bet you're thinking of plenty of exceptions to the above points right now. It's true that not all women think and behave alike, and neither do all men. But just as young adult writers research the specific needs and behaviors of teens and tweens, and romance and sci-fi novelists work to understand what makes their audiences different from the rest of the reading world, all of us should consider gender issues before tapping out those first few words on our keyboards. When you do, remember these words, from Edward Abbey: "It is the difference between men and women, not the sameness, that creates the tension and the delight."

LEIGH ANNE JASHEWAY is the author of fifteen books and the winner the Erma Bombeck Award for Humor Writing.

FOCUS ON THE WRITING LIFE: RESEARCHING YOUR WORK

RESEARCHING YOUR IDEAS

BY THE EDITORS OF WRITER'S DIGEST

The lengths that writers can go to understand their subjects may be best exemplified by James Alexander Thom, a former journalist who has written a number of acclaimed and best-selling books about the American frontier experience. When Thom decided to write the story of Mary Ingles for his book *Follow the River*, he actually retraced parts of the route Ingles followed when she escaped Indian captivity in 1755.

Following the completion of the book, Thom said he could only write Ingles's story after he had walked in her steps. Thom couldn't trace Ingles's entire six-week trek through the woods along the Ohio and Kenawha rivers, but he made five separate trips to key spots along her route. At times Thom even ate what Ingles had eaten, and at one point he fasted for a week.

For the rest of his research, Thom visited Ingles's descendants, read detailed family accounts of her life, and studied historic documents. In the long run Thom's research only made his job easier, and it made his account more believable.

This kind of dogged pursuit of authenticity can make your work stand out, whether you are writing a historical novel or an article on historic cars. To convince readers—and editors—that you know what you are talking about, you must first spend the time to understand the subject yourself.

As you outline your book or article, the idea of research may sound like drudgery, a necessary evil you must go through before you can get to your real work—the writing. Yet what many of us would consider drudgery is actually the most important step in the writing process. Consider, for a moment, that good research is what makes your finished work come alive with realism and truth. Each interview, Google session, or trip to the library adds excitement and authenticity to your finished piece. Research enlightens you and enables you to enlighten your audience. Research is nothing less than the heart and soul of what we do.

In reality, there are only so many subjects you can write from personal experience. And there are only so many subjects that you can learn firsthand, as Thom did. Fortunately, to learn everything else you can rely on others' expertise through interviews. The Internet has made millions of information sources instantly available to anyone who can afford a high-speed connection.

Whether your research is based on personal experience, interviews, document searches, the Internet, or any combination of the above, approach it with the same dogged professionalism. In the end, the quality of what you write will be based on the quality of what you know and learn. This is true whether you are writing fiction, nonfiction, or magazine articles. In all these cases, research adds the critical element of realism. This chapter provides you with the tools needed to approach research in a time-efficient and thorough manner.

The quality of what you learn is determined not just by the quality of your source material, but also by the mind-set you bring to the project. Approach your research with a real desire to learn. Find enough sources to obtain as many points of view as possible. Don't just accept the things you read or hear; ask questions and make your judgments based on factual information. At the same time, challenge your own assumptions. Be willing to consider other ideas and opinions even if it means reevaluating your work or redoing what you have done so far (which is admittedly painful).

FINDING THE RIGHT INFORMATION

The task of research is somewhat like that of writing. More important than where to start is the need to start. You can't know exactly what an article or book will be until you write it. Similarly you can't know all the information you need or where your search will lead you until it is underway. You can, however, narrow your choices with some foresight and good planning. From libraries and the Internet, to business and government sources, there's no shortage of places to find the right information on any subject. Begin with the places that will be of most benefit for your topic.

THE INTERNET

These days, your research should definitely start online. (If you haven't done this before, get someone to help you.) Hundreds of millions of Web pages are maintained by government agencies, universities, libraries, corporations, organizations, and individuals. Some experts estimate that the amount of information online is expanding at several pages per second. You can read and download government reports, newspaper and magazine articles, research studies, even the full text of books. While it can't supplant libraries and other sources of detailed information (at least not yet), using the Web for research is like shopping at a flea market. Every page is valuable to someone, but finding what is meaningful to you often requires sorting through a lot of junk. Not every source you find is reliable. Knowing a few shortcuts can save you valuable time.

Search Engines

No doubt you've already discovered the first major shortcut: search engines. Search engines help you find more specific information on a subject. They constantly scan the Web to create indexes of information. When you type in a word or phrase and hit the search button, the search engine creates a list of Web pages that relate to your subject. Some popular search engines include:

Google (www.google.com)

This is the granddaddy of them all, and the most comprehensive. When you look something up on Google, you'll find links organized from the most to least relevant. Frame your search parameters carefully: "Julia Roberts as Erin Brockovich" will find those pages that list the two names together. If you're writing an article on how Julia Roberts's starring role as Erin Brockovich transformed her image from toothsome movie star to serious actress, you don't want to have to wade through the hundreds of fan pages you'd find by just typing in "Julia Roberts."

Google's ambitious drive to be one-stop shopping for all conceivable information on the Internet has led it to create several initiatives that may also prove useful for your research:

- Google Alerts allow you to choose any phrase and receive a daily digest e-mail of all of the links to pages where that phrase has been used in a day. Authors may wish to put a Google Alert on a subject or individual they are currently researching to monitor any developing stories. If you're working on a profile article about an innovative Wall Street entrepreneur, for instance, you will want to put a Google Alert on her name to receive any news stories that mention her. www.google.com/alerts
- Google Book Search allows you to search millions of books that Google has scanned and posted online. This effort started with the classics—older, out-of-print books in the public domain—but soon mushroomed to include just about anything with printed words between two covers. Can't find the quote you put into your article but know you need to give a citation for it? Try typing it verbatim into the Book Search: Google will show you a facsimile of the page where it can be found and all the bibliographic information, so you

don't have to spend two hours frantically searching for the quote in every book you own. http://books.google.com

- Like Google Books, Google Scholar gives you access to nonbook research information, especially more academic and specialized sources like journal articles, theses, dissertations, abstracts, and the like. http://scholar.google.com

- Google Translate is precisely what it sounds like: an instant translator. It's not quite up to the futuristic standards of Star Trek's Universal Translator, but it's getting there, with more languages being added all the time. This can save you tremendous time and expense if you're doing historical research and some of your documents are in German, or you're writing a travel guide to Botswana and never mastered Setswana. The prose Google spits back may not be elegant, but you will get the basic meaning. http://translate.google.com

- Google Maps and Google Earth can help you in unexpected ways with your writing. What if you're writing a novel set in Paris but can't quite remember the street layout from your character's hotel to the café where she first encounters her soul mate over crème brûlée? Use Google Maps (http://maps.google.com) to get your heroine from place to place and Google Earth (http://earth.google.com) to zoom in on the café, reminding yourself of the sights, buildings, and flower vendors all around it. These tools are fantastic for helping to evoke a setting.

- Google Blog Search allows you to search the blogs of ordinary people for your research. This is especially useful if you want to add a personal component to a story you are writing. For example, if you were doing a piece on Lyme disease for a health magazine, you would of course research your topic in science journals, medical websites, and the like. But if you also want to hear from ordinary people who are suffering from the disease, you could run a blog search on Lyme disease and hear what individual people have experienced. This can be a great way to find interview subjects, too, since people who are willing to blog publicly about a subject are often also willing to talk about it with a writer. http://blogsearch.google.com

- Google Images is a search engine specifically designed for JPEGs, TIFFs, and other art formats. This is where you go if you want to find a photograph of someone, a book or album cover, or clip art. (Remember that most of these images are copyright protected, so you will need to double-click on the picture to find out where it came from and then contact the rights holder listed.) http://images.google.com

Yahoo! Search (www.search.yahoo.com)

Yahoo may not be quite as big as Google, but its boast of "twenty billion web objects" is certainly nothing to sneeze at. You can find just about anything you want to with this tool, as with Google. Yahoo also has some special tricks up its sleeve:

- Yahoo People Search is like the white pages and yellow pages combined in a national database. If you know the last name and state of the person you're seeking, you will probably be able to find him. But what makes the Yahoo tool particularly helpful is the e-mail search feature. If your quarry has an e-mail address that is publicly listed anywhere (e.g., at the university where he teaches or the law firm where she practices), Yahoo People Search will come up trumps. http://people.yahoo.com

- Yahoo Video, like Google Images, is a specialized search engine—in this case, one that is designed specifically to trawl through streaming video. Want to find an interview with an author or celebrity? A clip of the president giving the State of the Union address? This is where you want to be. http://video.search.yahoo.com

Specialized Search Engines

In addition to the general, big-picture searches you can do with Google and other engines, there are also subject-specific search engines. They can help you hone in on Web pages more likely to cover your topic in detail. Some popular specialized search engines and directories include:

Academic Info (www.academicinfo.net). This site provides educational information, online courses, and comprehensive subject guides on an enormous range of topics.

Infomine (http://infomine.ucr.edu). Like Academic Info, this emphasizes scholarly resources like journal articles but also includes government documents and more.

LawCrawler (www.lawcrawler.com). Does your mystery novel have characters embroiled in a last-will-and-testament court battle? Find legal precedents, case briefs, and even expert witnesses at this site.

U.S. National Library of Medicine (www.nlm.nih.gov). Run by the National Institutes of Health, this site offers comprehensive medical information, including fascinating details on the history of medicine in America, current research and treatments, and public health.

LIBRARIES

For most topics, a library is a great place to conduct research. After all, libraries hold the cumulative written knowledge of our entire history and civilization. Practically nothing is known that cannot be found in a library somewhere. Best of all, there are guides (research librarians and reference librarians) to point you in the right direction. Thanks to interlibrary loans, virtually no volume is beyond your reach. With directories on the Internet, searching for reference materials in the library system has never been easier.

There are three types of libraries: public libraries, college libraries, and specialized libraries maintained by industries or special interest groups. The federal government is another leading source of information, but many of its publications are also available in larger libraries.

Public Libraries

These are usually the best places for conducting research. The selection of material is unmatched by any suburban branch location (though if you know what you want you can often have it sent from the main library to the branch near you). The reference librarian at your local library is a valuable source of information. Many accept phone calls and e-mails from patrons asking research questions, so long as the questions are specific and can be answered quickly.

College Libraries

A library at a large institution will have more resources available than most branches of your public library. Colleges and public university libraries are usually open to the public, though you may not be able to withdraw a book unless you are affiliated with the school. In addition to the central campus library at most universities, many of the academic departments have their own specialized libraries, which may be open to the public.

Specialized Libraries

There are thousands of special libraries throughout the United States. While their collections may be limited to certain subjects, many offer an unparalleled amount of information on their specific subject matter, be it medicine, engineering, history, or art. Most are open to the public at least on a limited basis, though you will probably need permission in advance to gain access. Even those that aren't normally open to the public likely will allow you access if you explain the nature of your research. You can find out about special libraries in the Directory of Special Libraries and Information Centers or in the Subject Directory of Special Libraries and Information Centers. Both volumes are available at larger public libraries. The Special Libraries Association (www.sla.org) also may be of assistance.

BUSINESS AND GOVERNMENT SOURCES

Businesses

Businesses routinely make information available through their public relations offices, customer service departments, and sales staffs. Many trade associations also can provide you with valuable material, including chambers of commerce and tourism offices at the state and local level. In fact, many exist primarily to disseminate information and are often eager to provide writers with information. Don't hesitate to contact these people; they can be an enormous help. Three books that list thousands of these viable information sources include *Encyclopedia of Associations: International Organizations*, *Encyclopedia of Associations: National Organizations of the U.S.*, and *Encyclopedia of Associations: Regional, State and Local Organizations*.

Federal Government Information

There are several sources for government publications. You can contact the authoring agency directly or use any number of government outlets that serve as information clearinghouses. In many instances, the cost to purchase government documents can be prohibitive. Fortunately many documents are available for free viewing at public libraries or at thousands of other depositories throughout the country. The Monthly Catalog of U.S. Government Publications, published by the U. S. Government Printing Office, is one way to find what you need. The GPO's Subject Bibliography Index lists thousands of publications by category. To inquire about government documents, try the following agencies:

> The Federal Citizen Information Center (www.pueblo.gsa.gov) serves as a single point of contact for people who have

questions about any federal agency. Its information specialists can also help you locate government documents and publications.

The U.S. Census Bureau (www.census.gov) has thousands of reports about the U.S. population and economy. It offers statistics on such diverse subjects as fertility, education, mining, ancestry, income, migration, school enrollment, construction, and international trade. You can access data through more than two thousand libraries and other locations that serve as data centers and federal depositories.

The U.S. Government Accountability Office (www.gao.gov) is the investigative arm of Congress that compiles reports on all aspects of government. All of GAO's unclassified reports are available to the public. Known as the "watchdog" of the U.S. Government, the GAO is a good place to go if you need information about government spending, fraud, legal decisions, or other controversies, from salmonella scares to aviation crash reports.

The U.S. Government Printing Office (www.access.gpo.gov) is the largest distributor of government documents. The GPO provides information to designated libraries and other locations throughout the country, where you can view the information for free.

The National Technical Information Service (www.ntis.gov) distributes scientific, technical, and engineering documents.

RESEARCH TIPS AND TRICKS

While it's fairly easy to write out a list of places to get information, what to do when you get there is another story. There is more than one path to the same point, and some are quicker than others. Think of unique ways to get the information you need, and think of unique ways to use the information you get. In other words, be as creative in your research as you are in your writing. Use the tips and tricks listed below to help you find the best research path possible.

- Work from the general to the specific. Look for general background information first. Use that to better define your search and begin to look for more specific information.
- Develop a rapport with the reference or research librarians at your local library. They live to help people find information. (Be sure to hit the highlights yourself first; it would be a real waste of a librarian's time if you haven't so much as Googled your topic yet. Save the librarian as your backup plan when you've exhausted your options or hit a wall with your research.)
- Scan the table of contents of books you think might be relevant. If you are doing this online, try using Amazon.com's "Look Inside" feature to give you a sense of the book before buying.
- To get a quick overview of a large book or document, check the index for a list of illustrations, charts, tables, or graphs. Lengthy, complicated subjects are often summarized with charts and graphs. This is especially true of government and scientific documents. If you find a graphic that is of particular interest, scan the text pages around it for related details. Also look for an executive summary or introduction at the front of the document and conclusion statements at the end of each section.
- If you have trouble finding information on your subject, it could be you are using the wrong search words. Check your words against the subject heading list in the directory you are searching.
- When retrieving your books from the library shelves, browse nearby books to see if any others might be useful. Library

shelves are arranged so that nonfiction books about the same topic are generally kept near each other.

- Keep a list of what you find and where you found it. You may need to go back to it later.
- A volume number usually refers to the year that a periodical was published. Volume 10 refers to a magazine in its tenth year of publication.
- When you need facts, assume that there is a reference source that has what you need. There nearly always is.
- Most books and many articles themselves have bibliographies that list additional sources of information. By following these leads you can amass a body of information quickly.

PART 7:

REVISION:

HOW YOUR STORY COMES TOGETHER

CHAPTER 34

HOW TO GAIN PERSPECTIVE ON YOUR WORK

BY ELIZABETH SIMS

Throughout my childhood my mother gave me dolls and my father gave me puzzles: a typical parental dichotomy.

I ignored the dolls and went for the puzzles, in spite of not being very fast at figuring them out. Which led my dad to give me still more of them: jigsaws, table mazes, wire contraptions and carved wooden figure puzzles. Whenever I'd get frustrated and throw one down, Dad would just say, "Try it again later." Feeling hopelessly dumb, I'd run outside to ride my bike or find a friend to harass.

Hours or days later, I'd pick up the puzzle again. To my invariable surprise, this time I'd get further. I could see it better. Suddenly it would seem obvious that this double-wedge piece of wood was the key to the whole little elephant, or that if you twisted your fingers just so, the heart would detach from the ring all by itself.

What had happened? The puzzle hadn't changed; I was the same kid.

Wasn't I?

Yet somehow I had become less dumb (as I saw it). I never knew what to make of the phenomenon until I became a writer and had to work out problems I found in my stories—in other words, to revise.

Revision, every writing coach will tell you, means "to see anew" or "to visit again."

But what does that really mean?

We all instinctively know that when you work on a thing for a long time, your feeling for it can get stale, and eventually your efforts reach a point of diminishing returns. And we know that when you walk away temporarily, you give yourself a chance to come back to the work with a new eye—a fresh eye. When you do that, your work now looks somewhat different. You're seeing it from a new angle. You've gained perspective.

How do you know when you need perspective on a particular piece of writing?

- You've submitted your piece a bunch of times and it's gotten nowhere.
- Your revision has lost energy and direction, but still feels incomplete.
- You're getting consistent feedback that your writing needs work. (Notice I say "consistent." More on that later.)

You've come down with CRD—Creeping Rot Disease, which strikes all authors now and then, making us feel as if what we have spent so much time and effort on is nothing but junk.

Gaining perspective may well be the most important part of revision—and it can often be the most difficult. Fortunately there are several methods that can guide you, no matter what type of writing you do.

GETTING DISTANCE

The most obvious—and easiest!—way to gain perspective is to put your work away for a while.

The truth is, no one knows *how* taking a break frees up the mind, but it does: Somehow it freshens our little neurons, or perhaps it prompts the brain to create more cleverness molecules.

If you can bear to let a short piece sit a week and a book-length work a month, do so. Longer is fine, too; some authors have abandoned manuscripts for years before unearthing them and realizing, *Hey, this isn't bad*, and renewing their energy for the project.

But even just a couple of days totally away from your first draft can help. Your brain needs a rest from the whole damn thing. Therefore, physically getting away from your project isn't enough; you also need to stop yourself from thinking about it. If you spend your "break" reflecting on it, obsessing about it, turning over the same problems in your mind, you're not going to be fresh when you come back to it.

How do you take your mind off your work?

Trying to force thoughts out of your mind rarely goes well, but you can seek a state where you're not judging things as good or bad, but allowing everything simply to be.

Directing your attention to something else works wonders for this. Which brings me to a second key aspect of gaining perspective and preparing to revise.

SHARPENING YOUR SAW

You may have heard the expression "sharpening your saw."

That is, you can keep sawing away with a blade that's becoming duller and duller the more you bear down on it, or you can stop your work, step away, and sharpen your blade so that when you use it again, the work goes better and with less effort. Sometimes we are reluctant to sharpen our saw because we don't want to leave the work—we confuse stopping to do essential maintenance with quitting. But really, it must be done. Your writing mind gets dull, even fragmented. Sharpening your saw is a vital step to take between writing "The End" and beginning revisions. You need to regain your keenness.

What are some ways to sharpen your saw?

Seek. I'm a big believer in getting outdoors, as were Thoreau, Hemingway, and many other authors. If you can afford to take a few days entirely away, spending time in the natural world reconnects you with your calm, clear inner core. A backpacking or camping trip, either solo or not, can help center you and restore your mind to wholeness. Alternatively go for a day hike, engage in your favorite sport, or just take a walk around your neighborhood.

CLEAN. Tidy up your writing space. Throw out junk paper, file the rest, and act on the pending tasks you've been putting off. Vacuum the crumbs and open the window.

ORGANIZE. Shape up your books. Shelve the ones that are lying all over the place, cull some to sell, and make room on your shelves for new ones. Clearing stuff out in general has metaphorical value as well as practical.

READ SOMEBODY ELSE. When in need of perspective, I find it both comforting and refreshing to pick up a favorite book from the past, be it a classic like *Wise Blood* or a trash masterpiece like *Valley of the Dolls*, and take a spin with a friend I can trust.

DO SOMETHING ELSE CREATIVE. Draw or paint, even if you haven't done it since way back in art class. The act of putting up an easel and squeezing some colors onto a palette is a tremendously exciting thing to do. Grab a brush and lay on some paint. You'll be using a totally different part of your mind. Alternatively try your hand at a new craft project. Or if you play a musical instrument, pick it up.

BEGIN. Start a completely different writing project. It doesn't matter what, as long as it's new. Sometimes writing a short story is the perfect follow-up to finishing a novel. Or if you've finished an essay or article, you might just have the momentum to grab a fresh stack of paper and boldly throw down the words "Chapter One."

BRAINSTORM. If you don't want to begin a new project, just consider ideas for new material. Do character sketches, dream up a list of heart-clutching moments, ask yourself what you *want* to write about. What ideas, themes, or grudges have been banging around inside you?

No matter how you do it, when you give your conscious mind a break from the writing you'll soon revise, you turn over your work to your subconscious. That's good because your subconscious is where your magic lives. While you're trying to outsmart a trout or swinging your staff along a trail or stopping to watch a flock of kids on the playground, your story is still inside you, taking shape, settling, flying, settling again, resolving.

And when you bring your conscious mind back to it, you'll see things you didn't see before. You'll perceive better how to exploit the strong parts, and you'll see more clearly what to cut, what to fix, why and how. You'll gain confidence.

When you're finally feeling ready to return to your work, don't start with page 1 just yet. As we know, the main reason you get dull is you've gotten too familiar with your material. So, just before you begin revising, try reading parts of your work out of sequence. This takes away context, which allows you to see the writing from a new angle. It's the difference between meeting a new person at some fancy function, all dressed up and scented, and meeting that same person in the sauna at the gym. Context can distract us from essence.

GAINING AN OUTSIDE PERSPECTIVE

The most time-honored way to gain perspective is to borrow another set of eyes. To beta test—a term from the computer world—means to try out a not-final version on volunteer end users. The ideal beta reader is someone who: a) you know is a discriminating reader, and b) cares about you. That is, someone who at heart wants you to succeed as a writer.

The main, open-ended question you want to ask a beta reader is, "What did you think of it?" Make it clear that you want to hear it straight, good or bad. Sometimes you'll hear vagueness like, "It was different!" or, "I really liked it," or, "I don't know, I couldn't get into it." Such feedback is essentially worthless. To avoid this, coach your beta readers in advance by saying, "I'm just going to want to know wherever you went over a bump." That way they'll feel free to say they were uncomfortable with a scene, or felt something didn't work, without fearing that you're going to expect a step-by-step dissertation.

Then, when you sit down to get feedback, ask directed questions, questions that get your readers to comment on specific aspects of what they've just read.

Let's say you're in doubt about a particular scene or chapter. Ask:

- How did you feel when you read this scene?
- What did you like about it?
- What didn't you like about it?
- Did you ever get bored? Where?
- What part made you feel the most emotion? How come?

Then you can dig deeper into their gut reactions on the work as a whole. Readers love stories that make them *feel.* So zero in on their emotions:

- Did you feel dread anyplace? Horror?
- Did you get grossed out by anything? Was it a good gross-out or a bad gross-out?
- Did you feel stirred romantically? Whether yes or no, tell me more.
- Did you stay up reading later than you intended?
- Did you learn anything new?
- Was it ever a slog?
- Did the characters come alive? Which one seemed most alive? Which least? Do you feel you can clearly see them?

And then: What is X character like? (I have found this question to be especially rewarding. Readers have different takes on characters, and there have been times I've learned that my characters are coming across in ways I hadn't known, sometimes quite differently than I'd intended. Sometimes a reader sees depth in a character that I myself missed! With unique feedback like that, you'll be able to populate your fiction more realistically.)

Needless to say, be receptive. You don't have to agree with everything, but don't waste time defending or explaining your work. A useful response is, "Thank you, I'll think about it. What else?"

Remember earlier I mentioned consistency of feedback?

The responses you receive may be all over the map. You will hear variation after variation, and some of those variations may be exactly contradictory.

For example, from Reader A: "I like how your beginning gradually builds speed, but you didn't play fair with that random explosion at the end."

Reader B: "The beginning was slow, but you ended with a terrific bang!"

If you start rewriting in response to the specifics of every critique you receive, you risk eventually being driven to put a bullet through your brain. Be a bit cagey when taking comments. But if you start hearing similar criticism from multiple sources, sit up and pay attention. If, after considering the feedback, you think it has merit, go ahead and revise your work accordingly.

Still, you must trust your own internal writerly core above all.

I've kept notes from a years-ago phone conversation with a powerful figure in publishing who told me my novel was awful. I'd better stop submitting it, she said, and get some remedial training in storytelling.

I didn't listen. I knew in my heart that she was wrong, that my novel was publishable—if not the next *Light in August*—and, moreover, the other feedback I'd gotten on it didn't remotely reflect what she'd said. I soon sold the manuscript to another publisher.

On the other hand, when my agent talks, I listen, even though she's only one person. I listen very hard. Why? Because: a) she's made a career out of distinguishing great writing from the mediocre, and b) she can articulate exactly why a particular plot point or passage of writing works or doesn't work for her. We don't always agree, but I give her opinions a great deal of weight.

In the end, consider what Jack Kerouac told *The Paris Review*: "I spent my entire youth writing slowly with revisions and endless rehashing speculation and deleting and got so I was writing one sentence a day and the sentence had no *feeling*. Goddamn it, *feeling* is what I like in art, not *craftiness* and the hiding of feelings."

Then he wrote *On the Road*.

Don't make too much of revising.

ELIZABETH SIMS (elizabethsims.com) is a contributing editor for *Writer's Digest* Magazine. She's the award-winning author of seven novels and many short stories, poems, and articles.

CHAPTER 35

FIRE UP YOUR FICTION: FOUR TECHNIQUES

BY DONALD MAASS

Many fiction manuscripts submitted to my literary agency feel lackluster. Much genre fiction feels tired. Many mainstream and literary novels also strike me as stale. Even when well written, too often manuscripts fail to engage and excite me.

What is missing when a manuscript hugs the wall and refuses to dance? Originality is not the key. It can't be, otherwise no wounded detective would ever have a chance and every new vampire series would be dead on arrival. Even overpublished clichés can sometimes break out and sell big. The same is true of look-alike mainstream and literary fiction.

The issue, then, is not whether a story has a cool new premise. Whether hiking a well-worn trail or blazing uncharted wilderness, when a manuscript succeeds it is invariably fired by inspiration. Passion comes through on the page.

How does that passion get there? Here are some exercises to apply to your novel-in-progress. They are designed to dig up what matters in your story and infuse it in your manuscript in effective—but not obvious—ways.

FIND THE UNCOMMON IN COMMON EXPERIENCE

To get passion into your story, do it through your characters. What angers you can anger them. What lifts them up will inspire us in turn.

Even ordinary people can be poets, prophets, and saints. That's true in life, so why not in your fiction?

Here is an exercise designed to discover and utilize what is universal in the experience of your characters, especially when they are regular folk like you and me.

Write down what comes to mind when you read the prompts below.

1. Is your story realistic? Are your characters ordinary people?
2. What in the world of your story makes you angry? What are we not seeing? What is the most important question? What puzzle has no answer? What is dangerous in this world? What causes pain?
3. Where in the world of your story is there unexpected grace? What is beautiful? Who is an unrecognized hero? What needs to be saved?
4. Give your feelings to a character. Who can stand for something? Who can turn the plot's main problem into a cause?
5. Create a situation in which this character must defend, explain or justify his actions. How is the plot's main problem larger than it looks? Why does it matter to us all?
6. Find places in your manuscript to incorporate the emotions, opinions, and ideas generated in the prompts above.

FIND THE COMMON IN UNCOMMON EXPERIENCE

What if your protagonist is already a genuine hero? If your hero or heroine is an above-average, courageous, principled and unstoppable doer of good, then you may believe that you don't have a problem. Cheering will begin automatically, right?

Wrong. Perfect heroes and heroines are unrealistic. Readers know that. They will not strongly bond with such characters. To connect, they need to feel that such paragons are real.

That is also true for the world of your story. The rarefied stratosphere of national politics, international intrigue, or any other out-of-the-ordinary milieu will not draw readers in unless there they find some way to relate to it.

The following are steps you can take to humanize your hero and make the exotic world of your story real for us ordinary mortals.

1. Is your story about uncommon events? Are your characters out of the ordinary?
2. Find for your hero a failing that is human, a universal frustration, a humbling setback, or any experience that everyone has had. Add this early in the manuscript.
3. What in the world of the story is timelessly true? What cannot be changed? How is basic human nature exhibited? What is the same today as one hundred years ago and will be the same one hundred years ahead?
4. What does your protagonist do the same way everyone else does it? What is his lucky charm? Give this character a motto. What did she learn from her mom or dad?
5. Create a situation in which your exceptional protagonist is in over his head, feels unprepared, is simply lost, or in any other way must admit to himself that he's not perfect.
6. Find places in your manuscript to incorporate the results of the steps above.

DEVELOP THE MORAL OF THE STORY

What if your novel already has a driving message? Suppose its purpose is in some way to wake us up? That's great, but your message will harden your readers' hearts if you lecture or preach. To avoid that, let your story itself be your lesson. The teacher is your central plot problem. The students? Those are your characters.

Here are ways to use those elements to get across your point.

1. Is there a moral or lesson in your story?
2. When does your protagonist realize she got something wrong?

3. Who in the story can, at the end, see things in a completely different way?
4. At the end, how is your hero or heroine better off?
5. At the end, what does your hero or heroine regret?
6. Who, in the midst of the story, is certain there is no solution, nor is there any way to fully comprehend the problem?
7. Why is the problem good, timely, universal, or fated?
8. Find places in your manuscript to incorporate the results of the questions above.

BUILD THE FIRE IN FICTION

Did you ever get lost in the middle of writing a manuscript? Have you ever wondered, deep in revisions, if your story holds together or any longer makes sense? Have you ever lost steam?

Steal from life. That's what it's for, isn't it? How often, when something bad happened to you, did you think to yourself, *at least this will be good material for a story some day*?

Well, now's your chance. What has happened to you, its details and specifics, are tools with which you can make every scene personal and powerful. Use the following prompts whenever you are stuck, or if inspiration simply is low.

1. Choose any scene that seems weak or wandering. Who is the point-of-view character?
2. Identify whatever this character feels most strongly in this scene. Fury? Futility? Betrayal? Hope? Joy? Arousal? Shame? Grief? Pride? Self-loathing? Security?
3. Recall your own life. What was the time when you most strongly felt the emotion you identified in the last step?
4. Detail your own experience: When precisely did this happen? Who was there? What was around you? What do you remember best about the moment? What would you most like to forget? What was the quality of the light? What exactly was said? What were the smallest and largest things that were done?

5. In this experience from your life, what twisted the knife or put the icing on the cake? It would have stirred this feeling anyway, but what really provoked it was … what?
6. What did you think to yourself as the importance of this experience struck you?
7. Give the details of your experience to your character, right now, in this very scene.

DONALD MAASS is the founder of Donald Maass Literary Agency, which sells more than 150 novels every year. He is the author of *Writing the Breakout Novel, The Fire in Fiction,* and *The Breakout Novelist*.

CHAPTER 36

WHAT TO DO WHEN YOUR NOVEL STALLS

BY JOHN DUFRESNE

There are precious few experiences quite as exhilarating as diving headlong into your new novel. You write your opening sentence, and you're off. Immediately you're imagining a brave new world and creating goodly creatures to inhabit it. You find yourself an inquisitive stranger in this newfound land. Your job here at the outset is to wonder and to wander, to make yourself susceptible to the provocations of this exotic place, to absorb the rich and telling details, to welcome interaction with all these fascinating made-up people, and to follow your curiosity wherever it leads. You can't wait to see what's around the next corner, behind the next door, or over the next mountain. The world opens itself to you for its unmasking, as Kafka said it would.

You give your darlings one problem after another, because you know that writing a novel is taking the path of most resistance. You trail along behind your characters, writing down what they do. They surprise you, they delight you, and they alarm you. The story intensifies, the themes resonate and the mystery deepens. You think, *This novel-writing business is such a blast!* Not all of the writing has made it to the page just yet, but it's all there in your copious notes.

You're writing serenely every day. You're coming to know your characters' secrets, their dreams, and their shame. You're feeling clever, invigorated, and beneficent. But writing a novel is a marathon, and it can be difficult to sustain the composure, drive, and passion that inspired and launched the project. Today you're sputtering a bit. That subplot you constructed isn't panning out the way you had hoped it would. Bit of a dead end, really.

Not only that, now you realize that all of those problems you slapped your hero with need to be addressed, if not resolved. You put down your pen and scratch your head. Here you are in the middle of your novel, and you're not sure where it's going. And that character who you were certain was going to shine so brightly has dimmed, hasn't he?

Your graceful and sleek narrative turns out to be ragged and shapeless. It's just one thing after another, isn't it? You need a plot. You knew you would. You do know what a plot is—a central character wants something, goes after it despite opposition, and as a result of a struggle, comes to win or lose—so why can't you write one?

There is no experience quite so humbling and disheartening as the inevitable creative slump that arrives in the middle of writing your novel. It's the price you pay for your hubris. You're in the doldrums now, adrift, and you're starting to panic because you've invested so much time and energy, and you'd hate to see it all go to waste. (It won't, of course, because everything you write today informs everything you will ever write. But that's no consolation because right now you're thinking you may never write again.)

Your confidence flags, your resolve weakens. You're losing faith in your material. You're intimidated by the magnitude of the undertaking, shamed by your vaulting ambition. What had seemed like an exciting and noble endeavor now seems foolish and impossible. And so you put pressure on yourself, which leads to your reliance on habitual thinking and rational problem solving, neither of which will get your novel written. Because a novel is not a quadratic equation. You're not solving for *x*.

This setback is part of the process. So relax. Remember that no matter how much you have revised and polished as you've been going along, if you haven't reached the end—and you haven't—you're still writing a first draft. And first drafts are explorations and are for your eyes only. Don't expect to get it right; just try to get it written. Expecting too much from an early draft results in frustration and disappointment. You write a first draft in order to have something to revise. It will be a failure. Writers are the ones who don't let failure stop them.

Beginnings are relatively easy because they come out of nowhere. You start writing before you even know where you're going. And even endings can seem to write themselves, following as they do on preceding events and having nothing to foreshadow. It's here in the middle where things get dicey. The muddle in the middle is what separates writers from those who want to have written.

When you're mired like this, slog on! The only thing you can't do is stop. If you're lost, don't wait for rescue: No one's coming. Get moving! Write, don't think! If your car won't start, you don't go back into the house, have a coffee, read the paper, stroll back out and expect the engine to fire. No, you look under the hood. You get your hands dirty. So let's look under the hood.

1. PUT IT IN PARK

First, this might be a good time to take a short break from your manuscript. Try this: Reread a novel by an author you admire, if for no other reason than to remind yourself of the significance, beauty, and nobility of what you're trying to do. It's your favorite novel or it's the novel that made you want to be a writer in the first place. Read with a pen in your hand and take notes on scenes, characters, language, point of view, and so on. Keep a list of everything this writer did that you can emulate in your novel. When you finish reading, write down what you've learned from the novel and what you will apply to your writing. And then get back to work.

2. RECHARGE THE BATTERY

Turn your attention back to your own work-in-progress. What you need in order to persevere is enthusiasm. You have to be excited again by your characters and themes, and by the nut of the nascent narrative. You should enjoy and relish what it was in your characters that first aroused your fervor, the qualities that struck you about them and to which you felt your enthusiasm respond from the get-go. Any time you start to feel your creative spirits fade, stop and remember why you started this journey in the first place: You wanted to get to know these people who intrigued you. What was so beguiling about them? Why were you fascinated? Go there. If you don't already have a notebook where you record notes for your work, designate one now, and write your answers to all these questions in its pages.

3. RUN DIAGNOSTICS

Now it's time to dig deeper. Ask yourself why you're bogged down, and answer honestly—in writing.

Maybe you think you don't know your hero well enough to know what she'll do next. Well, here's your chance to spend some time with her. Ask her what's on her mind, and write down what she tells you. Are you buying it? Is she holding back? Why would she do that? Ask her to tell you something about herself that you don't know, a secret about a secret. Ask the questions provoked by her revelation, and answer those questions as specifically as you can. Send her on a trip. Where does she choose to go? Why there? Does she travel alone or with someone? Talk about movies, discuss politics, gossip about the other characters in the novel. Ask her, "Why do *you* think Bob hasn't returned your call?"

Or maybe you think what you're writing about is not important enough, and irrelevance is giving you an excuse to quit. You don't *care* whodunit anymore! Not so fast. Return to your notebook. Write about what keeps you up at night, what you're afraid of, what you don't want to know about yourself. Write about what you're ashamed of. If you think there is evil in the world, give that evil a shape. Write about what makes the world a miserable place. And then, once you've realized that you do care after all, work what you've unearthed into your draft.

Another common reason for stalling midnovel is that not knowing the ending is making you crazy. The key is to recognize that often the ending is implicit in the beginning. Go back to your opening chapter and see if you've left yourself any clues. Then make an exhaustive list of possible endings. Pick the most surprising one and write toward it, staying flexible as you go.

4. TAKE A TEST-DRIVE

Start reading your manuscript, beginning with your opening scene, and look for moments there that are begging for embellishment, exploration, and resonance, for opportunities that you wrote into the scenes but have yet to exploit. Now you get to open those scenes up, not close them down. Often these moments are those when you were surprised by what a character did or said. Or there might be something, an image, a notion, a theme that you started in the opening that fades away, fails to resonate. You need to see where you might reintroduce that something.

Take note of places where you forget you're reading and enter the world of your book—the parts that are working. Examining the good passages will help you strengthen the weak ones.

Each time you read the manuscript over, you'll see something new. Note the thematic connections, the narrative tangents. Listen to your story. Listen with a pen in your hand and jot down notes. What is the novel trying to tell you?

5. REV THE ENGINE

Every novelist is a troublemaker, so make some trouble. Follow Raymond Chandler's advice and bring in a man with a gun. Actually any weapon will do. Your man with a gun might, in fact, be a teenage girl armed with sarcasm. Or a golden retriever that lopes up to your hero with a human foot in its mouth. As you write about what happens next, you're looking for moments that are beyond what you thought was going on in your book. Let the phone ring at three in the morning and have your hero answer and get the alarming news. Or maybe he's in his doctor's office, and the doctor closes the door, sits back in her chair, picks up the results of the biopsy, taps the file on the desk, clears her throat.

Ask yourself what else could possibly go wrong in your hero's life—his car breaks down; he loses his health insurance; his child is caught dealing dope; he's falsely accused of a crime; his mom's been in an accident—any of the trouble you've had in your life or that you are afraid will happen to you or to someone you love. That's exactly what makes a plot compelling—things that you would not want your family to suffer through.

6. KEEP IT RUNNING

Now it dawns on you that writing a novel is itself very much a plot. Novels are about characters who want something. And you want something, too—to understand the lives of your own characters, which means resolving the trouble in your protagonist's life, which means completing the novel—and you want it intensely. If you don't finish, your life will be significantly diminished. And so you pursue your goal and battle every obstacle, not the least of which is your lack of confidence, your obstructionist tendencies, the world calling for your attention, the chaos of the characters' lives, those elusive words, the befuddling muddle, and so on. You sit day after day. You struggle and at last you finish your novel. Plot's resolved.

JOHN DUFRESNE is a fiction teacher and author of *Is Life Like This? A Guide to Writing Your First Novel in Six Months.* as well as several novels and short-story collections.

CHAPTER 37

KEEP YOUR STORY MOVING AT THE RIGHT PACE

BY JESSICA PAGE MORRELL

Pacing is a tool that controls the speed and rhythm at which a story is told and the readers are pulled through the events. It refers to how fast or slow events in a piece unfold and to how much time elapses in a scene or story. Pacing can also be used to show characters aging and the effects of time on story events.

Pacing differs with the specific needs of a story. A far-reaching epic will often be told at a leisurely pace, though it will speed up from time to time during the most intense events. A short story or adventure novel might quickly jump into action and deliver drama. Pacing is part structural choices and part word choices, and uses a variety of devices to control how fast the story unfolds.

When driving a manual transmission car, you choose the most effective gear needed for driving uphill, maneuvering city streets, or cruising down a freeway. Similarly, when pacing your story, you need to choose the devices that move each scene along at the right speed.

DEVICES FOR SPEEDING THINGS UP

You need speed in the opening, middle, and climax of your story. Sure, you'll slow down from time to time, especially to pause for significance and to express characters' emotions, but those times will usually appear just before or after a joyride of skin-tightening speed.

There are lots of tools to hasten your story. Some are better suited for micropacing—that is, line by line—and some are better suited for macropacing—pacing the story as a whole. Let's take a closer look at each device.

- **ACTION.** Action scenes are where you "show" what happens in a story, and, when written in short- and medium-length sentences, they move the story along. Action scenes contain few distractions, little description, and limited transitions. Omit or limit character thoughts, especially in the midst of danger or crisis, since during a crisis people focus solely on survival. To create poignancy, forgo long, descriptive passages and choose a few details that serve as emotionally charged props instead.
- **CLIFF HANGERS.** When the outcome of a scene or chapter is left hanging, the pace naturally picks up because the reader will turn the page to find out what happens next. Readers both love and hate uncertainty, and your job is to deliver plenty of unfinished actions, unfilled needs, and interruptions. Remember, cliff hangers don't necessarily mean that you're literally dangling your character from a rooftop as the scene ends. If your characters are in the midst of a conversation, end the scene with a revelation, threat, or challenge.
- **DIALOGUE.** Rapid-fire dialogue with little or no extraneous information is swift and captivating, and will invigorate any scene. The best dialogue for velocity is pared down, an abbreviated copy of real-life conversation that snaps and crackles with tension. It is more like the volleying of Ping-Pong or tennis than a long-winded discussion. Reactions, descriptions, and attributions are minimal. Don't create dialogue exchanges where your characters discuss or ponder. Instead, allow them to argue, confront, or engage in a power struggle.
- **PROLONGED OUTCOMES.** Suspense and, by extension, forward movement are created when you prolong outcomes. While it

may seem that prolonging an event would slow down a story, this technique actually increases the speed, because the reader wants to know if your character is rescued from the mountainside, if the vaccine will arrive before the outbreak decimates the village, or if the detective will solve the case before the killer strikes again.

- **SCENE CUTS**. Also called a jump cut, a scene cut moves the story to a new location and assumes the reader can follow without an explanation of the location change. The purpose is to accelerate the story, and the characters in the new scene don't necessarily need to be the characters in the previous scene.

- **A SERIES OF INCIDENTS IN RAPID SUCCESSION**. Another means of speeding up your story is to create events that happen immediately one after another. Such events are presented with minimal or no transitions, leaping via scene cuts from scene to scene and place to place.

- **SHORT CHAPTERS AND SCENES**. Short segments are easily digested and end quickly. Since they portray a complete action, the reader passes through them quickly, as opposed to being bogged down by complex actions and descriptions.

- **SUMMARY**. Instead of a play-by-play approach, tell readers what has already happened. Because scenes are immediate and sensory, they require many words to depict. Summary is a way of trimming your word count and reserving scenes for the major events. You can also summarize whole eras, descriptions, and backstory. Summaries work well when time passes but there is little to report, when an action is repeated or when a significant amount of time has passed.

- **WORD CHOICE AND SENTENCE STRUCTURE**. The language itself is the subtlest means of pacing. Think concrete words (like prodigy and iceberg), active voice (with potent verbs like zigzag and plunder), and sensory information that's artfully embedded. If you write long, involved paragraphs, try breaking them up.

Fragments, spare sentences, and short paragraphs quicken the pace. Crisp, punchy verbs, especially those with onomatopoeia (*crash, lunge, sweep, scatter, ram, scavenge*) also add to a quick pace. Invest in suggestive verbs to enliven descriptions, build action scenes and milk suspense.

Harsh consonant sounds such as those in words like *claws, crash, kill, quake,* and *nag* can push the reader ahead. Words with unpleasant associations can also ratchet up the speed: *hiss, grunt, slither, smarmy, venomous, slaver,* and *wince.* Energetic, active language is especially appropriate for building action scenes and suspense, and for setting up drama and conflict.

A fast pace means trimming every sentence of unnecessary words. Eliminate prepositional phrases where you don't need them: For example, "the walls of the cathedral" can be written as "the cathedral's walls." Finally, search your story for passive linking verbs and trade them in for active ones.

DEVICES FOR SLOWING THINGS DOWN

If your story zips ahead at full speed all the time, it might fizzle under this excess. There are plenty of times and reasons for slowing down, especially to emphasize a moment so readers can experience its emotional impact. There are also times when a sedate or dignified pace is called for, or you want to build a scene slowly to maximize the payoff. Readers want to relish lovemaking or wedding scenes, especially if they come after hundreds of pages of the characters being too afraid of their feelings to venture into the bedroom or walk down the aisle. Readers also want to spend time at celebrations, funerals, and births, and with characters who are gossiping or struggling with decisions.

Your job is to vary moods, tension, and pace. Readers don't want to feel intense emotions throughout the story. Too much intensity (and violence) creates a kind of shell shock—readers shut down their emotions as a self-protective measure. Provide readers with slower moments where emotional highs and lows can be savored. Here are the perfect tools for just that:

- **DESCRIPTION.** Description is an important tool for causing a reader to linger amid the story world. But there is a fine line between just the right amount of description and overkill. When possible, put description in motion, as when a character is walking or driving through a place.
- **DISTRACTIONS.** There are times when you want to distract the reader with small actions, such as a character cooking or gardening, or with weather or setting details. Distractions can be used to engage your reader's emotions. In the middle of an emotionally charged or pivotal scene, give your character another task, such as applying makeup or looking out the window.
- **EXPOSITION.** Exposition breaks away from action to dispense information. It can provide context and perspective, such as biographical or geographical information, character descriptions, and time references. Because straightforward exposition is so slow, trim it down to the essentials. Blend in facts. Delivering exposition via dialogue, when it's not stilted, can accelerate the pace.
- **FLASHBACKS.** Flashbacks halt the momentum of the front story. They can be risky because they can slow the story too much or too often. If flashbacks go on for pages or are not clearly linked to front-story events, they can be especially troublesome. Deliberately place flashbacks to pause and add insights.
- **INTROSPECTION.** A viewpoint character's thoughts or musings are another device for slowing a scene. Avoid putting

thoughts in quotation marks or making references, such as, "Marty thought long and hard about what do next." Instead slip the thoughts in without announcing their presence, so they mimic the character's dialogue and reflect his mood.

- **ONE STEP FORWARD, ONE STEP BACK.** Protagonists need to stumble, make mistakes, experience reversals, and hit dead ends. If your protagonist succeeds again and again, the story becomes both predictable and too quickly paced. Troubles and setbacks slow the pace, increase suspense, and keep readers interested.

- **SEQUELS.** A sequel is the aftermath of an action scene. Sequels are staged so your character can sort through her feelings, assess the changing situation, and make decisions about what to do next. Not every scene requires a sequel, but if characters never react to events or devise plans for the future, the story will feel episodic and lack depth.

- **WORD CHOICE AND SENTENCE STRUCTURE.** You can also slow down a story on a word-by-word and sentence-by-sentence basis. Think of the texture of sentences and call on all the senses for your purposes. In soft-sounding words, especially verbs (*soothe, simper, stroke*), the soft *s* and vowels slow the pace. Repetition, lengthy sentences, and long paragraphs also slacken the speed.

JESSICA PAGE MORRELL is a writing coach, freelance editor, corporate trainer, columnist, and author of *Between the Lines*.

REVISING TO IMPROVE PACE

One of your first editing tasks is to make certain your story contains all the scenes and information necessary to tell the tale, and to be sure the pacing is varied and fast enough to hold the reader's interest. Use these tools to improve your pace as you revise:

- Evaluate the length of your flashbacks. You want to enter a flashback at the last possible moment, then leave as quickly as you can.
- Analyze individual scenes that drag. Try tightening the dialogue and adjusting the tension by adding surprises and tweaking details.
- Examine the plot for places where you can withhold or delay the release of information the reader needs to know. This can increase suspense and accelerate the pace.
- Scrutinize your final scenes, making certain they are trimmed of extraneous information and don't introduce new characters.
- Make certain you have not used too many short sentences, because when overused, they act like a series of speed bumps, slowing the story.
- Heighten the emotional impact of scenes and influence the pace of your story by using imagery, symbols and metaphor.

CHAPTER 38

PUT YOUR FICTION TO THE PLAUSIBILITY TEST

BY STEVE ALMOND

I'm afraid I'll have to start my discussion of plausibility with a student story that remains vivid to me after some five years.

I should preface my thoughts by noting how generally awesome my students are. The notion that a 21-year-old would even attempt to write a short story, let alone subject such work to the unpredictable blandishments of a workshop, strikes me as ridiculously courageous. I didn't work up the nerve to write fiction until I was nearly thirty.

There's very little a student can do in a story that would actually make me angry. But I do get, uh, frustrated when I feel a student is failing to take his characters seriously on some level. The chief symptom being that I just stop believing them. They, and their world, become implausible.

This brings me to the story in question (I've forgotten the title), which was about a teenager named John who tries—and fails—to commit suicide. He wakes up in a hospital with his brother by his side.

The following things then happen:

1. John begins wisecracking with his brother.
2. His brother describes John's suicide note as "funny."
3. A nurse appears and treats John with blistering scorn.
4. His brother jokingly threatens to "tell mom and dad" about the suicide attempt.

5. John and his brother sneak out of the hospital.
6. John commits suicide.

I'm not sure where to start.

There are technical implausibilities (the story is told from John's perspective, and yet he winds up dead) and practical ones (the authorities would be legally bound to inform the parents, and John would be placed on suicide watch). But more disturbing are the emotional issues. Would John and his brother actually crack wise in the wake of a suicide attempt serious enough to require hospitalization? Would a nurse verbally abuse him?

Of course, John and his brother might engage in sardonic banter as a way of keeping their true feelings at bay. But the story contains no trace of those true feelings. The story is a tragedy posing as a farce.

COMMON PLAUSIBILITY FLAWS

The question of plausibility is central when it comes to fiction. Can you induce the reader to believe? More precisely, to suspend her disbelief?

All readers come to fiction as willing accomplices to your lies. Such is the basic goodwill contract made the moment we pick up a work of fiction. We know Elizabeth Bennet isn't a real person. But because Jane Austen describes her world (both internal and external) with such fidelity and elegance, Ms. Bennet comes to feel real.

If the reader stops believing, even for an instant, you've broken the spell. As I suggested earlier, there are several common types of plausibility flaws that can cause this.

FACTUAL: Simply put, you don't do your research. You place the Grand Canyon in Nevada. Or you write a story about an indigenous Amazonian culture based on "a cool article" you read a decade ago that's now hopelessly outdated. These are mistakes born of laziness (my favorite attribute!) that are relatively easy to correct.

LOGISTICAL: Here the problem isn't research but an insufficient immersion in the fictional world. If your hero is a poverty-stricken dreamer, that kindly bank officer simply isn't going to lend him money—no matter how much you'd like him to.

TECHNICAL: These flaws are the result of basic misunderstandings about craft. If your story is written from the point of view of a sexually frustrated mailman—as so many of mine are—your narrator can't suddenly leap into the mind of his ex-wife without losing the reader.

EMOTIONAL/PSYCHOLOGICAL: This is by far the most serious breach of plausibility, and the most common. The question here is motivation: why your characters do the things they do. The essential failure of the story about suicidal John is that the author never provided us any sense of why the kid wanted to take his life. John acted not because he had a complex, tortured internal life, but because the author made him act. He wasn't a person. He was a puppet.

And it's not enough to tell the reader about a character's feelings. We must be made to share in those feelings. The key to ensuring a reader's undying devotion is to implicate him in the fears and desires of your characters. The unnerving power of a novel such as *Lolita* is that we conspire in Humbert Humbert's illicit (and illegal) passion for his pubescent paramour.

SECRETS TO SUSPENDING DISBELIEF

This is all fine and well, but isn't there a risk to fretting over plausibility—namely that you inhibit your imagination? What about magical realism or science fiction? What about those stories that joyously throw conventional reality out the window?

I say more power to them, actually.

One of my favorite books on Earth is Kurt Vonnegut's *Slaughterhouse-Five*. It's a book about the horrors of war, specifically the firebombing of Dresden during World War II. But it's predicated on the premise that our hero, Billy Pilgrim, has become "unstuck in time" after being abducted by space aliens.

Clearly Vonnegut didn't give a damn about "plausibility" in his books, right?

Wrong. Vonnegut goes to great pains to ensure that the alternate world he's constructed is believable. We learn about the aliens, their physiology and moral philosophy, why they've come to Earth and why they've chosen to abduct Billy. Billy's life on Earth is portrayed in meticulous and convincing detail.

The same is true of the remarkable Gabriel García Márquez short story "A Very Old Man with Enormous Wings." The triggering event is the appearance of a very old man with enormous wings who falls from the sky and lands in a small village. Márquez provides no final explanation for this event. But what's most important is that the villagers treat the event as real, a source of genuine bafflement and wonder.

The lesson is this: Readers will happily suspend their disbelief (even in the face of space aliens and angels) if they feel their emotional and logistical questions have been addressed, and if the world they encounter feels internally consistent. In the end, plausibility in fictionisn't about adhering to the facts of the known world but the imagined world.

This should be taken as a cause for liberation, but not a license to indulge in feckless motivations, absurd plot twists, and too-convenient coincidences. We get enough of those from Hollywood. Writers of literary fiction have a sworn duty to pursue the truth, even (and especially) when it involves lying through their teeth.

STEVE ALMOND is a short story writer and essayist and is author of 8 books including *Not that You Asked.*

EXERCISES

1. Look at a draft of your most recent story. Compile a list of the assertions you're asking your readers to accept. Do any feel shaky? How might they be made more solid?
2. Think about your favorite piece of science fiction or magical realism. Consider the ways in which the author has tried to

preserve internal consistency. How can you apply them to your own work?

3. Think about a recent Hollywood film you found unbelievable. Make a list of the moments where you "stopped believing," and why. (Action/adventure movies are best for this exercise.)
4. Write a realistic scene in which a supernatural event occurs. What measures do you have to take to ensure plausibility?

CHAPTER 39

TRANSFORM THAT OUT-OF-SHAPE FIRST DRAFT

BY LIN ENGER

Novelists are the distance runners, the long-haul truckers, the transoceanic captains of the literary world. There is no sprinting through a novel, at least not for the novelist; there are simply too many characters, too many scenes, too many story lines and pages and sentences to be written—and then rewritten, revised, and polished. Endurance is key to completing the task. Yet endurance is not enough, not nearly. Because *reading* the novel is also a marathon experience, and that means the primary goal of your revision process should be to take pains to create a human pace for the reader, a pace that alternately rushes, strides, saunters, and lingers, according to the story's—and the reader's—needs. It's no small task to keep those narrative wheels rolling, but that's what you have to do, all the way from the title page to *The End.*

As a novelist, you need concrete strategies to sustain you on that long haul—and to transform your first draft into a work that can stand up to the task. Here are four rules you can use to make sure your readers won't fall asleep, burn out, or just give up before they finish the final chapter of your masterpiece.

1. WRITE THE WHOLE FIRST DRAFT FIRST—AND FAST

This first rule deals not so much with revision, but with resisting the impulse to revise as you write. This is difficult in large part because it means forgiving yourself for writing terrible prose. There's no way around it. Fast means sloppy—sloppy diction, syntax, grammar. Any damage suffered by your writer's ego, however, will come at a small cost compared to the benefits gained.

Truth is, a quickly written draft produces a narrative with a clean trajectory. Think of it as a carpenter's chalk line, the graph of your story's arc. Your characters might remain undercooked and your subplots unexplored in this first go-through, but in working fast you have little choice but to hew close to the basic story line. As a result, you're saved from the tempting side trails and seductive tangents that can derail your progress. (You can come back to those later, when your task is to spice up and thicken your characters and plot, to pursue all of their wonderful complications.)

Here's the point: Once you've blasted through to the end of a book, you have a much better sense of what belongs in the beginning and middle sections. And to your great advantage you won't have wasted your time writing, revising, and polishing unnecessary scenes that will only end up on the cutting-room floor.

How fast is fast, you ask? Depends on the writer. My natural habit is to work slowly, but I wrote the first draft of my current manuscript in six months, an hour a day, five or six days a week. My objective was to write two pages each time I sat down, not so daunting a task once I absolved myself in advance for committing every writer's sin there is, many times, in every session. If you do the same—if you dedicate yourself to writing without self-editing—you'll be amazed at how soon that draft is finished. Then it's time for the rewrite, starting with the element that will sustain your readers on their own marathon: the action.

2. EVALUATE THE DRAMATIC FUNCTION OF EVERY SCENE OR UNIT OF ACTION

Readers can tell if a passage fails to advance the story in some way. If that's the case, they begin to skim, or worse, they toss the book aside. Therefore the best way to start revising is to begin rereading your first draft and ask yourself this essential question at the opening of every chapter or scene: "What exactly happens here, and how does it surprise my character or offer some new perception to the reader?" Be sure every dramatized incident, whatever it is a fight, a conversation, or merely a silent moment in which a character ponders some issue—moves the story to a new place. When you find scenes that don't, you've found the first targets of your revision.

In Kent Haruf's *Plainsong,* a small-town Colorado teacher goes out to visit a pair of old bachelor farmers/brothers and stuns them (and the readers, too) by asking if they'd be willing to take in a high school girl who's been kicked out of her home because she's pregnant. The two old men, understandably, are struck dumb. It's a lively scene, and the teacher's request sets into motion a key element of the novel's plot.

The next passage, however, is quiet. The teacher has left the farmhouse kitchen, and the two men put on their coats and go outside into the winter night to fix a broken water heater. An entire page is spent describing how they chop free the heater from ice that's formed in the water tank and how they relight the pilot—nearly 300 words during which the men don't say one thing to each other! Nor does the narrator offer insight into their thoughts. Can such a passage justify itself? Listen to how it ends and to how Haruf transitions into the inevitable conversation:

> So for a while they stood below the windmill in the failing light. The thirsty horses approached and peered at them and sniffed at the water and began to drink, sucking up long draughts of it. Afterward they stood back watching the two brothers, their eyes as large and luminous as perfect round knobs of mahogany glass.

It was almost dark now. Only a thin violet band of light showed in the west on the low horizon.

> All right, Harold said. I know what I think. What do you think we do with her?

The passage in question may not advance the plot directly, but it does demonstrate the particular way these brothers communicate with each other: silently, through side-by-side labor. Also, its evocative language makes us feel as if the horses themselves are grateful, a feeling the reader—consciously or not—brings to the discussion the brothers are about to have concerning the girl.

Scenes don't have to be highly dramatic in order to perform valuable work. Yet it's important that you examine them one by one, satisfying yourself that each will deepen your readers' connection to the story and urge them to turn the page.

Failing that test, scenes need to be cut—or reworked until they pass.

3. IDENTIFY LULLS IN ACTION WHERE YOU CAN INSERT MINI SCENES

As novels progress, they inevitably alternate between the modes of scene and summary. Scenes, of course, depict moments of decision and high emotion, turning points that demand a full dramatic rendering, complete with dialogue, action, and vivid descriptions. But intervening periods of time, lulls between episodes of heavy weather, character histories, and complicated relationships also must be accounted for. Summaries—long passages of exposition—are a necessary evil. (All that densely packed prose, with no white space for the eye to rest upon!)

One way to help your readers persevere through spots where the pacing lags is to spice up the passages with bits of live action, with mini scenes.

In the first chapter of Jon Hassler's *Staggerford,* the narrator spends pages describing a typical day in the life of Miles Pruitt, a high school English instructor—a tedious approach had Hassler not interjected several mini-scenes into the long summary. Notice how smoothly Hassler moves from exposition to a moment of dry humor. All it requires is a single transitional sentence with the marker *had* indicating the shift backward in time:

> William Mulholland was in this class. In the Staggerford Public Library every book having to do with physics, chemistry, statistics, or any other sort of cold-blooded calculation contained on its check-out card the name William Mulholland. ... Only once had he spoken in this class. On the opening day of school Miles, taking roll, had said, "Bill Mulholland."
>
> "My name is William," he replied.

Toni Morrison uses a similar strategy throughout *Beloved,* a novel with a complex structure and wide scope that requires frequent use of summary. In this passage Sethe, a former slave, is reminiscing about her lost husband, Halle, and about other slaves she knew on the plantation. Morrison doesn't use transitional language at all. She simply plugs in a bit of uttered speech:

> Hidden behind honeysuckle she watched them. How different they were without her, how they laughed and played and urinated and sang. All but Sixo, who laughed once—at the very end. Halle, of course, was the nicest. Baby Suggs' eighth and last child, who rented himself out all over the country to buy her away from there. But he too, as it turned out, was nothing but a man.
>
> "A man ain't nothing but a man," said Baby Suggs. "But a son? Well now, that's somebody."

Be on the alert, then, in your own work for long paragraphs consisting of backstory, physical description, and character analysis. The information in such passages may be necessary, but unless you sprinkle in memorable scenic elements—snippets of dialogue, little clips of movement— your readers might lose patience.

4. VARY YOUR METHODS OF BEGINNING CHAPTERS

Chapter breaks and other pauses allow readers to catch their breath, ponder what they've read, and anticipate what might be coming next. As you revise your novel, don't miss the opportunity to look at them collectively and make sure you're offering a variety of chapter kickoffs to pique your readers. Sometimes you'll want to give them what they expect—but a good novelist walks the line between keeping readers comfortable and making them crazy, so other times it's best to startle them.

The most common method of getting a chapter started, one that takes readers by the hand and gently guides them into the next section of the story, is to position a character in time and instantly establish the dramatic situation. There's nothing flashy about this strategy, but it gets the job done.

> On the morning of the twenty-second I wakened with a start. Before I opened my eyes, I seemed to know that something had happened. I heard excited voices in the kitchen—grandmother's was so shrill that I knew she must be almost beside herself.
>
> —Willa Cather, Chapter 14 of *My Ántonia*

> After Ty left, it took me half an hour to get myself down to my father's.
>
> —Jane Smiley, Chapter 16 of *A Thousand Acres*

Another method sketches out a period of time, rendering its mood and general character as a way to place coming events into context. Use this strategy when your novel calls for a moment of reflection, requires a bit of backstory, or needs to make a chronological leap forward. Here's a writer at his evocative best:

> There was music from my neighbor's house through the summer nights. In his blue gardens men and girls came and went like moths among the whisperings and the champagne and the stars.
>
> —F. Scott Fitzgerald, Chapter 3 of *The Great Gatsby*

Other times, though—especially following chapters that move at a leisurely pace—you'll feel the need to shake things up, toss readers in over their heads, pitch them a curve. In other words, crank up the speed a notch or two. In my novel *Undiscovered Country*, chapter 13 begins with the appearance of the narrator's dead father in a moment for which neither the narrator nor the reader is prepared.

> This time he didn't smell like gunpowder and beeswax, but instead like he'd smelled on those nights when he got home late from closing and came into my room to check on me. ... He always reeked of cigarettes from his night at the Valhalla, but there was also a hint of his spearmint toothpaste and the soap he was partial to, a tangy brown bar soap peppered with mysterious black granules. It was this combination of smells that made me glance up now into the rearview mirror as Charlie and I neared the edge of town.
>
> Dad was in the backseat watching me.

Finally, a clever way to open a chapter is to offer some pithy observation that bears directly upon the events unfolding. My brother Leif Enger uses this method to good effect in his novel, *So Brave, Young, and Handsome.*

> Violence seldom issues a warning ...
>
> —from chapter 7

> It's an old business, it turns out, this notion that learning a person's true name gives you leverage ...
>
> —from chapter 4

Or consider this gem from Leo Tolstoy, at the opening of *Anna Karenina*:

> Happy families are all alike; every unhappy family is unhappy in its own way.

Remember that every new chapter offers the opportunity to reintroduce your story and reorient your readers to the world of your novel. So as you revise, be strategic with your chapter openings. Your efforts will stave off reader complacency and give your novel the chance to hook your readers again and again.

Are these all strategies you could employ while you write the first draft? I don't think so. It's not until you can stand back and look at that draft as a cohesive whole that you will be able to apply these rules effectively and give your manuscript the revision it requires.

Writing and revising a novel means hard work, months or years of it—all the more reason to keep your readers' needs at the forefront of your mind as you're working. The time and energy invested in your novel doesn't come to an end, after all, once you revise the last page, or even after the manuscript has been edited, produced, and published—because, finally, your readers pour *themselves* into it, lay their own claims to it. Keeping this in mind should inspire you to fashion novels that are enjoyable yet challenging, familiar yet surprising, and as free of unnecessary hindrances as you can make them.

LIN ENGER is the author of *Undiscovered Country*. He's won a James Michener Fellowship and a Minnesota State Arts Board Fellowship.

FOCUS ON THE WRITING LIFE:

GETTING PUBLISHED

SELLING YOUR FICTION

BY THE EDITORS OF WRITER'S DIGEST

After ten years of writing, Janet Evanovich decided to get serious about getting published. She had three novels written, all of which "had been sent to and rejected by a seemingly endless round of publishing houses and agents," she says. So she decided to abandon those projects—"big, bizarre books"—and try her hand at genre writing. Her first effort was rejected, but the second manuscript was accepted, and she was on her way to becoming the best-selling author of the Stephanie Plum mystery series. Rather than viewing the similarities of genre fiction as restrictions against creativity, Evanovich saw them more as the parameters of publication, and now her books regularly debut at the top of the best-seller lists.

Science fiction writer Walter H. Hunt waited fourteen years for his novel, *The Dark Wing*, to see publication. Written in the late 1980s, the book was sent to several speculative fiction houses—Ace Book, Baen, Warner, and others—and rejected, usually because the timing was wrong. "We like the book, but it isn't what we're doing right now," was a frequent comment from editors. But Hunt's patience paid off. "I waited fourteen years for the same editor to get a position at science fiction publisher Tor Books," he says. *The*

Dark Wing was published in 2001, followed by *The Dark Path*, *The Dark Ascent*, and *The Dark Crusade*. Hunt has finally found his readership.

As both Evanovich's and Hunt's experiences demonstrate, there are few straight paths to getting your fiction published. The process is fraught with circumstances a writer cannot control. Editors change publishing houses or get laid off. A short story from the slush pile too closely resembles another one just acquired. Imprints fold. Editorial focus changes. All of these circumstances and more can conspire to keep a manuscript from finding an editorial home. To increase your likelihood of success (publication!), it is important that you focus on the elements of the process a writer *can* control—the mechanics of fiction submission.

SELLING YOUR SHORT STORIES

As you probably know, the competition for publishing short fiction is fierce, and the days when a fiction writer could earn a respectable living writing short stories are long gone. Only a select few "slick" magazines today even publish literary short fiction (think *The New Yorker*, *Harper's*, *GQ*, *Esquire*, *Playboy*, and *The Atlantic*), and to get an acceptance letter from one of these publications you'll need to be writing at the level of the late John Updike. Traditional markets for more mainstream short fiction—swamped by a heavy volume of submissions—either do not accept unsolicited submissions or have quit publishing short stories altogether.

On the other hand, magazines that do publish fiction are always hungry for new voices, and if you're willing to investigate the field, you'll find there are still healthy markets out there for all types of short fiction, including short shorts and the interactive fiction called hypertext. Another encouraging development in the field is the proliferation of online magazines and journals. Finding paper costs high and subscription numbers too low to sustain production, many periodicals have either developed websites to complement their print publications or moved online altogether.

Research

One main key to selling to magazines and literary journals is reading them. You can tell a lot about an editor's sensibility by reading the short stories she chooses to publish and discerning whether or not your work is a good fit for that publication. It saves postage and time, and it'll increase your chances of publication because you'll end up targeting the right publications. Doing your research also gives you an opportunity to personally connect with an editor in your cover letter. Mentioning that you've taken the time to read a particular magazine or journal, and have found your work similar to the types of fiction they publish, will give you a definite edge over your competition in the slush pile.

It's also important to read several back issues of a publication you want to submit to, and keep track of editorial changes. Sometimes, a venerable literary publication can undergo a changing of editorial guard, and an incoming editor significantly changes the tone and feel of that magazine.

Find out what a magazine is looking for in fiction by checking its website. In addition, you can find detailed guidelines in market directories such as the annual *Novel & Short Story Writer's Market*. But your work is not finished once you've determined whether a publication wants romance, mystery, or literary short stories. It's not just what but how. With competition as fierce as in today's market, editors need methods for shrinking the slush pile, and one quick way is to reject outright any submission that doesn't follow guidelines. Writers are creative spirits, but in the submission process it's best to be an utter conformist and follow to the letter what an editor asks for in submissions. There are no bonus points for clever, attention-getting gimmicks. Pay attention to the details: What is the maximum word count? Does a publication accept multiple or simultaneous submissions, or neither? Will a journal accept electronic submissions? If not, does the editor want a disposable copy of the manuscript, or will she return yours? Do you need to enclose a self-addressed stamped envelope? The full list of particulars is long and important.

Jill Adams, editor of *The Barcelona Review*, says, "The best advice I can give is to read the guidelines carefully and take them seriously." Adams said she gets frustrated when writers ignore her electronic literary review's maximum word length of 4,000 words and send 10,000-word manuscripts, saying that they couldn't possibly cut the piece and retain its integrity. "Maybe not," Adams says. "But then it's not the story for our review, and my time—and the writer's—has been wasted."

Revise

Another major key to getting your short fiction published is remembering to revise. It can be easy in the afterglow of a finished story to want to rush it out into the world, to share your enthusiasm for your creation with readers. This is never a good idea. Phil Wagner, editor of the literary journal *The Iconoclast*, says, "Do all rewrites before sending a story out. Few editors have time to work with writers on promising stories; only polished."

Know that once you've finished your short story, what you have is a first draft, which Michael Seidman in *The Complete Guide to Editing Your Fiction* calls "your attempt to quarry a stone." A story can require an unlimited number of revisions to reach its full potential. Joyce Carol Oates is known to revise work of her own that has *already been published*. Give the manuscript time to become as polished as you can make it. Joining a writers' critique group can also be helpful. In addition to honors (and often cash prizes), contests offer writers the opportunity to be judged on the basis of quality alone, without the outside factors that sometimes influence publishing decisions. New writers who win contests may be published for the first time, while more experienced writers may gain recognition for an entire body of work.

Submit

When the story is ready and you've targeted a publication, it's time to submit. If you are submitting by e-mail, send a cover letter to the editor in question and note that you can send the story as an attachment if the editor requests it. This is now the standard method of submission, even for small publications, though there are some editors who still prefer an old-fashioned submission.

If that is the case, clip a brief cover letter to your short story and mail it to a specific editor, making sure your submission is addressed to the appropriate person. Because reading a flat page is simpler than one that's been folded in thirds and squashed into a business envelope, send submissions in a manila envelope, with a stamped, self-addressed return envelope. If the publication accepts e-mail submissions, follow the instructions carefully; sending an unreadable file is, obviously, self-defeating.

Cover letters are polite pieces of business correspondence simply acting as an introduction to your story. They should include the name of the story, a sentence or two on what it's about, its word count, a mention of why you're sending it to a particular magazine, and a paragraph about who you are. The cover letter won't make the sale. That depends on your story. But a sloppy or typo-ridden one can easily kill it.

Be prepared to be persistent, because magazines, online and on paper, report being inundated with submissions for fiction. At *The Barcelona Review*, only about one of the two hundred submissions it receives each month is accepted, and sometimes not that many. If your short story is sent back, send it out again. Always keep a copy for yourself and a record of where and when you sent it. A submission log can help you keep a record of where and when stories were sent, which were returned, editors' comments, and other pertinent information.

SELLING YOUR NOVEL

Finding a publisher for a novel is in many ways like finding a home for your short fiction—it's a matter of persistence, talent, and luck. Be aware that success is not easy in fiction. According to Donald Maass, literary agent and author of *Writing the Breakout Novel*, the discouraging fact is that "roughly two-thirds of all fiction purchases are made because the consumer is already familiar with the author."

Fiction readers gravitate toward novelists they already know and like, and it can be hard for a first timer to get a foot in the door.

Success may not be easy, but it is certainly not impossible. It involves first writing well, then researching publishers and agents, and then sending and resending material until it reaches someone who appreciates it as much as you do.

The Outlook

First-time novelists are well advised to learn what they can about changes in the publishing industry to understand how such changes might affect them. Before the book publishing industry became consolidated in the later part of the last century, editors established relationships with writers and cultivated their work. An editor had the time to recognize potential and coax out of the writer the best book he could produce. The writer-editor relationship was usually a long-term proposition, with the publishing company looking for its payoff later in the arc of a writer's career—on the third or fourth novel, say, when the writer began to fully realize his talent and develop a following.

Since that time, publishing houses have consolidated into roughly half a dozen major trade houses, including Simon & Schuster, Random House, HarperCollins, Macmillan, Penguin Group, and Hachette Book Group—all of which have numerous specialized imprints under their umbrellas. (Random House actually gives its sales reps a color flowchart explaining all of the different imprints like Bantam, Doubleday, Dell, Knopf, Harmony, WaterBrook, and so on.) Lots of analysis has been devoted to how these changes have altered the face of publishing and to the reasons behind these changes, but one thing is certain: At these houses, profit is king, and that has far-reaching ramifications for writers.

Editors at major houses do not have nearly the amount of time to spend with their writers as they used to. The result is what you may have heard called "the death of the midlist author," or a phenomenon in which blockbuster novelists continue to publish, and first-time authors are highly sought after as the next "big thing," but an author with a modestly selling first novel may well not get a second chance, at least not with her original publishing house. The publisher may want to make room in the list for a new author with breakout potential. This is actually good news for debut novelists, at least in the beginning of their careers. There is opportunity for writers with talent, determination, and no track record, who at least have the potential for a hit.

With an Agent

That said, it is increasingly difficult for a first-time writer to get a reading at one of the major New York houses without an agent. Unwieldy slush piles have caused the majority to decline unsolicited, unagented submissions, so in many cases you have to have an agent to even get in the door. There are obvious advantages to working with an agent. First, she will give you a leg up on finding the right editor for your manuscript. Agents are industry insiders who know the tastes of editors at both independent publishers and imprints of the big houses. Acting as business manager, an agent also handles contracts, rights negotiations, and royalties, which frees an author's time for writing. But of course it's a service you'll pay for—the average contract stipulates the agent earns 15 percent of your book's domestic sales, and the foreign sales percentage may be higher.

And Without

Many authors choose to work without an agent, and even with the closed nature of New York City's publishing houses, they can still succeed in going this route. Best-selling author Janet Fitch (*White Oleander*) chose to go it alone and sold her manuscript to the first editor she approached at Little, Brown. So it can happen either way. If you do choose not to work with an agent, remember you are your own business manager. You'll want to distance yourself from the passion of your writing and approach the submission process as completely different from the creative. You will need to precisely meet the submission specifications of each publisher you're sending your work to. This will accomplish the first and most important goal—it will increase your odds of getting your manuscript read. Don't make the novice's mistake of believing an editor will overlook sloppiness or inattention to detail to find the author is actually the creative heir to James Joyce. It just doesn't happen.

Research

When selling your novel, it is imperative that you research the markets thoroughly. Make a point to familiarize yourself with the industry by getting closer to it. Here are some ideas for educating yourself about the fiction publishing world.

- Regularly visit publishers' websites and review what titles are currently on their list, what titles are upcoming, and whether or not there are any changes that may affect how you submit your work (like a new imprint).
- Visit your public library and regularly read Publishers Weekly. You'll want to pay special attention to PW's First Fiction feature story every year, which highlights the success stories of debut novelists just like you. Who were their agents? Why did their novel hook an editor or agent?
- Check out the editors' blogs on www.writersdigest.com. These can be a great way to educate yourself, as the editors link to publishing news, discuss trends, and interview editors and agents.
- Sign up for the free version of Publishers Lunch, delivered every weekday to your e-mail in-box. (If you want more detail, you can also pay for a subscription to the full version of Publishers Lunch.)
- Bookstores also hold a wealth of information. Browse the stacks and familiarize yourself with the fiction being published today. What are you seeing a lot of? What is consistently popular? What trends are emerging?

- Booksellers can be wonderful resources for information about publishing trends.

Submit

Some book publishers want to see only a query first, but many want a letter with sample chapters, an outline, or sometimes even the complete manuscript. As we saw earlier, a query letter is the introduction of writer to editor or agent, but it is also a sales pitch. It tells enough about the book to intrigue the reader, mentions the title, offers the author's credentials and expertise, and asks for a chance to send in more of the manuscript.

Editors and agents say they look to the query not only for the idea, but also for a sense of how a writer uses words, and they say they usually can tell if a person cannot write simply by reading their letters or e-mails. When writers send an interesting query, Judith Shepard, editor-in-chief of The Permanent Press, says she also asks them to send the first twenty pages of the manuscript. "If someone wants to send me a query with the first twenty pages, that's more practical," she says. "What I prefer not to have, but what I get, are full manuscripts."

Before mailing or e-mailing anything, put yourself in the place of an editor. The Permanent Press, which publishes about twelve books a year, receives about seven thousand submissions annually. "We get so many submissions I almost hate to see the postman come," Shepard says. "But if someone is completely unknown, it's the letter that gets me. I'm very taken by the words that people use ... how people express themselves. I'm not as interested in the story line."

CRAFTING A FICTION PROPOSAL

As with nonfiction, there are several key elements to any strong fiction proposal.

Your Query Letter

Before you send the proposal, a query letter is your letter of inquiry. It serves two functions: to tell editors what you have to offer and to ask if they're interested in seeing it. Many editors prefer that you send the query letter either by itself or with a synopsis and a few sample pages from your novel. This is called a blind query or a proposal query, because you're sending it without having been asked to send it. No matter what you call it, it's your quick chance to hook the editor on your novel. If he likes your query, he'll e-mail back and ask for either specific parts of your novel proposal (a synopsis and sample chapters, for example) or the entire manuscript. Then he will decide.

Remember, your query letter is vital. You must make it compelling and interesting enough to hook your reader. Although every winning query works its own magic, all good queries should contain the following:

- A grabber, or hook, sentence that makes the reader want to get her hands on the actual novel.
- One to three paragraphs about your novel.
- A short paragraph about you and your publishing credentials (if you have any).
- A good reason why you're soliciting the person you're soliciting. Why this publisher instead of another?
- The length of the novel.
- A sentence or two about its intended audience.
- An indication that an SASE is enclosed, if you are not using e-mail.

Your Synopsis

If the publisher asks for a synopsis along with the query, you're lucky—you have another opportunity to hook an editor. The synopsis supplies key information about your novel (plot, theme, characterization, setting), while also showing how all these coalesce to form the big picture (your novel). You want to quickly tell what your novel is about without making the editor read the manuscript in its entirety. Remember that editors are extremely busy people. They are not going to want to read your entire manuscript, and if you send them a synopsis, you will get in their good graces by saving them valuable time.

There are no hard-and-fast rules about the synopsis. Some editors look at it as a one-page sales pitch, while others expect it to be a comprehensive summary of the entire novel. Many editors prefer a short synopsis that runs from one to two single-spaced pages, or three to five double-spaced pages. On the other hand, some plot-heavy fiction, such as thrillers and mysteries, may require more space and can run from ten to twenty-five double-spaced pages, depending on the length of the manuscript and the number of plot shifts. If you opt for a longer synopsis, aim for one synopsis page for every twenty-five manuscript pages. But try to keep it as short as possible.

When compiling your synopsis, be sure to include:

- A strong lead sentence.
- Logical paragraph organization.
- A concise expression of ideas with no repetition.
- An introduction of your main characters and their core conflicts.
- Plot high points.
- Narrative (third-person) writing in the present tense.
- Transitions between ideas.
- Strong verbs and minimal use of adjectives and adverbs.
- Correct punctuation and spelling.
- The story's conclusion. (Yes, you do need to give away the ending.)

Your Outline

An outline is often used interchangeably with a synopsis. For most editors, however, there is a distinction. While a synopsis is a brief, encapsulated version of the novel at large, an outline makes each chapter its own story, usually containing a few paragraphs per chapter. In short, you're breaking down the novel and synopsizing each chapter individually. Try to keep each chapter to about a page, and begin each new chapter on a different page.

Never submit an outline unless an editor asks for it. Fewer and fewer agents and editors want outlines these days. Most just request a cover or query letter, a few sample chapters, and a short synopsis. Outlines are most often requested by genre fiction editors, because genre books have numerous plot shifts.

In compiling your outline, keep in mind:

- Your outline is an extended, more detailed and structural version of your synopsis.
- Remember to explain how the plot and character development unfold in the chapter.
- Write in the present tense.
- Reveal how the chapter opens and ends.
- Make sure the chapters follow sequentially.
- Do not include dialogue or extended description.

APPENDIX A

FICTION GENRE DESCRIPTIONS

ACTION-ADVENTURE. Action is the key element (overshadowing characters) and involves a quest or military-style mission set in exotic or forbidding locales such as jungles, deserts, or mountains. The conflict typically involves spies, mercenaries, terrorists, smugglers, pirates, or other dark and shadowy figures.

BIOGRAPHICAL NOVEL. A life story documented in history and transformed into fiction through the insight and imagination of the writer. This type of novel melds the elements of biographical research and historical truth into the framework of a novel, complete with dialogue, drama, and mood. A biographical novel resembles historical fiction, except characters in a historical novel may be fabricated and then placed into an authentic setting; characters in a biographical novel have actually lived.

GOTHIC. Contemporary gothic novels are characterized by atmospheric, historical settings and feature young, beautiful women who win the favor of handsome, brooding heroes—simultaneously dealing successfully with some life-threatening menace, either natural or supernatural. Gothics rely on mystery, peril, romantic relationships, and a sense of foreboding for their strong, emotional effect on the reader. A classic early gothic novel is Emily Brontë's *Wuthering Heights*.

HISTORICAL FICTION. A fictional story set in a period of history. As well as telling the stories of ordinary people's lives, historical fiction may involve political or social events of the time.

HORROR. Howard Phillips (H.P.) Lovecraft, a master of the horror tale in the twentieth century, distinguished horror literature from fiction based entirely on physical fear and the merely gruesome. "The true weird tale has something more than secret murder, bloody bones, or a sheeted form clanking chains according to rule. A certain atmosphere of breathless and unexplainable dread of outer, unknown forces must be present; there must be a hint, expressed with a seriousness and portentousness becoming its subject, of that most terrible concept of the human brain—a malign and particular suspension or defeat of the fixed laws of Nature which are our only safeguards against the assaults of chaos and the daemons of unplumbed space." It is that atmosphere—the creation of a particular sensation or emotional level—that, according to Lovecraft, is the most important element in the creation of horror literature. Contemporary writers enjoying considerable success in horror fiction include Stephen King and Dean Koontz.

MYSTERY. A form of narration in which one or more elements remain unknown or unexplained until the end of the story. The modern mystery story contains elements of the serious novel: a convincing account of a character's struggle with various physical and psychological obstacles in an effort to achieve his goal, good characterization, and sound motivation.

POPULAR FICTION. Generally a synonym for category or genre fiction; that is, fiction intended to appeal to audiences of certain kinds of novels. Popular, or category, fiction is defined as such primarily for the convenience of publishers, editors, reviewers, and booksellers who must identify novels of different areas of interest for potential readers.

PSYCHOLOGICAL. A narrative that emphasizes the mental and emotional aspects of its characters, focusing on motivations and mental activities rather than on exterior events. The psychological novelist is less concerned about relating what happened than about exploring why it happened.

ROMAN À CLEF. The French term for "novel with a key." This type of novel incorporates real people and events into the story under the guise of fiction. Robert Penn Warren's *All the King's Men*, in which the character Willie Stark represents Huey Long, is a novel in this genre.

ROMANCE. The romance novel is a type of category fiction in which the love relationship between a man and a woman pervades the plot. The story is often told from the viewpoint of the heroine, who meets a man (the hero), falls in love with him, encounters a conflict that hinders their relationship, then resolves the conflict. Romance is the overriding element in this kind of story: The couple's relationship determines the plot and tone of the book, and the characters and plot both must be well-developed and realistic: Contrived situations and flat characters are unacceptable. Throughout a romance novel, the reader senses the sexual and emotional attraction between the heroine and hero.

SCIENCE FICTION AND FANTASY. Science fiction can be defined as literature involving elements of science and technology as a basis for conflict or as the setting for a story. The science and technology are generally extrapolations of existing scientific fact, and most science fiction stories take place in the future. There are other definitions of science fiction, and much disagreement in academic circles as to just what constitutes science fiction and what constitutes fantasy. This is because in some cases the line between science fiction and fantasy is virtually nonexistent. It is generally accepted that, to be science fiction, a story must have elements of science. Fantasy, on the other hand, rarely involves science, relying instead on magic and mythological beings.

Contemporary science fiction, while maintaining its focus on science and technology, is more concerned with the effects of science and technology on people. Since science is such an important factor in writing science fiction, accuracy with reference to science fact is important. Most of the science in science fiction is hypothesized from known facts, so in addition to being firmly based in fact, the extrapolations must be consistent.

TECHNO-THRILLER. This genre shares many of the same elements as the thriller, with one major difference. In techno-thrillers, technology becomes a major character, such as in Tom Clancy's *The Hunt for Red October.*

THRILLER. A novel intended to arouse feelings of excitement or suspense. Works in this genre are highly sensational, usually focusing on illegal activities, international espionage, sex, and violence. A thriller is often a detective story in which the forces of good are pitted against the forces of evil in a kill-or-be-killed situation.

MYSTERY SUBGENRES

CLASSIC MYSTERY (WHODUNIT). A crime (almost always a murder or series of murders) is solved. The detective is the viewpoint character; the reader never knows any more or less about the crime than the detective, and all the clues to solving the crime are available to the reader.

AMATEUR DETECTIVE. As the name implies, the detective is not a professional detective (private or otherwise) but is almost always a professional something. This professional association routinely involves the protagonist in criminal cases (in a support capacity), gives her a special advantage in a specific case, or provides the contacts and skills necessary to solve a particular crime. (Examples: Jonathan Kellerman, Patricia Cornwell)

COZY. A special class of the amateur detective category that frequently features a female protagonist (Agatha Christie's Miss Marple stories are the classic example). There is less onstage violence than in other categories, and the plot is often wrapped up in a final scene where the detective identifies the murderer and explains how the crime was solved. In contemporary stories, the protagonist can be anyone from a chronically curious housewife to a mystery-buff clergyman to a college professor, but she is usually quirky, even eccentric. (Examples: Susan Isaacs, Lillian Jackson Braun)

PRIVATE DETECTIVE. When described as hard-boiled, this category takes a tough stance. Violence is more prominent, characters are darker, the detective—while almost always licensed by the state—operates on the fringes of the law, and there is often open resentment between the detective and law enforcement. More "enlightened" male detectives and a crop of contemporary females have brought about new trends in this category. (For female P.I.s—Sue Grafton, Sara Paretsky; for male P.I.s—John D. MacDonald, Lawrence Sanders, Robert B. Parker)

POLICE PROCEDURALS. The most realistic category, these stories require the most meticulous research. A police procedural may have more than one protagonist, since cops rarely work alone. Conflict between partners, or between the detective and her superiors, is a common theme. But cops are portrayed positively as a group, even though there may be a couple of bad or ineffective law enforcement characters for contrast and conflict. Jurisdictional disputes are still popular sources of conflict as well. (Example: Ridley Pearson)

HISTORICAL. May be any category or subcategory of mystery, but with an emphasis on setting, the details of which must be diligently researched. But beyond the historical details (which must never overshadow the story), the plot develops along the lines of its contemporary counterpart. (Examples: Candace Robb, Caleb Carr, Anne Perry)

SUSPENSE/THRILLER. Where a classic mystery is always a whodunit, a suspense/thriller novel may deal more with the intricacies of the crime, what motivated it, and how the villain (whose identity may be revealed to the reader early on) is caught and brought to justice. Novels in this category frequently employ multiple points of view and have a broader scope than a more traditional murder mystery. The crime may not even involve murder—it may be a threat to global economy or regional ecology; it may be technology run amok or abused at the hands of an unscrupulous scientist; it may involve innocent citizens victimized for personal or corporate gain. Its perpetrators are kidnappers, stalkers, serial killers, rapists, pedophiles, computer hackers, or just about anyone with an evil intention and the means to carry it out. The protagonist may be a private detective or law enforcement official but is just as likely to be a doctor, lawyer, military officer, or other individual in a unique position to identify the villain and bring her to justice. (Examples: James Patterson, Michael Connelly)

ESPIONAGE. The international spy novel is less popular since the end of the Cold War, but stories can still revolve around political intrigue in unstable regions. (Examples: John le Carré, Ken Follett)

MEDICAL THRILLER. The plot can involve a legitimate medical threat (such as the outbreak of a virulent plague) or the illegal or immoral use of medical technology. In the former scenario, the protagonist is likely to be the doctor (or team) who identifies the virus and procures the antidote; in the latter, she could be a patient (or the relative of a victim) who uncovers the plot and brings down the villain. (Examples: Robin Cook, Michael Crichton)

COURTROOM DRAMA. The action takes place primarily in the courtroom; the protagonist is generally a defense attorney out to prove the innocence of her client by finding the real culprit. (Examples: Scott Turow, John Grisham)

WOMAN IN JEOPARDY. A murder or other crime may be committed, but the focus is on the woman (and/or her children) currently at risk, her struggle to understand the nature of the danger, and her eventual victory over her tormentor. The protagonist makes up for her lack of physical prowess with intellect or special skills, and solves the problem on her own or with the help of her family (but she runs the show). Closely related to this category is the romantic suspense. But, while the heroine in a romantic suspense is certainly a woman in jeopardy, the mystery or suspense element is subordinate to the romance. (Example: Mary Higgins Clark)

ROMANCE SUBGENRES

HISTORICAL. Setting is especially significant here, and details must be thoroughly researched and accurately presented. Some specific historical romance categories include:

> **GOTHIC.** Historical with a strong element of suspense and a feeling of supernatural events, although these events frequently have a natural explanation. Setting plays an important role in establishing a dark, moody, suspenseful atmosphere. (Example: Victoria Holt)
>
> **HISTORICAL FANTASY.** Traditional fantasy elements of magic and magical beings, frequently set in a medieval society. (Examples: Jayne Ann Krentz, Kathleen Morgan)
>
> **EARLY AMERICA.** Usually Revolution to Civil War, set in New England or the South, or frontier stories set in the American West.
>
> **REGENCY.** Set in England from 1811–1820.

CATEGORY OR SERIES. These are published in specific lines or imprints by individual publishing houses (such as Harlequin and Silhouette); each line has its own requirements as to word length, story content, and amount of sex.

SINGLE-TITLE CONTEMPORARY. Longer contemporary romances that do not necessarily conform to the requirements of a specific romance line and therefore feature more complex plots and nontraditional characters.

EROTICA. Deals mainly with the characters' sex lives and features graphic descriptions.

GLITZ. So called because they feature generally wealthy characters with high-powered positions in careers that are considered to be glamorous—high finance, modeling/acting, publishing, fashion—and are set in exciting or exotic (often metropolitan) locales such as Monte Carlo, Hollywood, London, or New York. (Examples: Judith Krantz, Jackie Collins)

ROMANTIC COMEDY. Has a fairly strong comic premise and/or a comic perspective in the author's voice or the voices of the characters (especially the heroine). (Example: Jennifer Crusie)

ROMANTIC SUSPENSE. With a mystery or psychological thriller subplot in addition to the romance plot. (Examples: Barbara Michaels, Tami Hoag, Nora Roberts, Catherine Coulter)

PARANORMAL. Containing elements of the supernatural or science fiction/fantasy. There are numerous subcategories (many stories combine elements of more than one) including:

> **TIME TRAVEL.** One or more of the characters travels to another time—usually the past—to find love. (Examples: Jude Deveraux, Diana Gabaldon)
>
> **SCIENCE FICTION/FUTURISTIC.** Science-fiction elements are used for the story's setting: imaginary worlds, parallel universes, Earth in the near or distant future. (Examples: Jayne Ann Krentz, J.D. Robb)
>
> **CONTEMPORARY FANTASY.** From modern ghost and vampire stories to New Age themes such as extraterrestrials and reincarnation. (Example: Linda Lael Miller)

MULTICULTURAL. Most currently feature African-American couples, but editors are looking for other ethnic stories as well. Multiculturals can be contemporary or historical and fall into any subcategory.

CHRISTIAN. Feature an inspirational, Christian message centering on the spiritual dynamic of the romantic relationship and faith in God as the foundation for that relationship; sensuality is played down. (Examples: Janette Oke, Karen Kingsbury)

APPENDIX B

RESOURCES

BOOKS

Beginning Writer's Answer Book edited by Jane Friedman

Bird by Bird: Some Instructions on Writing and Life by Anne Lamott

The Complete Handbook of Novel Writing, 2nd Edition edited by the editors of Writer's Digest

Dear Genius: The Letters of Ursula Nordstrom collected and edited by Leonard S. Marcus

Fiction: The Art and Craft of Writing and Getting Published by Michael Seidman

Fiction Writer's Workshop by Josip Novakovich

The First Five Pages: A Writer's Guide to Staying Out of the Rejection Pile and ***The Plot Thickens: 8 Ways to Bring Fiction to Life*** by Noah Lukeman

How to Write a Damn Good Novel by James N. Frey

How to Write & Sell Your First Novel, revised edition by Oscar Collier with Frances Spatz Leighton

If You Want to Write: A Book About Art, Independence, and Spirit by Brenda Ueland

Imaginative Writing: The Elements of Craft by Janet Burroway

The Indie Author Guide: Self-Publishing Strategies Anyone Can Use by April L. Hamilton

Novel & Short Story Writer's Market

The Playful Way to Serious Writing: An Anything-Can-Happen Workbook to Inspire and Delight by Roberta Allen

Yoga for the Brain: Daily Writing Stretches That Keep Minds Flexible and Strong by Dawn DiPrince and Cheryl Miller Thurston

Wild Mind: Living the Writer's Life by Natalie Goldberg

On Writing: A Memoir of the Craft by Stephen King

Poemcrazy: Freeing Your Life With Words by Susan Goldsmith Wooldridge

The Write-Brain Workbook: 366 Exercises to Liberate Your Writing and ***Take Ten for Writers: Generate Ideas and Stimulate Your Writing in Only 10 Minutes a Day*** by Bonnie Neubauer

Write Great Fiction: Plot & Structure by James Scott Bell

Write Great Fiction: Characters, Emotion & Viewpoint by Nancy Kress

Write Great Fiction: Dialogue by Gloria Kempton

Write Great Fiction: Description & Setting by Ron Rozelle

Write Great Fiction: Revision & Self-Editing by James Scott Bell

Writing the Breakout Novel by Donald Maass

The Writing & Critique Group Survival Guide: How to Give and Receive Feedback, Self-Edit, and Make Revisions by Becky Levine

You Can Write a Novel, 2nd Edition, by James V. Smith, Jr.

WEBSITES

Absolute Write (www.absolutewrite.com). Provides comprehensive information for writers—no matter what your skill level.

Agent Query (www.agentquery.com). Search over nine hundred reputable agents for free.

The Association of Authors' Representatives (www.aar-online.com). Find information about agents who meet professional standards and subscribe to a canon of ethics.

Author Buzz (www.authorbuzz.com). Get in touch with readers, booksellers, and librarians and partners with online publications like DearReader.com and Shelf-Awareness.com.

Authorlink (www.authorlink.com). An excellent site for news about publishing and articles about writing.

Book Docs (www.bookdocs.com). Provides manuscript evaluations, developmental and line editing, consultation on book proposals and conceptual development, and ghostwriting and collaboration.

Book Market (www.bookmarket.com). Lists book publishing statistics, free marketing advice, book promotion advice, Internet marketing resources, author resources, publishers resources, free downloads, and a subscription for John Kremer's Book Marketing Tip of the Week.

Booktalk (www.booktalk.com). Promising "all the buzz about books," this site offers connections to publishers and agents, and some news about the industry.

Library Thing (www.librarything.com). Create an author page, promote your books to potentially interested readers, and connect with readers. Plus, you can catalog your library, get reading suggestions, and participate in groups and discussions.

Editcetera (www.editcetera.com). Offers coaching and ghostwriting, crafting of book proposal and sample chapters, developmental editing of a first draft, and line editing of a late draft.

Guide to Literary Agents (www.guidetoliteraryagents.com/blog). Read interviews and articles from writers and agent.

Poets & Writers (www.pw.org). Offers links to workshops, services, and publications of interest to writers.

Red Room (www.redroom.com). Get an online home page, professional coaching and editing services, and a place to discuss and buy books.

Sisters in Crime (www.sinc-ic.org). A good site for mystery writers, male and female.

Writer's Digest (www.writersdigest.com). In addition to its own excellent information, this site also links to the 101 Best Websites for writers of all kinds.

Writer's Market (www.writersmarket.com). Like its print companion, *Writer's Market*, this site provides up-to-date listings of publishers and agents, with a tool that helps you keep track of where you've submitted and when.

Writers Write (www.writerswrite.com). Offers reviews, interviews, and articles on craft.

PERMISSIONS

"Amp up Dialogue With Emotional Beats." Excerpted from *Novelist's Boot Camp* © 2006 by Todd A. Stone, with permission of Writer's Digest Books.

"Balancing Description & Summary." Excerpted from *Write Great Fiction: Description and Setting* © 2005 by Ron Rozelle, with permission of Writer's Digest Books.

"Choosing Your Character's Profession" © 2006 by Michael J. Vaughn. Originally appeared in *Writer's Digest*, August 2006. Used with permission of the author.

"Craft an Opening Scene That Lures Readers Into Chapter Two." Excerpted from *Hooked* © 2007 by Les Edgerton, with permission of Writer's Digest Books.

"Create the (Im)perfect Heroic Couple." Excerpted from *On Writing Romance* © 2007 by Leigh Michaels, with permission of Writer's Digest Books.

"Create Vicious Villains" © 2006 by Charles Atkins. Originally appeared in *Writer's Digest*, August 2006. Used with permission of the author.

"Creating Your Story's Time & Place." Excerpted from *Writing the Breakout Novel* © 2002 by Donald Maass, with permission of Writer's Digest Books.

"Creative Lollygagging: Work Harder at Working Less." © 2006 by Michael J. Vaughn. Originally appeared in *Writer's Digest*, December 2006. Used with permission of the author.

"Depicting Convincing Relationships" © 2011 by Elizabeth Sims. Originally appeared in *Writer's Digest*, February 2011. Used with permission of the author.

"Draw Characters From the Strongest Sources." Excerpted from *Write Great Fiction: Characters, Emotions & Viewpoint* © 2005 by Nancy Kress, with permission of Writer's Digest Books.

"Emotion-Driven Characters" © 2011 by David Corbett. Originally appeared in *Writer's Digest* January 2011. Used with permission of the author.

"Fire Up Your Fiction: Four Techniques." Excerpted from *The Fire in Fiction* © 2009 by Donald Maass, with permission of Writer's Digest Books.

"Follow the Rules for Stronger Writing." Excerpted from *The Art and Craft of Storytelling* © 2008 by Nancy Lamb, with permission of Writer's Digest Books.

"Fueling Your Muse With Compost." Excerpted from *Page After Page* © 2009 by Heather Sellers, with permission of Writer's Digest Books.

"Get Off Your Butt & Write." Excerpted from *The Writer's Market Guide to Getting Published* © 2010 by The Editors of Writer's Digest, with permission from Writer's Digest Books.

"How to Build Suspense With Backstory." Excerpted from *On Writing Romance* © 2007 by Leigh Michaels, with permission of Writer's Digest Books.

"How to Gain Perspective on Your Work" © 2011 by Elizabeth Sims. Originally appeared in *Writer's Digest*, August 2011. Used with permission of the author.

"Keep Your Story Lean" © 2006 by Nancy Kress. Originally appeared in *Writer's Digest*, March 2006. Used with permission of the author.

"Keep Your Story Moving at the Right Pace." Excerpted from *Between the Lines* © 2006 by Jessica Page Morrell, with permission of Writer's Digest Books.

"Make Your Own Muse." Excerpted from *The Constant Art of Being a Writer* © 2009 by N.M. Kelby, with permission of Writer's Digest Books.

"Make Your Tone Pitch-Perfect" © 2011 by Adair Lara. Originally appeared in *Writer's Digest*, July/August 2011. Used with permission of the author.

"Map Your Novel With a Reverse Outline." Excerpted from *The Constant Art of Being a Writer* © 2009 by N.M. Kelby, with permission of Writer's Digest Books.

"Marry Your Life to Your Writing" © 2010 by Sheila Bender. Originally appeared in *Writer's Digest*, February 2010. Used with permission of the author.

"Mastering Multiple Points of View" © 2007 by Simon Wood. Originally appeared in *Writer's Digest*, February 2007. Used with permission of the author.

"POV Characters Who Overstep Their Bounds" © 2006 by Kristen Johnson Ingram. Originally appeared in *Writer's Digest*, April 2006. Used with permission of the author.

"Put Your Fiction to the Plausibility Test" © 2006 by Steve Almond. Originally appeared in *Writer's Digest*, April 2009. Used with permission of the author.

"Refine Your Setting Skill Set." Excerpted from *The 4 A.M Breakthrough* © 2005 by Brian Kiteley, with permission of Writer's Digest Books.

"Reinventing Your Relationship With Time." Excerpted from *The Productive Writer* © 2010 by Sage Cohen, with permission of Writer's Digest Books.

"Rescue Your Story From Plot Pitfalls." Excerpted from *Novel Shortcuts* © 2009 by Laura Whitcomb, with permission of Writer's Digest Books.

"Researching Your Ideas." Excerpted from *The Writer's Market Guide to Getting Published* © 2010 by The Editors of Writer's Digest, with permission of Writer's Digest Books.

"Selling Your Fiction." Excerpted from *The Writer's Market Guide to Getting Published* © 2010 by The Editors of Writer's Digest, with permission of Writer's Digest Books.

"Six Ways to Layer in Backstory." Excerpted from *Writing and Selling Your Mystery Novel* © 2005 by Hallie Ephron, with permission of Writer's Digest Books.

"Start Me Up" © 2006 by Elizabeth Sims. Originally appeared in *Writer's Digest* December 2006. Used with permission of the author.

"Story Trumps Structure" © 2011 by Steven James. Originally appeared in *Writer's Digest* February 2011. Used with permission of the author.

"Strengthen Your Scenes." Excerpted from *Write Great Fiction: Revision and Self-Editing* © 2008 by James Scott Bell, with permission of Writer's Digest Books.

"Three Techniques for Crafting Your Villain." Excerpted from *Writing and Selling Your Mystery Novel* © 2005 by Hallie Ephron, with permission of Writer's Digest Books.

"Transform that Out-of-Shape First Draft" © 2010 by Lin Enger. Originally appeared in *Writer's Digest* January 2010. Used with permission of the author.

"Avoid Writing Same-Old, Same-Old Conversations" © 2006 by Michael Levin. Originally appeared in *Writer's Digest*, January 2006. Used with permission of the author.

"Understanding Differences in POV." Excerpted from *Writer's Little Helper* © 2006 by James V. Smith Jr., with permission of Writer's Digest Books.

"Understanding Gender Differences" © 2010 by Leigh Anne Jasheway. Originally appeared in *Writer's Digest* May/June 2010. Used with permission of the author.

"Use Braiding to Layer Your Story Line." Excerpted from *Chapter After Chapter* © 2006 by Heather Sellers, with permission of Writer's Digest Books.

"Using Perception to Enhance Your POV." Excerpted from *The Power of Point of View* © 2008 by Alicia Rasley, with permission of Writer's Digest Books.

"Weave Action, Narrative, & Dialogue." Excerpted from *Write Great Fiction: Dialogue* © 2004 by Gloria Kempton, used with permission of Writer's Digest Books.

"Weave in Backstory to Reveal Character." Excerpted from *Breathing Life Into Your Characters* © 2009 by Rachel Ballon, used with permission of Writer's Digest Books.

"What to Do When Your Novel Stalls" © 2011 by John Dufresne. Originally appeared in *Writer's Digest* January 2011. Used with permission of the author.

"Why Backstory Is Essential." Excerpted from *Story Engineering* © 2011 by Larry Brooks, used with permission of Writer's Digest Books.

"Write a Five-Star Chapter One" © 2011 by Elizabeth Sims. Originally appeared in *Writer's Digest* January 2011. Used with permission of the author.

"The Write-At-Home Mom." Excerpted from *Writer Mama* © 2007 by Christina Katz, with permission of Writer's Digest Books.

"Write Well-Crafted Scenes to Support Your Story." Excerpted from *The Art of War for Writers* © 2009 by James Scott Bell, used with permission of Writer's Digest Books.

"Your Novel Blueprint." Excerpted from *From First Draft to Finished Novel* © 2008 by Karen S. Wiesner, used with permission of Writer's Digest Books.

INDEX